Studies of urban labour market behaviour in developing areas

Studies of urban labour market behaviour in developing areas

edited by Subbiah Kannappan,
Michigan State University

International Institute for Labour Studies   Geneva

Copies can be obtained direct from the International Institute for Labour
Studies, P. O. Box 6, 1211 Geneva 22, Switzerland.

CONTENTS

Foreword

by

Albert Tévoédjrè,
Director of the
International Institute for Labour Studies

Problems of rural-urban migration and urban unemployment are the subject of continuing attention from development specialists and a source of growing concern to developing countries. Studies conducted so far have demonstrated the need for a more detailed examination of urban labour market structures and for consolidating diverse empirical insights from different parts of the world. Theorising can be sterile without provision for feedback and refinement.

In this volume, the International Institute for Labour Studies (IILS) has brought together 17 technical papers exploring the interrelationships between labour market structures and their implications for unemployment and the distribution of economic opportunity in major urban areas of the developing world. The principal thrust of these papers is for more detailed knowledge and analyses as a basis for policy in this critical area. Not all readers may endorse, and some may in fact disagree, with the priorities indicated in the individual contributions. What is important is that individuals from vastly different national backgrounds and perspectives have marshalled arguments and evidence highlighting the importance of the institutional characteristics and heterogeneity of the urban labour markets. There are inevitably divergent emphases among the contributors as to the detail and breakdown that would be desirable but these are related to the predictive value of such exercises. The differences are not of semantics, ideology, purpose or (as indicated earlier) national affiliation. The IILS is happy that its "technical" and "academic" roof provided the encouragement for this volume, planned and edited by Professor Subbiah Kannappan.

PART I

EDITOR'S INTRODUCTION

Some issues in labour market research in developing areas: the editorial perspective

by
Subbiah Kannappan,
Michigan State University

INTRODUCTION

Studies of urban labour markets in developing areas have not yet come of age, although there has been a deep tradition of interest in problems of labour mobility and migration as well as the standard of living and welfare of workers. One reason for this is the tendency to proceed from general economic and demographic aggregates, rather than more detailed analyses and empirical studies. Whatever the basis for this inclination, there has as yet been little systematic attempt to bring together, within a framework of well-established theory, the rich variety of insights and knowledge concerning the pecuniary behaviour of households and employers in developing area urban labour markets. This volume, focusing on experiences in Africa, Asia, Latin America and Eastern Europe, is a small step in this direction. All utilise theoretical concepts and empirical measures which have no spatial limitation. There is a specialised bibliography at the end which testifies to the generality of the problems which arise and the need as well as the potential for further comparative investigations.

As there is a more detailed description elsewhere, we will introduce the contributors only briefly here. They have personal knowledge of the functioning of labour markets in several parts of the world, including those they report on. In many cases they are themselves from the developing nations. All have professional and research experience in the developing world and most, if not all, have held positions of responsibility in developed and developing nations alike. Although they touch on different areas and diverse experiences, a well-defined framework focusing on the economic aspects of urban labour market behaviour provides a common thread to their contributions.

The individual studies stand on their own merits and there is no need for further introduction as the titles are self-explanatory. However, the issues emphasised in the contributions may be sketched briefly before more detailed general commentary. All are concerned directly or indirectly with the utility of the theoretical constructs in vogue. Interestingly, misgivings with the so-called "Western" labour force concepts surface only occasionally, but there are more frequent and sustained exceptions to the levels of aggregation common in current analyses. Experiences analysed include the organisation and segmentation of labour markets, the relationship between the structured and more loosely organised components of this labour market (with a focus mainly on the supply side of the labour market), the diversities in urbanisation and employment patterns, the urban wage-earning structure, and the relationship of the functioning of the labour market to such policy goals as growth and employment generation, reduction of income inequalities, etc. While there is no pretension that this volume encompasses all of the interesting research currently taking place, the omissions represent largely the underdeveloped state of the arts of labour market analyses in development studies. In fact, a major purpose of this volume is to draw attention to this lacuna and to stimulate further studies in this tradition.

LEVELS OF AGGREGATION AND LABOUR FORCE CONCEPTS

A frequent concern is with the classification of urban labour markets. Nearly all identify a high-productivity urban subsector characterised by superior earnings. The debate over semantics should not detract from the importance of this consensus or divert attention from the analytical implications of the existence of this subsector. Any of the various and overlapping terms used to denote this subsector - "formal", "modern" or "organised" - would serve equally well.

The analytical problems with such classifications may be briefly indicated. There is first the issue of the reasons for the emergence and persistence of this high-wage or high-earnings sector (HWS or HES). Secondly, there are the contrasts and relationships with the rest of the urban economy implicit in such terminology. In question also is the utility of dualistic labour market models.

Dealing with the first issue, popular recent candidates include government practices favouring the better-off workers, trade union pressures, monopolistic market structures, colonial traditions, or ability to pay (for instance, foreign firms), etc. Dipak Mazumdar advances the alternative view that the wage structure is influenced much more fundamentally by the technology and organisation of the relevant productive activity - a view which finds independent support in other recent literature. This is consistent with a labour market equilibrium between a well-defined high-productivity sector and the rest of the urban labour force. Such an insulated or "protected" labour force (Mazumdar's term) may nevertheless be consistent with subtle forms of rationing and resultant queues in the labour market, which many authors note, and erosion of the protective boundaries, indicated in Kannappan's Sudan study. More on this later.

The relationship with the rest of the urban and national economy is more complex and is responsible for the diversity and even conflicting analyses. The simplest models contrast an urban "formal" with a residual "informal" sector, where the pressure of "unlimited" labour supplies keeps earnings down to the level of the countryside. "Informal" in that sense becomes a relatively superficial innovation, replacing other descriptive categories such as "traditional", "unorganised" and so forth. But on the whole, there is less confidence, and less agreement, about the appropriateness of a single descriptive measure. Even Dipak Mazumdar, who comes closest to an acceptance of a simplified dualistic framework, emphasises the heterogeneity of the unprotected or unorganised sector and the limits of present knowledge. All this is reflected in the diversity and perhaps even confusion in actual practice, in turn masking different ideas and hypotheses of how the labour markets actually function.

The term "informal" sector, for instance, has become a catchall term incorporating naïve hopes, despair and lack of analysis. But then it ceases to be a mere semantic innovation. Some see it as a dynamic sector with creative and latent entrepreneurial potential, held back only by various public restrictions and even petty harassment. Keith Hart, who gave it initial currency, was referring primarily to the self-employed with "informal" income opportunities rather than the successful traders, merchants or self-employed professionals.[1] Still others have understood this term to include all

---

[1] Keith Hart: "Informal Urban Income Opportunities in Ghana", _Journal of Modern African Studies_, Vol. 11, No. 1 (March, 1973).

of the urban poor, perhaps with the added assumption that this is
the material from which Keith Hart's viable "underground" or its
richer cousins emerge. Mazumdar argues, correctly, that the residual remainder is necessarily heterogeneous and it would not
advance analyses to equate it with any one of its component characteristics.

It is the interest in identifying the components, and analysing
their role in development, that leads many to go beyond the conventional dichotomies: formal-informal; organised-unorganised;
modern-traditional; large scale-small scale; and so on. Professor James G. Scoville takes a close look at industrial activity in
the traditional sector in this vein. Guy Standing distinguishes,
from those outside government and modern firm employment, a category
of "irregular" participants who "scratch" at this and "scratch" at
that but who develop no particular skills; these appear to correspond to Pang Eng Fong's "street" sector in Singapore. More, Standing
emphasises that this urban subsistence sector has no potential for
capital accumulation. Papola's categories in Ahmedabad, Kannappan's
in Khartoum, etc., are comparable.

But in Standing's model, there is also a component of the urban
residual with potential for expansion, and this contrasts with the
greater over-all stagnation in the dynamic growth path of Mazumdar.
Abstractions of a two-sector model, with concomitant assumptions (no
productivity growth in the unorganised or U sector, higher capital
coefficients, productivity and wages in the organised or O sector,
dependence of U sector income on O but independence of O and more
rapid increase in supply to O than the increase in O's demand for
labour) leading to a widening of differentials over time and to what
he calls "wage-gap underemployment". The lines of division are less
sharply defined in other contributions, notably Scoville, Standing
and Rempel-House. The factors which may lead to a less gloomy
assessment include formal sector consumption demand for urban services (Rempel-House), elasticity of substitution in the skills of
artisans and craftsmen (Scoville), potential for capital accumulation
elsewhere as a basis for successful involvement in the urban economy
outside of the HWS (Standing), and the flexibility of HWS practices
in taking advantage of cheaper sources of labour supply (as in
Khartoum). As for labour supply, the picture is at best mixed, even
when analysed in aggregative terms: some, like Sethuraman's study of
Jakarta, appear to support Mazumdar's model of urban labour supply,
although the data yield confusing results and are not available concerning worsening differentials; others, like Harold Lubell's comparative analysis of Calcutta, Abidjan and Jakarta, yield a more complex picture of matches between urban labour demand and supply.

Not surprisingly, researchers taking a closer look emphasise
results and structures of greater variety which blur simpler divisions
and establish new ones of their own. The pragmatic as well as the
theoretical cases for this are advanced by several contributors.
Professor Papola's study of the labour market in Ahmedabad (a major
metropolitan area of over a million inhabitants) and his study of
Bombay (one of the largest in the world) follow the dictates as much
of convenience (data availability) as of the need to understand the
functioning of a complex urban labour market. Such an approach has
a validity of its own, independent of whatever light it throws on
the urban-rural problem. In a similar vein, Scoville, Johri,
Rempel-House and others focus on occupational, industrial, rural-
urban and inter-urban differentials and variations, all of which
yield a more complex picture and sometimes even surprising results,
rather than the single dominant high-low wage superiority of the

modern or urban sector.   The case for such a closer disaggregated
look is advanced by Scoville as follows:

> An immediate payoff of such amplification is to increase the
> number of subjects covered by our models.   The constellation
> of wage differentials and the multifaceted patterns of labour
> mobility are only two sets of variables which come to mind.
> ... In general, more detailed models with more variables should
> allow us to address ourselves to more interesting questions
> than the various dualities have afforded.

Before we examine these interesting possibilities, we should note
the issues raised by Professors Solomon B. Levine and Koji Taira in
their treatment of labour market segmentation and their wide-
reaching analytical implications.

LABOUR MARKET SEGMENTATION, INTERNAL
LABOUR MARKETS AND OPTIMALITY

Levine sums up the sweep of the Japanese development experience
in terms of the progress towards "openness" led by forces giving
rise to wage and salaried employment pitted against the "stubborn
matrix of family and community" and other traditional forces sus-
taining segmented or fragmented labour markets.   This segmentation
will persist until the Lewisian labour "surplus" is absorbed in
modern employment.   This is in line with many models which envisage
a progressive diminution of the traditional sector, but the implicit
equation of openness with efficiency raises some difficult questions.

The theoretical challenge is posed by Taira who contrasts a
closed and "pure" internal labour market (ILM) model with an open and
equally "pure" external labour market (ELM) model.   While the closed
ILM poses many restrictions and inefficiencies, and its entirely open
counterpart is intuitively appealing because it is seemingly closer
to the ideal competitive market, neither extreme may be optimal.
The ILM with its own criteria for recruitment, lines of progression,
and other "locking-in" features may be "a necessity if only for
neutralising the cost-raising effects" of such "external" conditions
as firm-specific technologies, labour turnover, union or public
pressures, etc.   In many developing countries, there is in fact a
need to employ workers under conditions which involve "adopting and
indigenising complex technologies".   Even where these are financed
by monopoly profits or social subsidies, given the decision to
develop these technologies, "inefficient internal labour markets may
not be socially inefficient at all".   ILMs meet the efficiency
criteria when employment practices correspond with the firm's long-
run profit objective, given the problems of dealing with the external
labour market.   The "optimal articulation" of ILMs with ELMs
requires that "no job within the firm acquires a queue of qualified
workers or sees the incumbent depart leaving a vacancy difficult to
fill at the existing wage and benefit standards".

The issues raised are critical for labour market policy in
developing countries, and are perhaps of even greater general relevance than indicated in Taira's paper.   Labour market information
channels and certifications are necessarily less universalistic than
in developed countries.   Product markets also have a high degree of
differentiation and this is probably as true in many categories of

construction and "investment" goods as in consumer "durables" and other items of consumption conventionally so regarded. Limited, local enterprises also are likely to have organisational require- ments of a specific nature. Inadequate transport and communica- tions also separate labour markets by time and space. These argue not only for a greater reliance by employers - even employers in the so-called "formal" or modern sector - on "informal" labour market channels, but the greater relevance of ascriptive criteria and hence segmentation in the labour market as a whole.[1] Such a per- spective may be useful in examining some common labour market pheno- mena: the complex co-existence of ascriptive and universalistic criteria in the modern sector (the emphasis on formal education in Khartoum's factories and preference for employee relatives in Atbara railway headquarters); ethnic characteristics governing labour demand and supply in construction in Calcutta (Lubell); the closed patterns of "informal" sector entrepreneurship, creating an ILM all its own, quite the opposite of the more hopeful assessments; and so forth. It also calls for caution and restraint from summary judge- ment concerning labour market criteria now in force. As Taira points out, the dividing line between the optimal and sub-optimal cannot be decided a priori when dealing with the complex "articula- tion" of the external with the internal, traditional and segmented with modern and universalistic, "paternalistic" with non-paternalistic and so forth.

It is, of course, easier to identify shortcomings when they fall in the extremes. Such sharp contrasts may be noted in both formal and informal sectors. A Ceylonese architecture student explains his preference for public sector jobs as due to the following reasons:

> (i) pensionable; foreign scholarships; (ii) no housing problems, quarters provided; (iii) travelling facilities in government vehicles; (iv) job is permanent, no matter what happens; (v) holidays; (vi) government servants are very free when compared with the private sector.

This is, of course, the basis for criticisms of government hiring policies in such geographically separated areas as Jakarta (Sethuraman), Jamaica, Kenya, India, Sudan and elsewhere. Practices criticised include automatic annual increments, guaranteed employ- ment for graduates (Sudan), etc. Leading modern private firms with hiring-in wages way above market equilibrium, out of proportion to any functional criteria (Taira and Standing), and practices of secure or covenanted employment are also in this category.

Criticisms of one such extreme should not, however, make us oblivious of conditions at the other end of the labour market spect- rum. Standing's irregulars who "scratch" at this and "scratch" at that are not among the secure and lackadaisical, but their scope for learning skills and increased productivity is virtually negli- gible. As Standing argues convincingly, these urban "peasants" have little potential for capital accumulation either. There is as little basis for generalising the hopes provided by their more successful cousins as there is for generalising the norms of modern sector employment.[2] At least not on an a priori basis.

---

[1] "Informal" channels refer to such practices as reliance on word of mouth, friends, relatives, etc., in circumstances where the quality and benefits of the additional information (as compared to information obtained more generally) seem worth-while given the costs.

[2] Kannappan (1966).

This is one reason for the disaggregated look for, whether it is income distribution or employment practices, most of the interesting action lies in between the limiting extremes. Studies of the urban wage structure, job search and mobility patterns, and breakdowns of unemployment are of particular relevance here. The studies presented here hint at some of the interesting aspects which merit further investigation.

ASPECTS OF THE FUNCTIONING OF URBAN LABOUR MARKETS

Thus we learn of considerable variety in wage structure, whatever specific comparison we have in mind. In an as yet uncommon investigation for developing areas, a tri-national team of Professors Pastore, Haller and Gomez Buendia examine the determinants of the wage structure of specialised personnel in the São Paolo manufacturing sector. Occupationally specific training, occupational rank (indicative of span and nature of responsibility) and age are significant variables, while seniority in the firm and years on the job count for little in comparison. The authors conclude that "the São Paolo industrial system appears to reward its most highly placed workers - here the top 6 per cent - according to rational principles appropriate to the most highly industrialised countries".

Other wage structure comparisons are less specific but no less interesting. The diversities and surprises yielded by modern and traditional industry comparisons (the differentials being fairly close in some cases) and rural-urban comparisons (greater than one in the case cited by Scoville and of considerable inter-country variability as noted by Koji Taira in an Asia-wide survey)[1] merit further investigation for they disturb the picture of monotonic regularity of flows from the country to the city and within the latter to the modern sector. Rempel-House's low inter-urban (and rural-urban) variation for Kenya implies a vigorous mobility to close prevalent gaps, the more lucrative urban opportunities being generally outside this orbit. Pretty much the same picture is yielded by the Khartoum analysis and the over-all low waiting periods for migrants. A similar picture of absorption with low unemployment rates has been developed for other metropolitan centres too. These make sense when we consider that people are too poor to afford the luxury of passing up low-paying jobs when there can only be minimal expectations of landing the good ones. Sooner or later, expectations are adjusted to the availability of opportunities, and that is why the major problem in developing nations is not unemployment but wage poverty.

But the pattern of flexible wages and adaptations is not generally true of course. A Delhi industry study by Johri examines the pattern of flows as taking place within an industry-wide framework of wage rates and job availability and internal labour market channels conditioning job change patterns.[2] This is one typology we should

---

[1] Taira (1973).

[2] C.K. Johri: "Labour Market Mobility and Wage Differentials in Delhi, India", paper presented at the Research Conference on Urban Labour Markets in Developing Areas, International Institute for Labour Studies, Geneva, September 1974.

expect where there is industry-wide employment and wage regulation as in India and many other countries. The Ahmedabad study (Papola) dealing with mobility in the metropolitan labour market indicates that the average factory worker changes jobs once every eight years, most of it being voluntary. As Papola indicates, a single change may incorporate inter-plant, inter-occupation, inter-industry and inter-area mobility. But occupational and industry mobility dominate due to a low specificity of skills. Over-all, the narrow spread of wage differentials were compatible with competitive equilibrium, with the usual allowance for non-competing groups, differences in occupational mix, costs of acquiring skills, and so forth. He concludes that "the functioning of the labour market does not show any significant qualitative difference from the urban labour markets in developed countries".

But there are also problems of adjustment and rigidities. The modern sector (government and the larger enterprises) is characterised by sticky wages and stiff entrance requirements. But there are qualifications as to what these imply. Its size varies from one urban area to another and, therefore, its significance as a drawing card for the potential urban labour market entrant. There are also blurred edges due to supplementary employment not governed by the rules of "permanency" or fixed wage schedules.

Queues for employment, mostly in the modern sector, also develop. As Pang Eng Fong points out, the unemployed young and females, not being heads of households, can find means of support to sustain their search. It is also generally agreed that the longer waits in the queue are more serious for educated workers and for workers with special skills or experience, for some of whom the employment exchanges become relevant. As Mazumdar notes, there is a distinct possibility that the educated entrant becomes a candidate in waiting without even going through the "informal" sector. Employment here may actually be prejudicial to better employment either because it impedes search or the experience is considered pejorative by the jobseeker or even the potential employer. Idleness may be preferable for, as one interviewee explained scornfully to Standing concerning his remaining unemployed, "Man, I want a job, not a work". This reaction says a great deal about the attractiveness of the jobs themselves, and Standing's distinction between work-intensive and time-intensive jobs adds to our understanding. Employment for the educated also implies more durable job commitment, and potential employers would consider it necessary to undertake a more thorough review prior to employment. Candidates for civil service appointments may find it profitable to stay off the labour force and prepare for the necessary tests. In lesser measure, these would be relevant for other workers with qualifications suitable for modern sector employment. It is necessary to add that such idleness, whether it takes the form of unemployment or being out of the labour force, does not imply that the jobseekers are lazy or anything like that. Rather the organisation of the labour market, particularly as it concerns modern sector jobs, is such that suitable jobs emerge only after some time-lags and it inhibits participation in the meantime.

On the other hand, the gaps in information seem to be more serious inhibiting factors for other urban jobseekers. These include migrants, particularly those without urban relatives, or similar workers who have paved the way, first-time jobseekers, etc. Even for such an urbanised economy as Singapore, kinship, village connections, etc., appear important in job search. Even within

the category of factory workers in Ahmedabad, despite an over-all
sophistication about job alternatives, there is "a predominance of
informal channels and the absence of an equitable dissemination of
information". Further, in "63 per cent of the cases the jobs were
secured on the basis of 'introduction by other worker' and this
'other worker' was related to the incumbent by blood, kinship or
community in 91 per cent of these cases". There are arguments
both for and against the established practices which restrict the
scope of the labour market pool from which recruitment is made but
assure the employers of a dependable labour supply, reinforcing the
complexities of the optimality criterion raised by Taira. They
also underscore the virtual absence of studies in the tradition of
labour market discrimination in developing areas, as study after
study points to the importance of ethnic clusters in urban labour
market organisation.

One point deserves particular importance as we consider the
importance of adjustments in the urban labour markets which seem
generally to be proceeding along rational and predictable lines.
The categorisation of the urban economy into two, three or even
more sectors tends to encourage a picture of unified decision-
making embodied in such statements as "the modern sector imposes
unduly high entrance requirements", "the informal sector provides
jobs for all new entrants", and so forth. They are particularly
misleading if the latter is referring to the diverse residual urban
economy with highly decentralised decision-making and the difficulties in practice of dichotomising between demand and supply influences. Further, such over-all categorisations tend to divert attention from the behaviour responsible for adjustment of numerous
households and enterprises of varying sizes. Such adjustments lie
as much in the sphere of scaling down of aspirations as in the
seizing of entrepreneurial and/or productive responsibility.

The importance of this point is clearer when we follow
Hendrick Thomas' analysis of enterprise associations of workers in
the labour-managed Yugoslav economy. Under self-management, there is
a large degree of freedom to set wage rates and levels internal to
the firm. It is clear that an objective is superior earnings, but
the case is to be distinguished from a trade union intervention in
the wage determination process on two grounds. Although, as in the
union case, the self-enterprise may set wages above the labour market equilibrium, the associates also have an interest under self-
management to raise productivity. Further, the maximand becomes
the highest average product of labour, the downward-sloping marginal
product of labour function below the average product of labour curve
being largely irrelevant. Much more is needed to be known about
the economic aspects of small-scale, especially own-account, enterprises in developing urban labour markets before we can generalise.

Thomas' study also raises the interesting possibility that wage
structures are likely to be compressed under self-management and
elasticities of substitution fairly large for different categories
of workers. This may be true also in many small enterprises in the
residual urban economy for reasons of family management and low
specificity of skills.

Modern sector adjustments to changes in supply conditions is the
focus of Teshome Mulat's study of Ethiopian manufacturing employment
elasticities. He advances the view that the manufacturing sector
firms, operating under conditions of excess capacity, do not increase
employment as output increases and do not translate improved demand
conditions in the product market into additional employment. The
wage employment elasticity, apart from being less than unity, is positive, which contrasts with the usual and more recognised negative
association. Here again, the compelling need is for further empirical study.

CONCLUDING REMARKS

This essay began by referring to the fact that labour market studies in developing areas have not yet come of age. However, as one reviews the studies incorporated in this volume, and perhaps this introduction highlighting some of the major issues, the lines of further effort seem remarkably clear. There is little doubt that conventional labour market constructs of modern economics have widespread applicability - and utility. To be sure, there will be need for modification and adaptation of concepts to identify entities of decision-making, etc., as stressed by the authors themselves in their contributions here and elsewhere.

There is also no doubt that such exercises become increasingly necessary if we are to more effectively sort out the puzzles yielded by the more aggregative data sources and constructs. This is strikingly revealed for instance in the contrasting and puzzling picture yielded by Jakarta from demographic and survey sources, leading the author to suggest that urban labour demand, rather than supply, be regarded as the adjusting dependent variable. Others see supply as the over-responsive dependent variable, a picture not uniformly supported by Lubell in his comparative analysis.

One or the other of these may be more valid, or they may all be valid in different circumstances. What is clear is that well-defined labour market studies can help us handle some of these puzzles and yield a consistent picture. They are not going to cumulate to a uniform pattern of rights and wrongs, but will enable us to pinpoint more effectively where things are going wrong and what one may expect from proposed measures of amelioration. This is surely necessary if we are to make some further headway in the quest for development with equity.

PART II

CONCEPTUAL AND THEORETICAL ASPECTS

Analysis of the dual labour markets in LDCs

by

Dipak Mazumdar,
London School of Economics;

International Bank for Reconstruction
and Development

INTRODUCTION

The formal-informal sector distinction applied to the urban labour market is an aid to the study of income distribution in the urban economy. It ultimately boils down to a theory of personal income distribution which stresses "structural" factors in explaining earnings differentials as against rival explanations in human capital terms. Low earnings, in other words, are not to be explained solely in terms of factor supplies affecting the earning capacity of the worker, but an essential element in the story is his location in an institutionally determined part of the labour market. The formal-informal sector dichotomy is not by any means the only "structural" factor which has an effect on the distribution of earnings. Another important distinction may be between the salaried and wage workers within the formal sector. But the informal sector is expected to be a significant factor in explaining differences in the lower end of the distribution.

There are at least three aspects to the problem of income distribution which the theory of the informal sector is expected to illuminate.

First, there is the question of the levels of earnings in the two urban subsectors at a point of time.

Secondly, we are concerned about the lifetime performance of a worker, and it is sometimes suggested that workers in the informal sector - whatever their earnings at the point of entry - would typically produce a flat age earning profile (or, at any rate, significantly flatter than the profiles of workers in the formal sector). The reasonings behind this proposition are very similar to those encountered in the literature of the dual labour market in the United States. Low wages discourage the attachment of workers to an individual firm, and instability prevents acquisition of skill and perpetuates low wages.

Thirdly, the theory of the informal sector suggests hypotheses about the changes in the distribution of income over time.

In this paper, in section I, after discussing some conceptual issues about the definition of the informal sector, we refer briefly to the empirical problem of the identification of the sector. The predictions from the model about earnings at a point of time are discussed in section II. The dynamic analysis of the dual urban labour market is discussed in section III.

An important point to bear in mind throughout the discussion is that the formal-informal sector dichotomy in the urban market is related to, but quite separate from, the particular migration function used in the paper to describe the response of rural to urban migrants. As will emerge in the course of the paper, the inferences drawn from the use of the particular migration function are distinct from those dependent on the dichotomy of the urban labour market as such.

I. DEFINITION OF THE TWO SECTORS

Conceptual basis of the distinction

It is sometimes maintained that the characteristics which constitute the basis of the formal-informal sector distinction represent a pattern of continuous variation in a typical LDC labour market and, therefore, the dichotomy is unwarranted. There are two reasons for rejecting this contention:

(a) Whether the relevant characteristics represent a continuum or not is itself a subject of research and, if we are to go by casual empiricism, then certainly the view that the "formal" sector is separated sharply in some ways from the rest of the urban market is more valid than the contrary one for many LDC urban markets.

(b) Even if the difference between two types of employment is one of degree rather than of kind, so long as it is of marked degree the methodology of economics can be applied successfully by operating with models which assume that the labour market is split into two different sectors.

The basic distinction between the two sectors turns on the idea that employment in the formal sector is, in some sense or senses, protected[1] so that the wage level and working conditions in the sector are not available, in general, to the jobseekers in the market unless they manage to cross the barrier of entry somehow. This kind of "protection" may arise from the action of trade unions, of governments, or of both acting together. Examples of such institutional practices are widespread in the less-developed world. It should be stressed that in many cases the impact on wage levels would not be the most important part of such institutional factors; the effect on fringe payments and working conditions would probably turn out to be more substantial.

The development of protection from labour in the recent history of the LDCs is tied up quite closely with the development of import substitution as part of a policy of fostered industrialisation. The protection granted to factory-industry in many countries from foreign competition led to an inflation of profits in the sector which, in varying degrees, had to be shared by labour both on grounds of equity and political stability.

But it should be stressed that the play of free market forces, rather than institutional factors, could lead to the development of a "protected" sector within the urban market. This is because of a varied group of factors which establishes a direct relationship between the efficiency of a worker and the wage level.[2] Up to a certain point, an increase in the wage per worker increases efficiency more than proportionately to the increase in the wage, so that the wage cost per unit of work supplied falls. After a point, of course, the increase in wage will lead to a less than proportionate increase in efficiency, and there will be no incentive for management to set the wage level for an individual worker than this level. Thus, even in the presence of an excess supply of labour, it will not pay management to set the wage at the lowest level possible. The established wage will be that which ensures the minimum wage cost per unit of effort supplied.

---

[1] Harberger (1971).

[2] Liebenstein (1957), Mazumdar (1959a) and Harris (1971).

Why does not this mechanism apply to all firms in the urban economy?   First, the strength of the functional relationship between wage and efficiency will generally be more important for enterprises with modern technology employing a large number of workers. Secondly, management can adopt this type of wage policy only if it is dealing with a stable body of workers attached to the firm.   To the extent that labour with high turnover is found in some sectors of the urban market, the link between efficiency and wage for this body of workers is broken.   In fact, a high wage policy may have to be pursued by some firms to promote stability of labour; and once the stability is achieved, further wage increases would be forth-coming because the link between wage and efficiency has now been more firmly established.

Thus, even under free market conditions, the wage level in some types of enterprises will be established at a level higher than the alternative wages in other sectors of the same market.   This wage level is "protected" because jobseekers who will be very willing to accept employment at this wage are unable to bid down the wage, and can only be employed in the sector after going through a process of selection involving aptitude tests as well as rationing.

A specific example of this type of labour market behaviour has been studied by Mazumdar for the Bombay Textile Industry (1959b and 1973).   Alongside a stable core of workers, with a relatively high wage, the industry employed a sizeable proportion of employees on casual day-to-day contract which provided it with a pool of potential recruits.   The historical research published in 1973 proves conclu-sively that the two-tier labour market was established well before the era of trade unions and government intervention.

Recent post-colonial labour legislation in India has sharpened and institutionalised this division in the market for textile labour. In studying the impact of institutional factors in labour markets in other parts of the world, care should be taken to see if observed conditions today similarly reflect a continuation of processes which originated under free market conditions.

The arguments of the last few paragraphs give a hint of another idea lurking behind the concept of the formal sector besides that of protection.   In our discussion of both the institutionally deter-mined and market determined emergence of a protected sector for labour, there was a reference to the development of firms employing modern technology and with the high labour productivity associated with it.   Such firms would typically also have much more formal work arrangements for their employees than other types of units in the labour market.   The implication of the formal-informal sector dis-tinction in the labour market is then that workers in units with modern technology enjoy a type of "protection" which is qualitatively different from the protected market structures, hawkers, pedlars and other groups in the "informal" sector of the market are sometimes said to evolve.[1]   The quantitative impact on earnings of the protec-tion of the formal sector can accordingly be expected to be more significant.   This is, of course, a testable hypothesis and not a statement of fact.

---

[1] Lisa Pettie (1974).

Identification of the informal
sector empirically

We can now turn to the problem of identifying the two sectors empirically in a particular labour market. To start with a simple point, it is not possible in LDCs to identify the formal sector by locating the employees who are unionised.[1] Union organisations are not widespread enough for this purpose. We could then look at the aspect of government regulation. Enforceable welfare and wage legislation would presumably be confined to the formal sector, and the State would generally keep a list of establishments for this purpose. The boundaries of this so-called "enumerated" sector would probably conform fairly closely to that of the formal sector. It is well worth using this criterion in some cases, but two poten- tial problems exist: (1) sometimes the cut-off point for the size of establishments enumerated may be at too high a point (e.g. in India it is at those having more than 25 workers for units not using power); (ii) if we want to find out about the size of the informal sector, we can do so only by deducting the employment in the enumer- ated sector from the total labour force in the city. Information about the latter will, however, be available only for a census year, and thus most of the analysis of the labour market can be carried out for census years (cf. Joshi).

We need, in fact, some way of separating the two sectors from the usual type of information available in household surveys. To begin with, most groups of the self-employed clearly belong to the informal sector. Professionals and those in government services should, however, be excluded from the sector since their work arrangements and conditions of work would be most likely regulated. Additionally, in most LDCs small firms will not have the character- istics of formal work arrangement, modern technology and the protec- tion as discussed above. In many countries, there is a strong positive relationship between employment, size of establishment and labour productivity. The inclusion of employees of small firms in the informal sector, however, does mean that we have to be arbitrary to some extent. The cut-off point must be determined by the judge- ment of the researcher in the particular labour market concerned.

A third possible criterion of classification exists in some labour markets in which the workers of a certain type participate in social security schemes with wide coverage. In Brazil, for example, contributions to social security are shared by employers and employees. The persons included in the scheme are involved in work arrangements in which a written contract exists, and will generally belong to the formal sector. Thus, in one study (Merrick), workers were assigned to the formal or informal sectors accordingly as they did or did not pay social security dues. The information on this point was available from a question included in the household survey. A valid criticism of using this criterion, however, is that it tends to preselect the low-income groups as belonging to the informal sec- tor. Among the self-employed in particular, those who pay income taxes will also be paying social security dues, and thus the higher- income earners among these will be excluded from the informal sector. There is a danger in a case like this of circularity. One of the

---

[1] We do not go into further questions as to when a worker should be considered to have been unionised - e.g. when did he last pay his union membership fee?

objectives of our investigation should be to see how the relative levels of earnings in the two sectors behave in different circumstances - and we cannot define the employed in the informal sector as those with low earnings.

It is our judgement that the criteria discussed in the penultimate paragraph would probably be the useful ones in most situations.   Care should, however, be taken to collect information in a disaggregated way, particularly for the self-employed, so that more pragmatic screening might be undertaken at a later stage for identifying the workers in the formal sector.

II. THE STATIC MODEL OF THE LABOUR MARKET AND ITS EMPIRICAL TESTING

The model of job search

The division of the labour market into two sectors does not in itself carry any implication about the process of migration and job search.   But the informal sector is expected to be characterised by relative ease of entry for new workers.   This is partly a result of the unprotected nature of the sector.   The lack of long contractual relationship in employment, which characterises important parts of the sector, also encourages high turnover of labour, favouring ease of entry into the sector.   Finally, it is expected that many types of self-employment will require very little capital or other co-operant factors for new workers to set up on their own.

The idea of easy entry plus variable hours of work leads to the hypothesis that the informal sector serves as a point of transition for new migrants to the urban labour market who want to break into the formal sector.   The migrant wishing to get a formal sector job has to spend some time searching in the urban market.   The income he gets by participating in the informal sector finances his period of search, and the fact that his participation is less than full time (because of the prevailing condition of underemployment) enables him to search for an opening in the formal sector even while he is earning a livelihood in the informal sector.   As set out formally in the model of the Appendix, migrants with this type of behaviour would respond to a function of expected wages in the urban market which includes two components: the expected earnings in the informal sector, and the probability of getting a formal sector job at the going (high) wage.   If we assume that, in equilibrium, in the absence of the second factor, the earnings in the informal sector would equal the alternative income in agriculture, then this model leads to a prediction that the level of earnings in the informal sector would be below that in agriculture.   Migrants, in other words, are willing to incur a "loss" during the period of search in the urban market in expectation of getting a high-wage formal sector job later on.

Before we come to a discussion of the testability of this model of job search, we should look at a couple of important theoretical points.   First is the question of open unemployment.   The model suggests that, while underemployment and low average earnings in the informal sector would be significant features of the market, the rate of open unemployment would generally be not very high.   Certain urban labour markets do, indeed, have this feature.   Indian data generally conform to this picture.   The National Sample Survey, defining the unemployed as those "who were not employed during the reference week and were looking for full-time work", consistently showed a very low rate of measured unemployment in urban India. In 1961, for example, the proportion of the labour force wholly unemployed was only 3 per cent in towns, compared to 4 per cent in villages.[1] A much larger percentage of the urban labour force, however, worked less than full time in the reference week. As much as 12 per cent, for instance, worked less than 28 hours in the week. This result was generally borne out by the surveys done for individual cities under the auspices of the Planning Commission.[2] However, there are many urban markets in other countries in which the totally unemployed constitute a much larger proportion of the labour force. Does the conclusion of the job search model need to be modified if we include open unemployment as an important element of the labour market? The answer is largely no. Migrants who are seeking to break into the formal sector and are openly unemployed may have greater opportunity for searching than those who participate in the informal sector. Open unemployment in this view would be a conscious choice in which the higher probability of obtaining a formal sector job is balanced against the loss of earnings from work in the informal sector. But as long as participation in the informal sector does not reduce the probability of obtaining a formal sector job to a negligible value, the conclusion of the two-sector model stands: equilibrium earnings in the sector will be below the marginal supply price of migrants from agriculture. It should be emphasised that the unemployed do not _necessarily_ have an edge on the informal sector workers in searching for entry into the formal sector. It depends very much on who the unemployed are and how long it takes to break into the formal sector. If the unemployed, for example, are largely young persons looking for their first job, they would not necessarily be the type of workers preferred by the formal sector even if they are able to search full time for some weeks.

A second theoretical issue relates to the participation of two distinguishable types of workers in the informal sector. There is the type discussed so far who are using the informal sector to finance their period of waiting before they break into the formal sector. (We could call them "regulars".) But there will be another group who are interested in informal sector employment as an end in itself. Even if we retain the assumptions of easy entry and absence of differentiation of earnings within the sector, we can think of at least two broad groups of workers who will be employed primarily in this sector: (i) among the migrants, there will be those who come to town as individuals without any thought or plan of extended stay - the seasonal migrants, the target workers, or those who can be away from the family farm for short periods of their working life without affecting the productivity of the farms too much; (ii) among the native born, the groups employed principally in the informal sector will include the secondary workers whose participation in gainful activity outside the home is sporadic - as is probably true of married women, or whose entry into the informal sector

---

[1] Pravin Visaria in _Employment and Unemployment Problems of the Near East and South Asia_, Vol. I (edited by R.G. Ridker and H. Lubell).

[2] J.F. Bulsara: _Problems of Rapid Urbanisation in India_ (Bombay, 1964).

is severely restricted for one reason or another - as is true of non-prime age male workers in many labour markets.[1]   Generally, the supply price of these groups (call them "visitors") will be different from that of the regulars and can generally be expected to be lower for the farmer for the same volume of labour.

The regulars are interested in both sectors of the urban market and they will, in equilibrium, equate their marginal supply price (E_w^r) to the expected earnings which will be the <u>sum</u> of the expected earnings in the formal sector and the expected earnings in the informal.   The visitors, by contrast, are interested only in the informal sector, and the equilibrium condition for them will be given by their equation of their marginal supply price (E_w^v) to the expected earnings in the informal sector only.[2]   If the supply function for both groups is upward sloping we will, in normal equilibrium, have both types in the informal sector, and the visitors will have a lower expected wage than the regulars.   This situation is depicted in figure 1.   Since both types have the same <u>actual</u> earnings in the informal sector $(P_u W_u)$, the conclusion reached above still holds for the regulars: their actual earnings continue to be lower than their marginal supply price.   The only difference is that there is now a group of workers in the sector whose actual earnings are equal to their marginal supply price.

However, the visitors, many of whose participation in the labour market is short term or intermittent, are much more likely to have an elastic supply function than the regulars.   If it is near to being perfectly elastic we have the situation portrayed in figure 2.   The invariant supply price E_w^v for visitors determines the level of earnings in the informal sector by determining P_u (the degree of underemployment) given W_u.   This level of earnings in its turn determines the volume of regulars participating in the informal sector.   In fact, if, as already discussed, the regular has a greater probability of finding a job in the formal sector if he is wholly unemployed (call it P_f) than if he is working part time in the informal sector (P_o), then along with a volume of OA of regulars in the informal sector there will be a volume AB unemployed in the urban market.

---

[1] This statement does not mean that no prime-age male worker is ever employed in the formal sector, but that the barriers to entry for these groups are sufficiently strong for them to evaluate their probability of getting into the sector as fairly small.   Such barriers could be due to conventional discriminatory practices or due to rational employer response to legislation determining minimum wages and other working conditions.   For evidence on age and sex selectivity of workers found in the informal sector see Mazumdar (1974).

[2] The conditions are, for the visitors and the regulars, respectively:

$$E_w^v = P_u W_u \quad \text{and} \quad E_w^r = P_o W_o + P_u W_u$$

when P_o and P_u are the probability of getting a day's work in the formal and informal sectors and W_o and W_u are the respective wage rates (cf. the model of the Appendix).

Figure 1

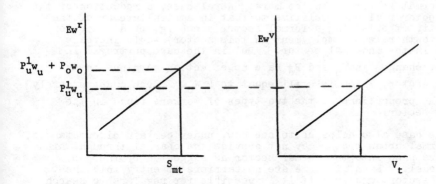

Figure 2

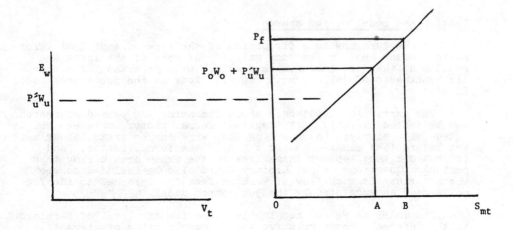

The interesting point about this case is that, unlike in the more general case portrayed in figure 1, the level of earnings in the informal sector is independent of conditions of employment and wages in the formal sector. In the more general case, a reduction of the formal sector real wage relative to that in agriculture or of the probability of obtaining a formal sector job (e.g. by a reduction of the growth rate of employment in this sector) would <u>increase</u> earnings in the informal sector. But in the case portrayed in figure 2, changes in W_o and P_o have no effect on earnings in the informal sector, which is still equal to $P_u W_u$. Such changes merely affect the proportions of the two types of workers found in the informal sector.

This case also helps us to see how, under certain circumstances, the informal urban sector may not provide the channel through which jobseekers pass into the formal sector as suggested by the job search model. Even if there are no barriers to entry into the informal sector, and even if it is possible for regulars to search for formal sector jobs while working part time in the former, only a few regulars may be willing to do so. The level of earnings in the informal sector may be so low, as determined by the low supply price of "visitors", that most regulars may value their opportunity for searching full time as greater than the earnings foregone (OA in figure 2 may be small compared to AB).

Testing the model of job search

Let us turn now to a discussion of the type of empirical information we may need to test the validity of some of the ideas and results of the dual labour market model, with or without the specific hypothesis of job search. We will look at the job search model first.

The particular hypothesis about financing the period of search can be tested directly. A sample of formal sector employees can be asked quite simply: (a) how long they were in the urban labour market before they managed to get a job in the formal sector; and (b) how did they support themselves in the urban area during this period? Questions on job history could also be included to see whether there is much flow of workers from the informal to the formal sector as suggested by the job search model.

The model as we saw has implications for the level of earnings in the informal sector relative to the supply price of migrants. In particular, the prediction is that earnings in the sector will be below the supply price of "regulars". However, the notion of a unique supply price is a simplification. What we will be comparing is a distribution of earnings in the urban informal sector with the distribution of earnings in the rural sector from which the migrants generally come. It is important to avoid the pitfall of comparing <u>average income</u> in the two sectors: the informal sector has been demarcated in such a way that it will contain the relatively lower earnings groups in the urban labour market. To compare the average earnings of this group with the average earnings of the rural population as a whole is to commit the mistake of comparing the earnings of non-homogeneous socio-economic groups. What is required is looking at the distribution of earnings of that section of the rural population which predominantly supply the migrants to the urban area.

In the absence of any evidence about the selectivity of migrants by income levels, it is probably best to compare the tail of the earnings distribution of the two groups. We may, for example, compare the first quartile (which would, one expects, be quite close to the mode) of the earnings distribution in the rural sector with the first quartile of the distribution of incomes in the urban informal sector. If the difference is larger than any plausible cost-of-living adjustment can account for, then the prediction of the job search model is contradicted.

The presence of "visitors" in the urban market in any significant proportions may create complications. As discussed, the visitors' supply price would be very much lower: it is likely to be geared to the (low) marginal product of individual workers in farms with an especially excess supply of labour or in seasons when the demand for agricultural labour is slack. Earnings in the urban informal sector, in other words, may be lower than the average income of the relevant rural population group, not because of the mechanism described by the job search model but because of the prevalence of the temporary visitors in significant numbers.

Testing for differences in earnings
between the urban subsectors

Leaving aside the model of migration and job search, are there any special points to remember if we are just interested in measuring the earnings difference between the formal and informal sectors of the urban economy? Because of the importance of self-employment in the informal sector as well as the expected prevalence of underemployment among the workers in the sector, it is the difference in average earnings over a period of time rather than the differenc in wage rates which is of interest.

The main problem in measuring the differential in earnings comes from the selectivity of workers found in the informal sector. As already mentioned, they are likely to be the young and the old; a disproportionate number of them would be females; and they will be the less educated. Now age, sex and education are the most significant variables determining earnings, whether in the formal or the informal sector. Thus if we try to estimate an earnings function by regression techniques including age, sex, education and, additionally, location in the market (formal or informal sector) as the explanatory variables, the estimated coefficients would probably be unreliable because of the intercorrelation between the formal-informal sector variable and the age-sex-education variables. We are better advised to estimate a series of ratios of actual earnings in the two sectors for different groups of workers of a particular age, sex and educational category.

A more serious problem arises because of the selectivity with respect to migrant status. Many of the migrants working in the informal sector may be single migrants whose supply price would be at a lower level than that of migrants with their families who would be found more commonly in the formal sector. Also the migrants found in the informal sector may contain a disproportionate (and significant) number of temporary "visitors". It is not easy to sort out the effect on earnings due to differences in migrant status. But if we have adequate information from household surveys, it is desirable that the differences in earnings between the two sectors should be studied separately for different types of migrants.

There are at least three groups of factors which will determine migrant status: (i) the duration of stay in the city; (ii) lone or family migration; and (iii) extent of connection with the area of origin, e.g. frequency and period of visit to the native area. These factors should, wherever possible, be introduced as explanatory variables in addition to the formal-informal sector variable in the earnings function for the standardised age-sex-education groups. But here too the problem of intercorrelation among the variables will be a serious one, and we may be forced to rely on the presentation of a detailed series of earnings ratios, rather than the much more compact analysis of estimated coefficients of an earnings function using regression techniques. Even with all the relevant data in his possession, the researcher will be left with hard problems of deciding how best to estimate the combined effect of the several variables on the difference in earnings between the two urban subsectors.

III. THE DEVELOPMENT OF THE URBAN LABOUR MARKET OVER TIME

An important aspect of the study of the dual urban labour market in LDCs is its usefulness in the dynamic analysis of changes in the distribution of income in the urban economy over time. The latter will be a function of the trends in (a) employment and (b) the level of earnings in the two sectors of the urban market. The problem can be broken down into three main areas: (i) the relationship between the rates of growth of income in the formal and the informal sectors; (ii) the determinants of the rates of growth of productivity and wage rates in the two sectors; and (iii) the changes in the degree of underemployment (and the changes in average earnings, given the wage rate) in the informal sector.

(i) The rates of growth of income
     in the two urban subsectors

We start with the observation that in the urban labour market the informal sector sells its output entirely to the population in the urban area, who derive their income from the informal (U) as well as the formal (O) sectors. The O sector, however, sells most of its output to the population outside the labour market. Consequently, U-sector output is dependent on the income of the O sector, but O-sector output is autonomously determined.

Let Y = the income of the U sector at a point of time

   P = the income of the O sector at a point of time

   α = the marginal propensity to consume U goods on the part of the U sector

   β = the marginal propensity to consume U goods for the O sector.

Then we have

$$dY = \frac{\beta}{1-\alpha} dP. \qquad \ldots\ldots (6)$$

From which we get

$$\frac{dY}{Y} = \frac{\beta}{1-\alpha} \cdot \frac{P}{Y} \cdot \frac{dP}{P} \qquad \ldots\ldots (7)$$

or

$$\sigma + z = \frac{\beta}{1-\alpha} \cdot \frac{P}{Y} (\gamma + v) \qquad \ldots\ldots (7a)$$

where σ, z represents the proportionate rates of growth of employment and labour productivity respectively in the U sector, and γ
and v those in the O sector.   It should be noted that much of the
activities in the unorganised sector use highly labour-intensive
techniques with minimal application of non-labour factors.   In the
case of the large service subsector there is hardly any independent
notion of "product" apart from the earnings of labour engaged in it.
Thus we can expect the value of z to be negligible.

It would appear from (7a) that $\frac{P}{Y}$ will play an equilibrating
role in the relationship between the rates of growth of the income
in the two urban sectors.   When the rate of growth of O-sector
income is higher, the increase in $\frac{P}{Y}$ will tend to bring (σ) up (with
γ and β remaining constant) until the rates of growth of income in
the two sectors are equalised.   On the other hand, if ($\gamma + v$) is less
than (σ), the latter will fall in value and tend to equal ($\gamma + v$).
Two points should be noted about the mechanism just described.
First, the strength of the equilibrating relationship depends on α
and β having relatively high values.   This in turn depends on the
importance of the traditional sector in the urban economy of the LDC
in question.   It is, however, unlikely that both α and β will have
very low values in any LDC.   If the modern urban sector in a particular LDC is of the "enclave" type, its marginal propensity to consume traditional goods - β - will be relatively small.   But it is
precisely in this type of urban economy that the unorganised sector
will tend to be relatively self-sufficient with a high value of ∞.

Secondly, the working of the equilibrating mechanism depends on
the values of ∞ and β remaining unchanged over time.   In fact, if
α and β do change, barring short-run fluctuations, they are likely
to have a downward trend, as the U sector comes into greater contact
with the O sector, and there is a reduction in the propensity to
consume traditional goods due to the "demonstration effect" of the
O sector.   If this is the case then the equilibrating mechanism
will work when (σ) exceeds ($\gamma + v$), but will be dampened if the O sector is growing at a higher rate.

This last argument suggests that there is a greater possibility
for growth rate of income in the O sector exceeding that of the U
sector over a stretch of time than there is for it being the other
way around.

(ii) Changes in labour productivity
      and wages in the O sector

Given the rate of growth of income, what happens to the distribution of income in the urban economy depends crucially on the rate
of growth of labour productivity and hence employment in the O sector.   The development which will produce the most favourable outcome

from the point of view of urban income distribution is a
capital-widening type of development à la Lewis with constant productivity and wages.   The rate of growth of employment in the O
sector is thus maximised, and although workers in the sector are
better off than they are in much of the urban economy to the extent
of the initial wage gap,[1] the disparity between the two groups is
not increased over time.[1]   But the historical experience of several
countries suggests that the sequence of development in the O sector
would be rather different.   Generally the rate of growth of labour
productivity is high, the growth of employment is small and wages
increase <u>pari passu</u> with productivity.   Why should productivity and
wages increase when labour is available in elastic supply in the
same market at lower levels of earnings?   The process in operation
is not yet adequately understood.   But the following are components
of an interdependent set of relationships:

(a)   There is a continuous process of diffusion of modern technology
       going on in the organised sector as new firms improve their
       knowledge of the best (least-cost) production process in
       developed economies (cf. Nelson).   In other words, after a
       firm has been committed to a modern production process it is
       some time before the possibility of reducing cost through learn-
       ing is exhausted.   Even without increased capital investment
       per worker this process of learning would tend to increase
       capital and productivity per worker, as labour would be used
       more efficiently.

(b)   The increase in labour productivity leads to rising wages both
       due to market-determined and institutional reasons.   Increase
       in capital intensity per worker can be expected to shift up-
       ward the wage level at which the cost per efficiency unit of
       labour is minimised (cf. page 15 above).   At the same time,
       the type of skilled labour firmly attached to an establishment,
       and in some way specific to the production process of the firm,
       is sufficiently irreplaceable to obtain bargaining power through
       unionisation.   Unions are also helped by political support
       which they tend to get because of their urban presence and dis-
       ruptive potential.   Well-meaning legislative programmes of the
       ILO type would also strengthen the tendencies for wages to
       increase.   Management of firms with increasing productivity
       per worker would, of course, be reluctant to cause serious slow-
       downs in resisting wage increases as long as they are kept with-
       in the limits of the increase in <u>quasi-rents</u>.

(c)   In some cases, institutionally determined wage increases would
       be responsible for the speeding up of the learning process, and
       may even encourage mechanisation to increase the capital and
       productivity per worker (cf. Reynolds and Gregory).   Often
       this process of productivity and wage increase is one of cumula-
       tive causation in which it is impossible to isolate the cause
       from the effect.

---

[1] Profits are reinvested in this process of development and the
rate of profit as well as the share of profits in total income do
not change.

(iii) The trend in earnings in the U sector

What happens to the course of earnings in the U sector?
Because of the prevalence of self-employment and variable hours of
work in this sector it is more relevant to consider the trend in
average earnings per worker rather than the wage rate as a predic-
tor of labour income. Given the rate of growth of income (as discussed in section (i) of this part), the trend of average earnings
will be determined by the rate of growth of labour supply in this
sector and the latter in its turn will be a function of the rate of
migration from the rural to the urban informal sector. The simple
theory of migration would suggest that migrants will come into the
sector until average earnings in the sector fall to the level of the
alternative income of migrants in the rural sector. The prediction
here is that the rate of growth of earnings in the urban U sector
will equal that of the agricultural (or rural traditional) sector.[1]

But when we are considering an urban economy with two distinct
subsectors, the simple theory of migration has to be modified to
take into account the fact that migrants respond not only to average
earnings in the U sector but also to the wage level and the probability of obtaining employment in the O sector. The results with such
a migration function are much more complicated and are worked out in
Mazumdar (1975). A short summary of the model is given in the
Appendix to this paper. The conclusion arrived at is that with the
most likely behaviour of income growth in the urban subsectors - the
rate of growth of income in the U sector being somewhat less than
that in the O sector - the rate of increase of average earnings in
the U sector, in equilibrium, will be lower than that in agriculture.
If the alternative income in agriculture is constant, U-sector earnings will decline over time. The intuitive argument for this result
could run as follows.

The rate of growth of labour supply to the urban U sector (ℓ)
will be a weighted average of the rate of growth of labour demand in
the U sector (σ) and the rate of growth of the wage bill in the O
sector ($\gamma+v$).[2] With σ being less than ($\gamma+v$), ℓ will lie between
these two values. Thus the supply of labour increases in the U sec-
tor at a rate higher than the demand ($\ell > \sigma$), and the average earnings
in the sector fall relative to the alternative income in agriculture.

Even if there is equilibrium growth in the urban economy with
the rate of growth of income equalised in the two subsectors, there
will be a tendency for U-sector earnings to decline, given the constancy of the alternative income of the migrants in agriculture.
This is because if $\ell < \gamma$ (which it will be in this case), the proportion of jobseekers in the urban area who get absorbed in the O sector falls over time, and more of them will be left to share in the
available employment and income in the U sector.

The predictions of the model of the urban economy discussed in
this part can now be summarised:

(a) The rate of growth of income in the U sector is dependent on
     the growth rate of income in the O sector, but can be expected
     to generally lag behind it to some extent.

---

[1] The assumption is that there is no marked change in the distribution of earnings in either sector.

[2] Cf. section (i) above.

(b) The rate of growth of labour productivity and wages in the O
     sector are very high, leaving the (residual) rate of employment
     growth in the O sector to be quite modest.

(c) The rate of growth of earnings in the U sector will lag behind
     that of average income in the rural traditional sector.

It is a picture of a widening disparity of income in the urban
economy, even with the working classes.

This model offers a framework for focusing attention on some
important issues in the development of the urban economy in LDCs
and on the variables affecting them.   National accounts data could
be organised to give the split between the urban subsectors, in
addition to the rural-urban split which already exists in the statistics of many countries.   The rate of growth of employment, value
added and wages over a period of time in the three sectors would be
important additions to our knowledge about the economy concerned,
whether or not they bear out the predictions of the model as outlined above.

REFERENCES

Harberger, Arnold G. (1971): "On the Social Opportunity Cost of
    Labour", in International Labour Review, Vol. 103, pp. 559-79.

Harris J. (1971): "Wage Rate Determination with Limited Supplies
    of Labour in Developing Countries", in Journal of Development
    Studies, Jan. 1971, pp. 198-200.

Joshi, Vijay and Hether (1975): "The Unorganised Sector of Bombay
    City", unpublished typescript.

Liebenstein, Harvey G. (1957): "The Theory of Underemployment in
    Backward Economies", in Journal of Political Economy, Vol. 65,
    pp. 91-103.

Mazumdar, D. (1959a): "The Marginal Productivity Theory of Wages
    and Disguised Unemployment", in Review of Economic Studies,
    Vol. 26, pp. 190-97.

_____, (1959b), "Underemployment in Agriculture and the Industrial
Wage Rate", in Economica, Vol. 26, pp. 328-40.

_____, (1973), "Labour Supply in Early Industrialisation: The
Case of the Bombay Textile Industry", in Economic History
Review, Vol. 26, pp. 477-96.

_____, (1974), "The Urban Informal Sector", in IBRD Mimeo, Oct.
1974.

_____, (1975), "The Theory of Urban Underemployment in Less
Developed Countries", in IBRD Mimeo, Jan. 1975.

Merrick (1975): "Employment and Earnings in the Informal Sector in Brazil", forthcoming in Journal of Developing Areas.

Nelson, R.R.: "A 'Diffusion' Model of International Productivity Differences in Manufacturing Industry", in American Economic Review, Vol. 58, pp. 1219-48.

Pettie, Lisa (1974): "The Informal Sector - A Few Comments from Bogota, Working Draft", Department of Labour Studies and Planning, Massachusetts Institute of Technology.

APPENDIX

A model of wage gap underemployment

In this section we shall build a model of the urban labour market with two sectors. Wages in the organised sector are held at a high level by institutional forces, and a certain proportion of the urban labour force are able to obtain employment in this sector. Those who are not accommodated in this sector are not totally unemployed but become potentially available to the urban unorganised sector, irrespective of source - whether they are old members of the urban labour force, fresh entrants through natural growth of the settled urban population or new migrants from the rural areas. It is assumed that employment in the unorganised sector is less than full time, and hence participation in this sector can be carried out simultaneously with the search for a job in the organised sector.

The most important component of the labour force found in the unorganised sector would be the self-employed. With free entry we can make the extreme assumption that the total income generated in the sector gets distributed equally among the workers in this sector. In order to make the mechanism behind this assumption a bit more explicit, and also to ensure that the formulation is applicable additionally to the case of casual daily workers (another important component of the unorganised sector in some markets), we can think of the average income of a self-employed as being the product of two terms: (i) the "net value" produced by him on average from a day's work (call it Wu); and (ii) the number of days of work secured by him over a period of time (call it Nu).

We assume that the labour market of the sector behaves like a perfect casual market and all workers are of equal endowment. Every worker then has an equal probability of getting a day's work as every other worker in the sector, so that over a period of time the available number of days of work gets equally shared out among the labour force in this sector. The degree of underemployment in the sector varies with the ratio of jobs available to the number of jobseekers in the market. It is recognised that, for the self-employed, the "output" from a day's work will vary from day to day but, in this case also, if employment is randomly distributed among the jobseekers, good days will be distributed with bad days equally for everybody, and the "net value" produced for a day's work will average out to be the same for everybody if the market works perfectly, and if labour is homogeneous. In the rest of the paper, Wu is referred to, for simplicity, as the unorganised sector's daily "wage".[1]

---

[1] This setting of the problem covers the case of wage labour hired on a daily basis in the urban casual labour market. Wu then is determined by the disutility price of a day's labour.

Assuming that the rural population is sufficiently large so that outmigration does not have a significant effect on rural wages and working conditions, we can set up a function relating the net flow of rural-urban migrants to the expected urban wage:

$$S_{mt} = f(Ew). \qquad \qquad \dots\dots (1)$$

The function is general enough to take care of transport and other psychological costs of migration as well as the alternative income foregone.

The expected urban wage, in turn, depends on the probabilities P_o and P_u respectively of getting jobs in the organised sector at wage W_o and in the unorganised sector at wage W_u. For simplicity of exposition, we consider only a one-period model, i.e. the migrants' decision is based on the time horizon of one period only:[1]

$$Ew = P_o W_o + P_u W_u. \qquad \qquad \dots\dots (2)$$

Define $U_t = N_{T,t-1} + S_{mt} + G_t,$

where $N_{T,t-1}$ is total unorganised sector labour supply at the end of period $t-1$ and G_t is the growth of the settled urban labour force through natural growth

N_o = the number employed in the organised sector

N_u = the number of days of employment available in the unorganised sector.

Then on the assumption that hiring is random, on a daily basis, in the unorganised sector, and for new jobs opening up in the organised sector, we have:

$$P_o = \frac{\Delta N_o}{U_t} \qquad \qquad \dots\dots (3)$$

and

$$P_u = \frac{N_{u,t-1} + \Delta N_u}{U_t}. \qquad \qquad \dots\dots (4)$$

---

[1] With a multi-period time horizon, the expected wage will be present values and we should use sequential probabilities for the migrant breaking into the organised sector. The author has worked out a model on these lines, but it is omitted because of consideration of space, particularly since it does not seem to add anything of substance. It could be made available to anyone interested.

The equations (1)-(4) are sufficient to determine the values of the four unknowns, S_{mt}, Ew, P_o and P_u. In the particular case in which the supply price of migrants to the urban area is given, i.e. if the migration curve is highly elastic, Ew is determined. Since ΔN_o and ΔN_u are exogenous (although, as we shall see, related to each other) the only variable to equilibrate the system is S_{mt} generating on both P_o and P_u.

The average earnings of workers in the unorganised sector will be given by:

$$Eu = \frac{P_u W_u}{1-P_o}. \qquad \dots \dots (5)$$

(Note that P_o and P_u do not add to unity.)

The equation (5) helps us to see how the phenomenon of low earnings in the urban unorganised sector arises as a direct consequence of a wage gap between the rural and the urban organised sectors. Putting $W_o = LE_w$ we have from equation (2):

$$Ew = \frac{P_u W_u}{1-P_o L}. \qquad \dots \dots (2a)$$

Comparing (2a) and (5) it is seen that the marginal supply price of migrants (Ew) is equal to the average earnings in the unorganised sector if L equals unity, i.e. there is no rural-urban wage gap. If L > 1, the average earnings are lower than the migrant's supply price. Migrants, in other words, are willing to incur a loss in the period of search because of the probability of gaining from the wage differential if they manage to break into the organised sector. This case of low earnings in the urban unorganised sector, associated with a significant rural-urban wage gap, has to be distinguished from another case, to be identified in section III, in which average earnings in the unorganised sector, although lower than the organised sector wage, are not below the supply price of temporary migrants.

The working of the model

We are now in a position to see how the model works over time. We make the following assumptions about the behaviour of wages/earnings in the different sectors:

(1)   The wage rate in the organised sector increases at the same rate as labour productivity in this sector (v). Institutional factors - trade unions or government legislation - ensure that the share of the labourer's income in this sector remains constant in spite of the conditions of labour supply in the labour market as a whole.

(2) The "wage" in the U sector - the net value produced by a day's work - remains constant at Wu. We have already argued that the rate of growth of labour productivity in the sector can be expected to be small.

(3) The marginal supply price of migrants from the rural sector (Ew) is unchanged over time. This assumption is made only for the simplification of the analysis which helps us to determine the course of the urban U-sector earnings relative to that of the rural sector.

The first two assumptions can be incorporated in the equation determining the supply of labour to the urban market by rewriting equation (2) as the following, using (3) and (4):

$$Ew^u(t) = \gamma N_o(1)W_o(1)e^{(\gamma+v)t} + W_u(1)N_u(1)e^{\sigma t}. \qquad \ldots \ldots (2b)$$

This equation says that the percentage rate of growth and labour supply in the urban labour market as a whole - call it ℓ - is a weighted average of the proportionate rate of growth of wage bill in the organised sector $(\gamma+v)$, and of labour demand in the unorganised sector σ.

Labour supply to the urban market being given by (2b), we can study the course of development of the labour market over time by taking the logarithmic differentials of equations (2), (3) and (5). Thus from (3), setting ΔNo equal to γNo, we have:

$$\frac{dPo}{Po} = \frac{dNo}{No} - \frac{dU}{U} = \gamma - \ell. \qquad \ldots \ldots (3^*)$$

From (2), with $d(Ew)/Ew$ constrained to zero:

$$\frac{dWo}{Wo} = -\frac{dPo}{dP} - \frac{dPU}{Pu}\left(\frac{PuWu}{PoWo}\right). \qquad \ldots \ldots (2^*)$$

or

$$\frac{dPu}{Pu}\left(\frac{PuWu}{PoWo}\right) = \ell - (\gamma+v), \qquad \ldots \ldots (2^*a)$$

using (3^*), and remembering that the percentage rate of increase of Wo is equal to that of labour productivity v.

From (5):

$$\frac{dEu}{Eu} = \frac{d\ Pu}{Pu} + \frac{d\ Po}{Po}\frac{Po}{1-Po}. \qquad \ldots \ldots (5^*)$$

The three equations (3^*), (2^*a) and (5^*) help us to classify the possible cases of labour market trends depending on the values of σ, γ and v.

If we have the equilibrium in the urban market as discussed in the text, we have $\sigma = \gamma+v = \ell$. Thus P_u remains constant, but P_o falls over time. Hence E_u declines.

It was suggested that marginal propensities to consume U-sector goods may fall over time, in which case we have $\sigma < \gamma+v$. Thus we will have $\gamma+v > \ell\sigma$. Hence P_u declines over time, and unless v is large P_o will also decline $(\gamma > \ell)$ reinforcing the downward trend in E_u. In the alternative case γ when v is not too small, $\gamma < \ell$ and P_o increases. But it can be shown that in this case E_u declines, even though P_u and P_o have opposite effects on the course of earnings.[1]

The conclusion is that with the alternative rural income remaining constant, within the migration function as postulated in the model, we will get a declining trend in earnings in the urban U sector, at the same time as wages in the O sector are increasing.

Urban workers and patterns of employment

by
Guy Standing,
Churchill College, Cambridge;

World Employment Programme,
International Labour Office

For many years development models have been dualistic in design despite the everyday observation that both the rural (subsistence) and urban (or modern) sectors can be divided into a number of distinct subsectors, the behavioural and productive characteristics of which differ significantly.

All this seems to have changed with the "discovery" of what has been loosely described as the informal sector in which the Singer-Jolly team placed so much faith in their analysis of Kenyan employment problems, despite the fact that the mission made no real analysis of the informal sector as such.   Moreover, since the work of Keith Hart - work which might be described as seminal were the literature on, say, British labour history not replete with similar observations - nobody has adequately conceptualised the sectoral distribution of the labour force, let alone traced the patterns of interaction between the various sectors.[1]

As far as the informal sector is concerned - however it is defined - the issue to be resolved by planners is the extent to which it is a potential dynamic growth point for employment-led development as opposed to a residual, underemployment-rife pool of surplus labour.   On this the ILO-Sussex team sent to Kenya had few doubts.   In their long report they asserted confidently:

> Informal economic activity - though often not formally recognised, and in some cases (particularly in Nairobi) restricted and actively discouraged - is often economically efficient, productive and creative.   In such activity people practise a variety of modern trades and crafts, just as in the formal sector, but without the formal sector's protection from competition or its favoured access to credit and sophisticated technology.[2]

Later they claimed:

> The sector can be a source of future growth as an integral part of an employment strategy.[3]

On that premise they recommended, in essence, a policy of laissez-faire towards the informal sector, while among their more specific proposals they suggested there should be no more slum clearance. There is something rather Canute-ish or perhaps merely desperate about such a strategy but, more relevantly in the present context, the composition of the informal sector was left somewhat vague.

The typology of sectors set out in this paper attempts to treat the informal sector less broadly than is suggested by Hart, whose work in Ghana inspired the ILO-Sussex mission to Kenya.   He distinguished formal from informal income opportunities, the latter

---

[1] Since writing this paper I have come across a recent article by John Friedmann and Flora Sullivan which to some degree rectifies this situation and in certain respects takes a similar line to the present paper.   See J. Friedmann and F. Sullivan: "The absorption of labour in urban economy", in Economic Development and Cultural Change, Vol. 22, No. 3, Apr. 1974, pp. 385-413.

[2] ILO: Employment incomes and equality: A strategy for increasing productive employment in Kenya, Geneva, 1972, p. 51. Emphasis added.

[3] ibid.

effectively encompassing all non-wage sources of income, whether legitimate or illegitimate.[1]   In effect, as defined by Hart, the informal sector is a highly heterogeneous grouping which, to be analytically useful, needs to be subdivided, otherwise one is forced into an ambivalent position.   In his recent interesting work on Calcutta, Harold Lubell commented:

> The informal sector constitutes the residual labour market of last resort, which persons enter as self-employed, low-income producers of marginal goods and services for lack of any other means of earning a livelihood.

He then covered his options by adding:

> In metropolitan Calcutta, it is also a reservoir of traditional and modern skills which can be made productive if effective demand for them is created.[2]

The question remains as to whether the informal sector is a residual or a reservoir.   If the informal sector is defined as every activity connected with economic survival that is not wage employment, it is neither a very novel nor a very useful concept: it is merely a fancy name for a host of disparate phenomena.

However, if the informal sector needs to be subdivided to become analytically useful, the other identified segment of the urban economy, the formal sector, is scarcely less heterogeneous. In fact, if the urban labour market is to be divided into sectors, the present dichotomous model should probably be discarded for a more finely divided spectrum of sectors.   This may mean that the whole sectoral approach would be open to the criticism that there is a continuum and that therefore the concept of an informal sector becomes redundant.   But this need not be the case if the conceptual distinctions facilitate a policy-oriented discussion of, say, the dynamic interaction between the several sectors and the changes that could be expected to follow specific developments.

So although empirically the dividing line may be hard or prac- tically impossible to determine, in a sectoral schema we can ident- ify a formal sector, which is subdivided into a core and a periphery; an informal sector;   and an irregular stagnant sector, which includes the scuffling unemployed and various fringe groups such as "criminals", beggars and the like.

In the urban areas the core of the formal sector is character- ised by wage and salary earners in private and public employment of a regular standardised type.   In the peripheral formal sector, labour is paid by capital, in that workers are working for an employer, often on a subcontracting basis, but the temporal alloca- tion of work time is often left to the worker and, sometimes, his family or other assistants.   This is akin to the great putting-out industries of the eighteenth- and nineteenth-century Industrial

---

[1] K. Hart: "Informal income opportunities and urban employment in Ghana", in Journal of Modern African Studies, Vol. 11, No. 1, Feb. 1973, p. 73.   "The distinction between formal and informal income opportunities is based essentially on that between wage earn- ing and self-employment."

[2] H. Lubell: "Urban development and employment in Calcutta", in International Labour Review, Vol. 109, No. 1, July 1973, p. 28.

Revolution in England and encompasses contract and task work of various types. Historically, this sector proved a vital contributor to the process of capital accumulation, fueling the expansion of the core formal sector. But in many underdeveloped countries today it has tended to be both weak and small.

The informal sector is characterised by the fact that, for the most part, work is neither paid nor regulated by capital, while the worker's allocation of his, or the family's, work time is almost entirely discretionary and is thereby akin to the traditional "natural rhythm" of rural life. The informal sector has much in common with Chayanov's peasant mode of production in which "the whole activity of the family unit" is determined not by expected net profitability but by "the internal economic confrontation of subjective evaluations".[1] To Chayanov the quantity of labour units supplied by the peasant household during the course of a year reflects the family's "degree of self-exploitation" which "is determined by a peculiar equilibrium between family demand satisfaction and the drudgery of labour itself".[2] But as will emerge in the ensuing discussion, the informal sector is by no means completely analogous to Chayanov's peasant model.

The informal sector consists of a variety of distinctive groups and should be clearly separated from the irregular stagnant sector "employment", which is unstructured and based on daily survival; it is unmistakably a residual.

In the following paragraphs some of the principal characteristics and behavioural patterns within each sector will be outlined, and the nature of the interactions between the sectors explored, paying particular attention to the viability of a strategy of expanding the informal sector as a means of combating urban unemployment and related employment problems.

THE FORMAL SECTOR

Within the formal sector the prestige, pacesetting jobs are found in the core, which tends to be what Mamalakis has called the dominant sector. In the productive part of the core, often dominated by multinational foreign-owned firms, the usually highly capital-intensive technology means that labour productivity is high and rising relatively rapidly. As trade unions usually flourish in such firms, wages tend to be high and to rise broadly in line with productivity growth.[3] At the same time, wage rates

---

[1] A.V. Chayanov: "The theory of peasant economy", edited by D. Thorner, B. Kerblay and R.E.F. Smith, 1966, p. 7.

[2] ibid., p. 5.

[3] Although the direction of causation has not been demonstrated, on some occasions institutionally determined wage increases may lead to a rise in productivity and sometimes vice versa. The increase in worker incomes may exceed productivity growth in so far as the core sector is subsidised by income transfers from other sectors.

are set with an eye to attracting a particular type of worker, one
who is not umbilically tied to the informal sector or rural peasan-
try and who can therefore be regarded as likely to be more indus-
trially stable.[1]   The remaining part of the formal sector core
consists mostly of government employment which, being on a par with
the private formal sector in terms of prestige, tends to adapt its
wages to those prevailing in the high-productivity segment of the
core.   As Lloyd Reynolds noted: "Government is expected to be a
'good employer' and even to function as a wage leader for the
economy."[2]

In the peripheral formal sector, product and labour markets
tend to be much more competitive.   While product prices may differ
only a little, except in so far as they are set to reflect lower-
quality goods and services, wage levels and fringe benefits tend
to be lower in the periphery than in the core, thus intensifying
the tendency for high-quality workers to gravitate towards the
core.   Indeed this tendency is such that it is not uncommon to
find skilled workers demanding a wage premium from employers for
working in what they consider a peripheral enterprise to compensate
for the greater degree of job insecurity or the lower status
attached to working for such a firm.   Moreover, although wage
levels and fringe benefits tend to be lower in the periphery, there
nevertheless exists a close relationship between the respective
wage structures, whereby productivity growth in the private core
sector raises worker earnings there which, in turn, pulls wages up
in the public and peripheral segments of the formal sector.   So,
in the main, wages are not determined by competitive market forces
but by institutional factors that include considerations of status,
custom, trade union strength in the core firms, institutionalised
qualifications in those firms, and consumption expectations.

Compared with the peripheral formal sector, the core has a
more clearly defined and developed division of labour based not so
much on ascriptive roles as on economic criteria.   Yet jobs in
peripheral firms tend to be more progressive than in the core formal sector, where a surprisingly large proportion are essentially
static jobs - coinciding with a proliferation of job titles and
pseudo-grades, as well as with numerous ports of entry into employment.   By "progressive" is meant not "better" in the sense of
involving higher productivity or socio-economic status - on the
contrary, many "static" jobs are high-productivity, high-wage and
high-status jobs - but jobs in which a worker can increase skills,
productivity and responsibilities with experience on the job.
Correspondingly, static jobs are those that do not involve broad
skill acquisition in this way.   A man working in the periphery or,
for that matter, in the informal sector tends to have greater
opportunities to learn and apply a broad range of skills and related knowledge than many workers in core formal employment.   Even
in senior grades of management in the private sector core the nature

---

[1] On this and related questions see Guy Standing and
Koji Taira: "Labour market effects of multinational enterprises",
in Nebraska Journal of Economics and Business, Vol. 12, No. 4,
Autumn 1973.

[2] L.G. Reynolds: "Economic development with surplus labour:
Some complications", in Oxford Economic Papers, Vol. 21, No. 1,
Mar. 1969, p. 95.

of the work has been increasingly static.   Thus, local managers
of affiliate companies of multinational enterprises are often
mere recipients of systems-programmes decided for them by the
parent company's board of directors, who expect them to concentrate on the relatively mundane practical implementation of pre-
determined policies without their having the opportunity to
develop either their own or their assistants' entrepreneurial
potential.   With the paucity of visible entrepreneurial expertise
in many underdeveloped economies, it is probable that the bureau-
cratic structure of employment in the formal sector core, geared
as it is to attract the best available manpower, effectively
stifles the capacity of indigenous entrepreneurship.   It is not
so much the wage rate that attracts the best labour, nor even the
status connected with working in a certain type of establishment,
though both these are important.   The greatest attraction of
core employment is its reliability and income regularity.   This
relative security not only helps concentrate the most efficient
workers in core establishments but deters many workers from
independent entrepreneurial activity, with all its attendant risks.

        The peripheral formal sector has none of the institutional
safeguards of the core sector.   Employment and earnings tend to
be much more erratic, and casual labour is used extensively.
Whereas in the core skills are often institutionally acquired off
the job, in the periphery those skills that are needed are
commonly learnt on the job, and when employers attempt to do otherwise, and even when they train workers themselves, they are unable
to prevent their newly trained labour from being poached by core
employers.   In addition, most wage workers in the periphery not
only receive low wages but are expected to work long working days.
This is partly because peripheral employers are forced to respond
to the cost and competitive pressures exerted by the presence of
the technologically superior core formal sector by increasing the
intensity of work, notably in sweat-shops or their equivalent.
It is also due to the fact that, in many peripheral enterprises,
relatively primitive techniques are kept going by cheap labour in
the form of women and children and casual labour, producing a low
and uncertain quality product.

THE IRREGULAR SECTOR - "THE STREET ECONOMY"

        The irregular, or stagnant-opportunistic, sector consists of
those involved in a variety of legitimate low-status fringe activities, notably begging, begging with favours, and various forms
of casual labour (e.g. gardening, car-washing, leaf-raking and the
like), as well as the full range of illegitimate-criminal activities.   As such, it encompasses the open unemployed who, in the
absence of unemployment benefits, invariably spend a portion of
their time in one or more of the fringe pursuits of the irregular
sector, a fact incidentally which does not mean they should not be
described as unemployed.   If you ask a man raking leaves about
his employment status he will tell you he is unemployed but is
obtaining the price of a meal.   In effect, irregular sector activities are an alternative to more systematic unemployment benefits.

        The "labour" of those in the irregular sector is non-
productive in the classical sense of the term and no increase in
effective demand can transform their pursuits into productive

activities because their "labour" is revenue-consuming. As a
rule, incomes in the irregular sector are trifling, consisting
largely of transfer payments enabling those trapped in the sector
to eke out a subsistence existence of sorts.[1] The term "trapped"
is valid, of course, for once inside this sector it becomes cumu-
latively harder to effect as escape. The ability to perform
regular sustained work tends to evaporate through lack of use,
and the poor diet and medical treatment available to those in the
irregular sector tend to undermine their physical and mental
capacity to do sustained work. Finally, those in the irregular
sector develop behavioural traits inimical to regular employment.
Rejected, they adopt the ways and means of rejects. And by mix-
ing with those who have become unemployable others also degener-
ate towards that state. Irregularly occupied, they lose their
sense of time, an attribute which is essential for successful
assimilation into the mainstream labour force.

In essence, irregular sector activities are unstructured and
non-productive, and whereas informal sector activities can facilitate primary capital accumulation the potential for this in the
irregular sector is non-existent. It is also likely that, faced
with a fall in the aggregate demand for labour in the formal sector, the irregular sector will tend to mushroom, and in particular
the elasticity of supply of criminal participants with respect to
changes in the "employment rate" is considerable. However, the
relationship between the size of the irregular sector and the
"employment rate" in the informal sector is not clear cut. A
decline in the "employment rate" due to a sectoral shift in output,
and/or a relative suppression of the formal sector, in itself might
increase income opportunities in the informal sector and thus attract
a certain proportion of the irregular sector participants into informal activities. This possibility highlights the need to explore
the patterns of interaction in considerable detail empirically.

The irregular sector is in fact endemic in all industrialising capitalist economies as it was in the nineteenth century in
Britain and elsewhere. Thus Marx succinctly classified the relative surplus population under eight headings: (i) the unemployed;
(ii) the partially unemployed; (iii) displaced workers of middle
age or more who, despite having a skill, were forced to join "the
ranks of the supernumeraries"; (iv) migrants displaced by capitalist production in agriculture; (v) the "stagnant" sector which
"forms a part of the active labour army, but with extremely
irregular employment"; (vi) paupers, the "dangerous classes" made
up of (a) those able to work, (b) orphans, etc., (c) "the demoral-
ised and ragged, and those unable to work, chiefly people who
succumb to their incapacity for adaption, due to the division of
labour"; (vii) the aged; and (viii) the "victims of industry".[2]
These comprise the irregular sector.

---

[1] Admittedly, in return, the effort price of "labour" tends
to be relatively small, which is important in tropical conditions.

[2] Karl Marx: Capital, Moscow, 1961 edition, Vol. 1,
pp. 641-44.

THE INFORMAL SECTOR

The informal sector (IS) consists of small-scale, non-wage economic activities commonly done by family concerns. But although the operations of IS work units are not dependent on wage labour, they sometimes hire workers, not only to meet peak demand but even when the amount of work to be done would not occupy the family workforce to anything like its full capacity. However, in the main, informal sector work units are structured according to ascriptive principles in that tasks and responsibilities are assigned to various members of the family according to their relationship to the family head. Though the internal structure of jobs is minimal in most cases there is a tendency, where the nature and size of the trade permit it, for the job structure to be vertically integrated (i.e. skills and responsibilities grow with age and experience in the business). When the informal sector is a dynamic one, as arguably was the case in Britain's Industrial Revolution in the eighteenth century, skill accumulates with on-the-job experience and is passed on inter-generationally. But in many underdeveloped countries, the informal sector has not been dynamic in this sense.

Activities undertaken within the informal sector tend to be risky, while the demand for the sector's output is characterised by severe uncertainty. Yet the extent of market competition is tempered by a number of institutional and socio-economic factors. For instance, one such constraint is the pressure often put on participants to conform to certain established norms. But perhaps a more important factor, one intending to limit the supply of competitors, is the very low status which many of the livelihoods in the informal sector entail.

In Kingston the informal sector dominates certain well-defined areas where there are numerous little shacks of wood and corrugated metal. Many of the stalls or workshops have sprung up as a result of squatting, although some spots have been inherited or rented. From these, men and women sell beer and fruit above everything else, though the streets are dotted with welding signs, shoemakers, bars, woodworkers and dressmakers. Although no official data have been collected, their income varies enormously and the distribution seems highly skewed. With an open unemployment rate of over 20 per cent, it might seem strange that new entrants to the informal sector do not rush in, given the attractive average income. Partly this is due to the licensing system, although this is almost certainly a minor reason. A second factor is locational, for the potential IS participant would probably not be able to set up his stall or workshop in a spot "where the action is". He or she would have to start up down the road where relatively few people are likely to stop or walk. What this means is that the potential entrant to a specific trade often has to consider not the average income but the income earned by the marginal traders. Even so, these market factors only partially explain the restrained competition. Part of the explanation lies in the considerable stigma, particularly among the young, attached to IS activities, notably traditional own-account pursuits. This was nicely summed up for me by an unemployed man in his twenties when I asked him why he did not try using his skills in self-employment. He looked at me almost incredulously and said: "Man, I want a job, not a work".

Usually profits or earnings earned by informal sector
participants are quite small, but it is a moot point whether they
aim at a high volume of business and turnover with a low profit
margin or a smaller volume with a higher per unit margin of profit.   From discussion with higglers in the outskirts of Kingston,
the latter principle seems to hold for them, in large part because
of the relatively high cost of transport and the perishable nature
of their goods.   Sidney Mintz, the anthropologist, argued some
years ago that Haiti market women sought to achieve a rapid turnover on the basis of the marketing precept to "keep capital working", but if transport costs are high and if goods are highly
perishable higglers may readily adopt a strategy that keeps the
volume of working capital to a minimum.   So the desire for a
rapid turnover does not necessarily entail low margins.   On the
other hand, in some trade-service activities the need to corner
a personal clientele induces the trader to operate on very low
margins, initially at least.

There tends to be a low income elasticity of demand for
informal sector products and services and, in many cases, they
are inferior, or Giffen, goods.   Investment tends to be small or
insignificant, partly because the typical IS participant is motivated by a "survival algorithm" rather than by any form of profit
maximisation.   Lacking wealth, he is a risk averter because any
bad decision is likely to spell disaster, and in the informal
urban sector, as among peasant farmers, "risk premium is an
increasing function of risk and a decreasing function of assets".[1]
But in emphasising the risk aversion propensities, it should not
be overlooked that some entrants to the IS are risk takers.   A
typical representative of this group may begin his career by working for wages for a while, then with his savings set up business,
risking almost everything.   The likelihood of someone doing this
is greater if the risk is reasonably low, which it is if he can
always return to wage employment if necessary.   However, if there
is chronically high unemployment, and if wage employment opportunities are an increasing function of wage employment experience, the
chances of re-employment are slim and, partly for reasons of age,
skill obsolescence, and loss of contacts, get slimmer with the
passage of time.

Directly related to this is the question of the route of entry
to the informal sector: are people driven into it out of despera-
tion, in which case they would most likely remain conservative risk
averters?   Or do they deliberately opt for the IS to maintain a
degree of autonomy as nascent entrepreneurs, in which case they
would more likely be risk takers?   In Kingston, risk-averting
tendencies have predominated, as has been explicitly recognised by
government planners who have tried to overcome this inclination by
attempting to reduce and collectivise the risk element by such
means as a Small Business Load Board and a medley of extension services, including training facilities and informational and advis-
ory services.   One of the problems with any such programme is
that limited success almost earmarks workers for recruitment by
formal sector enterprises.   But there is also a fairly pervasive
pressure to conform, which deters potential innovators;   an inno-
vator can become an outsider likely to forfeit some of the
community and informal social security benefits.

---

[1] Michael Lipton: "The theory of the optimising peasant", in
Journal of Development Studies, Apr. 1968.

Labour productivity and the intensity of work both tend to be
low, and although IS participants tend to be on the job for long
periods, or at least available in the immediate vicinity, they typically work a relatively small proportion of those hours.   Essentially, therefore, their livelihood is time extensive but not work
intensive.   Correspondingly, work patterns tend to be highly flexible, making the distinction between work and leisure time even more
problematic than it is in a highly industrialised environment.   If
you ask an independent artisan how long he works you are likely to
get the dusty response: "I am here whenever I need to be, and I work
however long it is necessary".   Similarly, many IS workers spend a
lot of time working to get work, partly because market informational
processes are so inadequately developed.

To the extent that IS participants are not merely bent on daily
survival, the family-based business and productive units tend to follow a life-cycle pattern, with investment and saving taking place
during the early formative stages of the family's life cycle, reaching a peak fairly quickly, and then proceeding through a process of
disinvestment.[1]

There is little inter-generational growth within the informal
sector because high-status and income opportunities are perceived to
be in the formal sector where incomes take on an aura of reliability
so valued by most workers, especially those geared to a credit-based
pattern of consumption.   It is often the lifetime goal of the informal sector family to get the children up the social scale, which means
into wage and salary employment in the formal sector.   For this
reason, the older generation will usually make no attempt to pass on
their skills but will instead encourage in their offspring those
traits which they consider to be essential for successful assimilation
into the formal sector.   For their part, the young often make little
effort to learn their parents' skills, seeing them as outmoded and
even contemptible, a tendency accentuated by the nature of modern formal education.

In certain respects, the life-cycle pattern exhibited by the
informal sector is analogous to Chayanov's peasant mode of production.
But whereas in peasant farming the process of disintegration, which
Chayanov not surprisingly attributed to demographic factors, produces
a self-perpetuating cyclical pattern, in the informal urban sector the
disintegration process takes two forms: those families that are relatively successful in the informal sector push their children into the
orbit of the formal sector, while those who are not successful tend to
sink into the irregular stagnant sector.   Either way, and this is
another interesting parallel with Chayanov's peasant mode of production, there is rarely a cumulative process of petty capitalist accumulation.

For this reason, inter alia, there is little long-run growth in
the demand for labour in the informal sector.   Whereas much of the
investment that does take place is geared to shift the family out of
the informal sector, the propensity to consume is extremely high, a
fact which serves to indicate that informal sector enterprises tend

---

[1] An important investment in the IS is the development of contacts and the securing of supply lines, a set of activities that
accounts for a large significant proportion of work effort and time.
Disinvestment involves not renewing such supply lines, or not
replacing those that are lost, not making repairs, or not replacing
worn-out equipment.

not to be geared to any long-run growth path.   Unfortunately for income/employment generation in the informal sector through multiplier effects, this propensity to consume is in turn geared to formal sector goods and services, often to imports.

Although there are certain generalisations that can be made about any particular sector, the informal sector contains a number of subgroups with individual, clearly distinguishable characteristics. The first of these - perhaps the most important of all - consists of those workers or work families who spread their risks by devoting time to a number of different work activities at the same time or over a period of time.   This multiple-activity work may involve several pursuits within the IS or it may involve wage labour and IS work.   Many people living in underdeveloped economies, both in rural and urban areas, combine IS activities with wage employment, sometimes splitting the working week or day between the two, sometimes over the year according to seasonal factors.   It is this probably more than anything else which produces the much-mooted instability of the labour supply to the formal sector, which in turn has contributed to the hastening of mechanisation and the resultant growth in open unemployment.   Census data give little or no information that might suggest how large a proportion of the labour force this group represents, but it is substantial.   The interesting question is whether the participation in wage employment is discretionary or necessary for subsistence purposes.[1]

For many workers there are, in effect, opportunities for job and skill arbitrage.   But it is important to distinguish three categories of multiple activity workers.   There are those who scratch at this and scratch at that simultaneously because they are only able to survive by such a combination.   Then there are those who have to seek wage employment because they earn insufficient in their IS livelihood (or vice versa).   And finally there are those who build their second, or even third, activity on the basis of some limited success in the first.   In any case many workers attempt to possess a portfolio of jobs and skills, however rudimentary those skills might be, and it is patently unsatisfactory to look at occupational statistics and conclude, as many observers do, that such-and-such a percentage of the workforce is unskilled, such-and-such semi-skilled, and so on.

The first category of multiple-activity workers, the "scratchers", essentially belong to the irregular stagnant sector, while the last-mentioned group represents an important component of the informal sector, deserving more analysis than it has received hitherto.   Living in the shanty towns of underdeveloped countries, the IS unit tends to survive by serving an economically and geographically limited market. Trade is precarious, partly due to an unpredictable supply of inputs or demand for the product, partly because potential demand is so limited, and partly because there is always the possibility of an intruder, either through a new recruit to the IS or from more efficient competition from the formal sector.   In these circumstances, the IS worker who has initial success will tend to buy a labour-saving, quality-improving piece of equipment, such as a lathe, a deep freeze that can save time in trips to the wholesaler, sharper, newer knives, and so on.

---

[1] In Jamaica, ever since full emancipation from slavery in 1838, employers and landlords have acted in such a way as to make wage employment increasingly necessary.

Or he may hire wage labour or entice a rural relative to assist in the work even though the existing family labour force is not fully employed. But this means the worker, or work family, frees a portion of his work time which he can devote to another economic activity, often facilitated by the savings from the income gained from the initial activity. By getting established in one, albeit limited, enterprise the worker can afford to diversify into other types of work. So, interestingly, in certain not uncommon circumstances productivity in one activity is directly related to the income and production possibilities in the secondary or derivative activity.[1]

It is perhaps instructive to compare this situation with that depicted for rural households by Hymer and Resnick in their 1969 article in the AER.[2] In their model, rural sector households produce food (F) and non-agricultural goods and services (Z activities). Whether or not food is produced in market gardens or outside the urban areas by urban residents, this two-activity approach can easily be extended to fit the urban informal sector, with initial activities equivalent to F and derivative (or subsequent) activities equivalent to Z. But in their model, Hymer and Resnick assume the production possibility frontier is of the conventional textbook type. In fact, it is likely for many IS units that a greater production of F, whether in volume or value terms, will be associated with - or be a condition for, greater production, income or time spent in Z-type activities. Indeed there will probably be a threshold before which only F activities will occupy the work time of this category of worker.[3]

Why, it may be argued, does the IS participant not specialise? The answer is straightforward: specialisation is limited by the extent of the market. And with barriers to entry minimal, the IS can be highly competitive and risky if the worker family concentrates on one source of income. Moreover, many activities are subject to seasonal fluctuations, even in urban areas, which helps explain the number of workers with more than two activities in their work portfolio.

The common combinations of work activities in Kingston are probably typical of many urban areas in low-income countries. Often an IS worker, or family, will combine a work-intensive activity with a time-extensive one. Another typical case concerns the worker who possesses a relatively expensive piece of equipment (e.g. a truck) which he uses whenever the demand materialises while he does something quite different for most of the time. The types of combination are numerous, but because the demand for specific goods and services within the IS is limited and because relative success in one activity can facilitate entry into another there can be a concentration of "underemployments" in the IS rather than a great many people being underemployed in single well-defined activities.

---

[1] The main activity, in terms of work or income, may only be taken up once some sort of subsistence base (guaranteed source of income) has been secured, but thereafter the derivative activity may become the primary one.

[2] S. Hymer and S. Resnick: "A model of an agrarian economy with non-agricultural activities", in American Economic Review, Vol. LIX, No. 3, 1969, pp. 493-506.

[3] Certain inferior activities may be important in the work portfolio at some stage but drop out subsequently, either temporarily or permanently.

Whatever the activity mix, ignoring the multiple-activity nature of work can lead to thoroughly erroneous conclusions. For instance, suppose, by virtue of increased productivity in the F activity, the IS worker spends more time in Z activities and less in the F activity. Then if, as is almost invariably the case, researchers study the employment patterns in terms of a one-activity labour "supply" schedule, the higher income accruing to work in the F activity would be depicted in terms of a backward-bending supply curve. Similarly, the emphasis usually put on "main activity" in censuses and labour force surveys can produce all sorts of statistical inaccuracies, most notably through inflating the degree of underemployment.[1] This leads to an under-recording of national income, as well as an overestimate of growth rates due to shifts in the proportion of total output and employment out of the IS into the orbit of the FS.

Besides the multiple-activity worker, an equally important phenomenon consists of the household which has one or more members in, or trying to get into, the FS while one or more members ensure that the household can survive by working in the IS. In this case, the IS participant is usually the woman or women of the household, and it is often on them that families come to rely. This has a number of implications, including the possibility that the existence of IS livelihoods for women enables men to become openly unemployed, with all that that implies. But in addition, because women play such a prominent part in the IS and because they are forced to perform the role of standby workers, the number of women seeking income opportunities tends to result in severe overcrowding and competition that lowers the average earnings. As a result many women are forced into unemployment and irregular sector activities. At the same time, participation in the IS is highly conducive to high rates of fertility, as many IS activities (e.g. bazaar trading, dressmaking and pottery making) are compatible with the maternal set of tasks.[2]

---

[1] The Jamaican Labour Force Survey is illustrative. The single-answer questions are asked: "What kind of work do you do?" "In what kind of business or industry do you work?" And for the unemployed "available" for work: "What kind of job (main)?" Such questions tend to induce answers in terms of what the individual would like to be his main activity. He might work eight months in market gardening and four months as a wage-earning mason. But, because he perceives the latter to have a higher status he comes to regard that as his main activity. As a result, certain statistical illusions can emerge from the survey - for example, the occupational tables may be biased "upwards", and the occupational earnings biased "downwards".

[2] For evidence showing the relationship between type of work and fertility, see A.J. Jaffe and K. Azumi: "The birth rate and cottage industries in underdeveloped countries", in Economic Development and Cultural Change, Oct. 1960; A.O. Zarate: "Differential fertility in Monterrey, Mexico: Prelude to transition?" in Millbank Memorial Fund Quarterly, Apr. 1967, pp. 213-29; C.A. Miro and W. Mertens: "Influences affecting fertility in urban and rural Latin America", in Millbank Memorial Fund Quarterly, July 1968, pp. 89-117; R.M. Weller: "The employment of wives, role incompatibility and fertility", in Millbank Memorial Fund Quarterly, Oct. 1968, pp. 507-26.

Many women working in IS-type activities did not intend to be labour force participants but were forced into IS work by the chronic instability or insufficiency in the earnings of their husbands and/or sons. Many higglers in Kingston, for instance, are in this position. A question I have been investigating is whether this pattern of standby work implies that, if more formal sector employment was created, open unemployment would fall, not only because of the direct employment creation, plus multiplier effect, but because a proportion of these secondary workers would withdraw into economic inactivity. It seems quite likely that those effects would be more than offset by the attraction of more people into the labour force looking especially for FS jobs, in which case increasing employment could increase open unemployment. On the other hand, if the IS is stimulated, more women will probably enter the labour force, possibly choking off any reduction in urban unemployment. This is an area urgently requiring research if informal sector expansion is to be recommended.

Internal labour markets, ability utilisation and economic growth

by
Koji Taira,
University of Illinois

INTRODUCTION

The raison d'être of an efficient "internal labour market" (to be defined shortly) derives from its contribution to the profitability of the firm making use of it. The spread of such "internal labour markets" over the whole economy where they are relevant may also be socially beneficial by promoting an equitable utilisation of human resources and by reducing social tension and political unrest arising from iniquities in opportunities for work and in rewards for merit. When objective circumstances determined by technology, economic structure, income level, social custom and political aspirations warrant the desirability of "internal labour markets", the failure to promote and make use of them may hinder aspirations for further economic development.

The concept of "internal labour market" had long been implicit in the discussion of the "internal" wage structure within the firm. It was given an explicit formulation by Doeringer and Piore (1971). Although the Doeringer-Piore definition of the "internal labour market" emphasises "administrative rules and procedures" which govern "the pricing and allocation of labour" within the firm (pages 1-2), one may start with the simplest possible case in which an "internal labour market" can be said to exist and elaborate the variations of the case to the extent that criteria for economic efficiency are always fulfilled. It may be proposed therefore that an "internal labour market" exists in the firm where workers can change jobs internally, whether or not there are explicit administrative rules and procedures. To what extent these intra-firm job changes are administratively elaborated then becomes a separate question that forms a part of the larger question as to whether or not the internal labour market is efficient and rational.

Conditioned by the history of methodological controversy concerning the nature of labour markets in the United States of America, Doeringer and Piore liken their concept of "internal labour market" to such pre-existing notions as "industrial feudalism", "balkanisation of labour markets", and "property rights in a job" (page 2). By saying this, the authors generate an unfortunate impression of the internal labour market as an antithesis of economic efficiency or of rational business behaviour. It is, of course, strange for anyone who uses the word "market" and accepts or respects its implications to side with those avowedly anti-market notions which deny an autonomous role to the labour market as an allocator of human resources. However, Doeringer and Piore struggle hard to free themselves from the spell cast on them by the foes of markets. This is evident in their discussion of the rational process of labour market "internalisation" (pages 27-34) and their analysis of internal-external labour market articulation under changing circumstances (Chapter 5).

It is this question of efficiency and rationality of the internal labour market that this article is concerned with. The emphasis on this question does not imply that the internal labour markets in actual firms are rational or efficient. Quite the contrary. Many internal labour markets are often irrational as evidenced by nepotism, discrimination and segmentation among the firm's workforce. They are also inefficient in the sense that some workers are paid too much and others too little for what they are doing and what they are capable of doing in the future. A normative concern about efficiency criteria implies a practical desire to detect and remove their

violations. Policy implications emerging from this article
therefore have to do with efforts to improve the labour market
system as a whole on the one hand and the synchronisation of
internal and external labour markets on the other.[1]

WHY INTERNAL LABOUR MARKETS?

Historically, firms have discovered the usefulness of internal labour markets under the impact of changing circumstances that
offer an incentive for such arrangements, e.g., technological
change and economies of scale that create firm-specific jobs, the
costliness of dependence on "external" labour markets (like high
labour turnover rates and long waiting time for filling certain
vacancies), the rigidity of workforce commitment (as may be insis-
ted upon by strong trade unions), or public policy that tends to
raise the cost of employing a worker (like safety standards, social
security contributions, legal minimum wages, and other statutory
benefits). A rational internal labour market becomes a necessity
if only for neutralising the cost-raising effects of all these
environmental pressures. Internal labour markets have also arisen
from management's anticipations about these pressures. "Paternalism" is the word that has often been applied to management's anti-
cipatory action leading to the institution and improvement of an
internal labour market. This last point has enormous implications
for workforce management in the firms of less-developed countries
(LDCs).[2]

"Internal labour market" is not a mere alias for conventional
workforce management. It signifies that the efficiency criteria
for the market are observed in the recruitment, training, utilisation and retirement of all workers in such a way that the firm's
long-term profit objective is served more adequately. Therefore,
when there are efficient "external" labour markets which can supply
workers with appropriate skills needed by the firm, it violates the
efficiency criteria for the firm to rely entirely on the internal
training and recruitment for filling vacancies. This raises the
question of optimal articulation of internal with external labour
markets.

---

[1] It would have been inevitable that Doeringer or Piore should
eventually come to grapple with policy issues of this kind. See
especially Doeringer (1974).

[2] The "paternalism controversy" with respect of Japanese management is particularly relevant to the discussion of internal labour
markets. Two latest works in the stream of publications related
to this controversy are Dore (1973) and Okochi, Karsh and Levine
(1973). Recently, a few of my students at the Institute of Labor
and Industrial Relations, University of Illinois, have responded to
my call for the examination of paternalism in the light of the internal labour market concept in their seminar or tutorial papers.
Among these is the paper by Miss Sumalee Paveanbampen (1974). The
effect of paternalism on the "internalisation" of labour markets is
also discussed by Myrdal (1968, II, Ch. 23) and Chirayu Isarangkun
(1969). All this is also related to the "commitment controversy"
evaluated by Kannappan (1966).

Since empirical information of the realities of internal
labour markets is not abundant enough to permit generalisations,[1]
it may be regarded as premature to raise issues that bear upon the
efficiency of internal labour markets. But there are good reasons
to do so. In LDCs, there are already public services and large
firms that have personnel structures resembling internal labour
markets. The military service structure in particular, with its
extensively developed administrative rules and procedures governing
recruitment, training, promotion and retirement, almost looks like
a well-ordered internal labour market. It may well be that, but
whether it is also an _efficient_ internal labour market is surely
subject to debate. The military service structure is at best an
"imperfect" labour market, and market imperfections in this case
have far-reaching consequences on resource allocation inside and
outside the internal labour market in question. In other words,
how a given internal labour market meets the efficiency criteria is
an extremely important question, although it has so far been neglected in the literature on internal labour markets.

In LDCs, the notion that the market criteria can be applied to
the evaluation of the workforce structure probably enjoys a far
lower degree of ethical or philosophical legitimacy than in more
developed countries. Deep-seated suspicions are often expressed
about whatever is implied by "market". Especially, the workforce
structure is also a structure of relations among human beings who
are the managers and workers. The social custom that fashions how
human beings should relate to one another in a given society often
interferes with the efficiency of the workforce structure as an
organisation of human capabilities for economic objectives. Since
this interference is also a part of the total circumstances under
which production takes place, the analysis of internal labour markets would eventually have to pay attention to the optimum relations
between the job structure and inter-personal relations among those
who hold jobs.

THEORETICAL CONSIDERATIONS

The internal labour market can be justified with a minimum of
violence to the competitive framework. The theoretical firm in
conventional micro-economics has no internal labour market as distinct from the external. More correctly, internal and external
labour markets function as one unified labour market system. The

---

[1] In the last few years, I have been conducting intermittent
interviews with managers of large firms in developing Asian countries.
I have now formed serviceable impressions of internal labour markets
in the firms of Taiwan, Thailand and the Philippines. My knowledge
of external labour markets in these and other Asian countries has
gone a step ahead of my understanding of internal (see Taira (1973)).
In fact, this article may be considered a generalised counterpart to
Taira (1973). Currently, I am collaborating with
Dr. Chirauy Isarangkun on a project concerning internal labour markets in Thailand with financial assistance from the Midwest Universi-
ties' Consortium for International Activities (MUCIA).

firm has a structure of jobs and, for each job, the capability to
do it is a portable commodity that can be bought and sold in the
labour market in the quantity agreed upon by buyer and seller.
Management structures jobs with the price of each job in mind in
the way that corresponds to the least-cost technology and follows
the dictates of profit maximisation. Any vacancy is filled by
the competitive process of the market. The speed of filling the
vacancy is in part the function of the price offered for the job.
(In this and the following few paragraphs, I paraphrase M.W. Reder's
perception of the theory of the firm that he proposes as a preliminary step for his theory of occupational wage differentials
(1955).)

One assumption about the external labour market makes the
internal labour market absolutely unnecessary in the sense that no
job vacancy need be filled by internal recruitment (promotion) and
that the least-cost principle for filling the vacancy is fulfilled.
This is where there is a "reserve army of unemployed" for every
job. Any vacancy can be filled by calling in an appropriate
worker from this "army". But there is no theoretical necessity to
assume this extreme situation.[1] The variable extent of availability
by job of the qualified unemployed creates the possibility that certain vacancies must wait a long time before they are filled and that
a worker best suited for the least-cost filling of a vacancy may be
trained and reassigned inside the firm. As soon as there are job
changes within the same firm among workers who are already in its
employ, our minimal definition suggests that an internal labour
market is at work. The extent of this market is the function of how
tight the market is for each job and how conscious management is of
the usefulness of internal recruitment.

One more assumption makes the internal labour market a theoretical necessity even in the face of management's indifference to
where the recruit for a vacancy originates. This is that a worker
usually has an array of job capabilities to sell. Naturally, he
desires to sell that capability which fetches the highest price.
Why a worker often settles for doing a job that is not the best he
can do is due to the cost of waiting for the best job to occur as
compared with the immediate income from a less advantageous job that
happens to be available. In other words, any employed worker is
potentially "unemployed" with reference to the best job he can do.
Therefore, a worker with this reserve capability, while doing his
second or third best job, is in search for the best job either inside or outside the firm he is working for.

An additional assumption strengthens the theoretical justification of the internal labour market. This has to do with what may
broadly be called "transactions cost" or, more commonly, the cost of
labour turnover. The latter expression usually refers to the
employer's cost. From the point of view of the inter-firm job
changer, the "transactions cost" includes the cost of breaking the
existing job contract and forming a new one with a different employer

---

[1] One suspects that this sort of extreme situation is implicit
in the two-sector models of economic development with surplus labour.
This suspicion arises from these models' absolute silence about relative wages for different skills in the modern sector.

as well as the cost of residential change. From the point of
view of the employer who has a vacancy to fill, the transactions
cost includes the cost of an unfilled vacancy, the cost of recruitment (either internal or external), and the loss of productivity
during the interim orientation period of the new worker even if he
is thoroughly qualified for the job. (See Scoville's analysis of
the turnover cost to the employer (1974).) If an equally qualified worker is available inside the firm, the transactions cost to
the employer may be much less than in the case of hiring from outside. The cost of job change is also lower to the worker when
done inside than between firms. If the vacancy occurs at a
higher (that is, more skilled) level of the job structure, the
internal filling induces a chain of vacancies and promotions
throughout the workforce necessitating the recruitment from outside
at some lower level. But the internal promotions probably have
minimal transactions costs, however extensive they may be, while
the transactions cost associated with recruitment from outside may
also decrease as the skill level goes down.

The preceding paragraph indicates that the emergence of
vacancies entails an increase in the labour cost to the firm.
Once this is realised, the control over the labour turnover rate
becomes a valid management objective. The objective is to retain
an employee as long as his job performance justifies his wage and
related benefits. Since his quitting calls forth the transactions
cost for filling the vacancy left behind, measures that help the
firm retain him are a trade-off against the transactions cost.
There are two classes of factors that help the firm retain a given
employee. One is the class of factors that makes the net advantage of staying on the current job at least as attractive from the
employee's point of view as the best alternative job he could find
elsewhere. Another is the class of factors which induces the
employee to feel that he can put his reserve capability to the best
use in the foreseeable future by staying with the current employer.
In other words, the probability that a given employee shows up for
work (that is, he supplies a day's labour) is a function of his
current wage relative to his best alternative opportunity outside
the firm and of the present value of all future wages he can reasonably expect from staying with the present employer compared with
other employers. The difference between unity and this probability·
is equivalent to the conventional measure of labour turnover rate
which is the fraction of total workforce leaving the firm per unit
of time. Naturally, the cost-conscious firm would be interested
in attaining an optimal minimum of the cost of labour turnover.
This would induce the firm to schedule an array of jobs over time
in association with the evolving capability of an employee. A
structured internal labour market thus comes into being. Rules
and procedures are then written down and continue to be elaborated
as the internal labour markets evolve.

IDEAL-TYPICAL ILLUSTRATIONS

An indicated above, a theoretical case can be made for the
raison d'être of intra-firm practices with respect to workforce
utilisation which one may cover under the rubric of "internal
labour market". This is so even when all the postulates of pure
competition are kept essentially intact. In reality, labour
markets are grossly imperfect by the standard of theoretical

markets. Since imperfections refer to all kinds of obstacles and
impediments that hinder the theoretically expected mobility in the
process of adjustment towards an equilibrium, the barriers that
separate internal labour markets of various firms from one another
and from the external labour markets can be expected to exist in
the real world. The strength of these barriers varies according
as the market system as a whole is more or less imperfect. Thus,
in a system where the external labour market is an inefficient
allocator of labour resources, one may reasonably expect that the
internal labour markets of some firms are "balkanised" and set
apart from the general labour market process. Likewise, as in the
theoretical world mentioned in the preceding section, there would
be little distinction between internal and external labour markets
in an efficient market system.

Thus we arrive at a definition of the "efficiency" of the
internal labour market. It refers to the situation in which the
pattern of jobs and workers successfully meets the challenge of
the external labour market when the internal labour market is pushed
open for interactions with the external. This means that no job
within the firm acquires a queue of qualified workers or sees the
incumbent depart leaving a vacancy difficult to fill at the existing wage and benefit standards. Since internal labour markets
tend to develop in large firms which enjoy all kinds of economic
privileges due to market imperfections of various kinds, the danger
of failing the efficiency test for internal labour markets is likely
to take the first type mentioned above - that is, most jobs will
acquire substantial queues of qualified jobseekers. In other
words, large high-wage firms are already enjoying a reserve army of
qualified workers for many of the jobs in them. This situation is
inefficient and irrational because the firm is paying too much for
all categories of labour services and not doing anything to modify
the practice.

In order to help visualise many conceivable internal labour
market types, I now offer illustrations of two extreme ideal-
typical situations. Intermediate situations can be imagined with
varying degrees of admixture of these polar cases. These illustrations have emerged from an exaggerated reinterpretation of the practices of British and Japanese factories described by Ronald Dore
(1973).

Type 1 is the case where the firm dogmatically rejects the use
of an internal labour market. Type 2, in contrast, is the case
where the firm dogmatically rejects the use of the external labour
market except at the entry-level of recruitment. Type 1 is a
caricature of the British factory, and type 2 that of the Japanese
factory. Neither is literally true, of course.

The firm has a structure of jobs corresponding to the technology it has adopted. In both types, these jobs can be arranged in
a hierarchy of job capability which is associated with relative
wages. However, in type 1, each job is independent of any other
job, although all jobs are integrated into a production process.
In type 2, the hierarchy is also a "line of progression" by which a
worker can move up to more-skilled, better-paying jobs with the
help of in-employment education and training.

In type 1, each job is filled by hiring a worker with the
necessary qualifications from the "external" labour market. If a
worker, after low-grade work experience, wants to acquire better

job capability, he can invest his own time and resources for its acquisition through the use of educational or training facilities available in society at large. The employer is thoroughly "colour blind" with respect to the identity of workers who fill jobs in his firm. Workers who used to be on low-grade jobs may now be back on higher-grade jobs via labour markets, but the employer does not care about their identity or personal history.

In type 2, education, training and experience relevant to job mobility within the firm are all internalised. Young and inexperienced but promising workers are recruited through a select-ive process with emphasis on aptitude, versatility and "train-ability". They are put to the lowest level of jobs after a minimum necessary training and promoted to better and more complex jobs through the combination of in-employment experience and training. In order to ensure the most orderly promotions over the job ladders, the employer makes efforts to hire workers of reasonably homogeneous capability at regular intervals. Each cohort of workers is then put through a uniform schedule of experience and training within the firm. Under the circumstances, promotions can be regulated fairly and automatically by seniority, occasionally qualified by proved differences in ability and other qualities. Workers are retired when their job capability has reached its maximum and their job per-formance begins to slacken. No doubt there are misfits who reach their maximum job capability before they encompass the full career available in the firm over their working lives or who fall short of standards of job performance somewhere along the line of progression. They are weeded out and ejected into the external labour market. But no workers are hired from the labour market for any intermediate job grade.

One would naturally ask how a system of workforce management resembling type 2 could ever obtain in the real world. Type 1 looks more natural in a market economy. Type 2 seems to infringe upon workers' freedom of occupational choice or to assume an unbelievable degree of prescience at the start of a working life. (These are some of the worries expressed by G. Becker (1964).) The "paternalism controversy" with respect to Japanese management has pointed up a constellation of certain crucial economic and tech-nological forces for making a management system come close to type 2. Generalising from Japanese historical experience (as described by Taira (1970)), these forces can be summarised as follows:

(1) The firm in question is a monopolist or an oligopolist in the product market. This ensures that whatever the firm does in the factor markets, it can usually manipulate the product mar-ket to cover the factor costs. (Any organisation that does not worry about its revenue may be likened to a monopoly. For example, the military establishment is a monopoly producer of national defence services.)

(2) Production is on a large scale and its technology requires a "lumpy" capital investment.

(3) The skill contents of jobs required by the adopted technology need many years of in-employment experience and training with the "line of progression" roughly equal to a man's working life. (When the nation's life expectancy was short, for example, shorter than 40 years as in pre-war Japan, the problem of getting stuck with too many older employees does not arise.)

(4) Skills are specific to the firm in question and largely
     non-transferable to the activities of other firms. This
     ensures that the longer a worker stays with the firm, the
     larger his losses are if he quits. This is because the next
     best job he can find outside the present firm is likely to be
     a low-paid, low-skilled one. This is a factor that weakens
     the worker's bargaining position vis-à-vis the firm. "Worker
     docility" may result from this factor. But if the right kind
     of worker should quit before his job capability is maximised,
     the firm not only loses the return to its past investment in
     his recruitment and training, but also has to forgo the bene-
     fits of the future improvement of his job capability which
     depends upon the continuation of his employment. This creates
     a curious situation where a worker enjoys a sort of bargaining
     power without the leverage of better alternatives elsewhere or
     even without wanting it.

(5) The preceding item suggests a zone of indeterminacy for the
     wage rate for each skill level. There are no "prevailing"
     market rates to guide wage determination in the firm. Wages
     are therefore subject to a large margin of employer discretion,
     subject to acceptability by the worker.

(6) The employer can readily see in this situation the possibility
     of a wage structure which is favourable to both him and his
     employees. It is favourable to workers if the expected life-
     time earnings at entry are visibly higher than elsewhere. It
     is favourable to the firm if workforce productivity covers the
     cost of operating the internal labour market and still leaves
     a rate of return higher than the same amount of investment put
     into physical and human capital may earn in alternative uses.

(7) That a wage structure of the preceding type can be made more or
     less favourable to workers at management's discretion implies
     the possibility of "paternalism", which may be defined as a
     management action that results in the choice of a wage struc-
     ture favourable to workers although the circumstances should
     enable management to get away with a much worse wage structure
     without demoralising or antagonising employees. But the oppor-
     tunity for "paternalism" can be abused. The same circumstances
     may allow the satisfaction of irrational whims on the part of
     management like preferences for diplomas, particular manners,
     pleasant looks, or certain ethnic backgrounds, not related to
     job capability as such.

(8) On the other hand, the zone of indeterminacy can be seized
     upon by workers if they succeed in organising themselves into
     a trade union. When the union becomes very strong, it may
     raise wages so much that the firm, after having maximised its
     monopolistic profits in the product markets, merely ends up
     with normal profits, handing over all excess profits to the
     union. (A rigorous theory of bargaining of this type may be
     seen in George de Menil (1971).)

(9) The trade union mentioned above tends to be an "enterprise
     union" comprising all the workers employed in the firm in
     question and scheduled to move over the line of progression.
     The hiring policy with emphasis on cohort solidarity and equal-
     ity (a micro-social democracy by default, which R. Dore (1973)
     idealises as the product of a plant-level social democratic

revolution) should also promote inter-cohort, that is, enterprise-wide, solidarity. But since there are no comparable firms and skills acquired in this firm are non-transferable, the union membership does not spill over beyond the confines of the firm.

(10) The trade union is not an inevitable outcome, however. If it fears the rise of a union, management can substitute its "paternalism" and counteract workers' need for a union by offering them what they are hoping to get with the help of a union. Anti-union paternalism literally follows the dictum that "Father knows best". Boulewarism in the General Electric Company of the United States, which eventually failed, was a variant of this type of paternalism.

(11) That unionism and paternalism are close substitutes despite the same cost of concessions to workers implies that management feels a "psychic" income from choosing paternalism against unionism.

It is clear that considerable inefficiency exists in the internal labour market of the type depicted by type 2. The surest way to cut down the margin of inefficiency in this case is to deprive the firm of its monopolistic or oligopolistic position in the product market. Since large firms are not likely to be numerous at an early stage of economic development, the discipline of competition may come from abroad via imports. The need for an internal labour market still exists, but the zone of indeterminacy in wage determination will be narrower, offering the incentive for management to think hard about alternative ways of structuring jobs and of manning them.

From a broader social point of view, an inefficient internal labour market like type 2 above may be regarded as a device for adopting and indigenising complex technologies in a limited number of industries. That private firms take on the burden of training for purposes of generating skills, attitudes and habits to operate these technologies is perhaps a logical course of action for LDCs. Of course, the burden is financed by monopoly profits. An alternative is a public facility for training and education, but it would not meet the specific needs of these firms adopting foreign technologies. Furthermore, the dropouts from the internal labour markets at various stages of skill acquisition may find their way into the general pool of skill supplies and contribute to the upgrading of society's technical level. The inefficiency of the internal labour markets of large firms at this stage of development may therefore be regarded as the price society at large pays for generating and augmenting the supplies of skilled workers of various grades. Since the price has to be paid somehow in the interest of economic development, paying it through inefficient internal labour markets may not be socially inefficient at all.

SOME PRACTICAL IMPLICATIONS OF
INTERNAL LABOUR MARKET INEFFICIENCY

Although the closure of the internal labour market in reality cannot be as thorough as in type 2, one may suppose that complete closure is the ideal in the internal labour market approach partly because civil and military services are such ubiquitous models for workforce structuring. In reality, this ideal is comprised

because of certain practical considerations, and there arise double
standards in how the firm relates to its employees by distinguishing
those on the line of progression from those who are not on it.   In
other words, "market segmentation" becomes a regular feature of the
internal labour market in practice.   The workers who are not on the
line of progression are those who have not been screened through the
entry-level recruitment procedure and who come in at various life
stages with various work experiences and qualifications.   Their
work capability not originally cut to the specifications by the firm
hiring them is considered suspect.   They are therefore employed on
a "temporary" basis.   For purposes of distinction, those who are
on the line of progression are called "permanent" employees.   In
addition to fixed short-term contracts for specified jobs, "temporary"
workers are often paid lower wages than the "permanent" employees for
the same jobs and entitled to inferior fringe benefits.   Where the
segmentation of the internal labour market is extreme, there is no
way for any "temporary" worker to be co-opted into the "permanent"
workforce.   The principle of equity is thus violated.   (Even in the
People's Republic of China, despite its commitment to the equality
and solidarity of all workers, fairly extreme internal market seg-
mentations are allowed to exist, as pointed out by Howe (1973).)
Naturally, an internal labour market segmentation is economically
inefficient because it is clear that the firm is employing the "permanent" employees for the jobs which "temporary" workers could perform equally well for lower pay and poorer benefits.   The availability of such "qualified temporary" workers in the external labour
market must eventually loosen the structure of "permanent" employment
within the firm unless maintained by non-economic forces like
employer paternalism or worker unionism limited to "permanent" employees.[1]

There is also reason to suspect that the existence of a small
number of large firms equipped with segmented internal labour markets
induces labour surpluses in the external labour market.   The extent
of these surpluses is the function of wage differentials between
these firms as a group and the external labour market.   Since the
internal labour markets of these firms are at least open to the
external labour market through recruitment at the entry level and the
hiring of "temporary" workers at various levels with varying possibilities of co-opting into the "permanent" workforce, there develops a
labour reserve from which selective recruitments are made.   The
higher the wages in the internal labour markets, the larger the
extent of labour reserve that presses down the wages and working conditions in the external labour market, accentuating the internal-
external wage differentials.   (For data on Latin American experience
and analytical inferences, see Gregory and Reynolds (1965) and
Standing and Taira (1973).)

Closed internal labour markets do not contribute to a full
utilisation of human work capabilities (as distinct from a "full
employment" of human resources).   Since ability or capability in

---

[1] The segmentation of a firm's workforce into the "permanent"
and "temporary" components almost amounts to a part of the natural
order of the universe, ubiquitous in many Asian countries.   The
differentials of pay, working conditions and security between the
two components evidently spur the commitment of the "permanent"
workers to their employers.   The labour turnover rate, for example,
may be a rough guide to the situation.   Japan's rate is about one-
half of the United States', while Thailand's is even lower than one-
half of Japan's.

general is not a uniform quantum equally shared by every worker,
but distributed with different frequencies over a scale ranging from
the most to the least capable, it is possible that, even with perfectly open internal labour markets, the firms which can afford the
longest lines of progression may be the first to pick the cream of
the labour force by means of the hiring standards that are geared to
the identification of the most durable, versatile and trainable
qualities of workers. As the size of the firm becomes smaller, the
lines of progression usually shorten and the hiring standards also
come down. Thus, smaller firms collect workers of lower qualities.
If the practices of all firms, large and small, strive to institute
the best feasible internal labour markets, this will have the effect
of matching jobs and wages with worker qualities as if jobs are cut
out to fit individual workers. The long-run equilibrium will therefore be the situation in which each worker has found the best
employer and is doing the best of all jobs he is capable of at the
moment while devoting an optimum amount of time, effort and resources
to preparing himself for the next, more sophisticated job that his
ability permits. (This kind of equilibrium is rarely examined in
the literature on labour theory, but Malcolm Fisher's ingenious
analysis of the individual labour supply function has opened up vast
possibilities in this direction (1966).) In the real world, disequilibrium is the usual state of affairs. But what is important
is that the efforts to move toward an equilibrium would generate a
tendency toward the maximum utilisation of the total stock of
worker capabilities (not merely "full employment" in the sense that
every one has a job regardless of how well the job matches his
ability) and as a byproduct make the total output of the system grow
faster than if this tendency is absent. In this sense, the widespread espousal of the concept of efficient internal labour markets,
commensurate with efficient external labour markets, would contribute
to economic growth.[1]

TOWARD A POLICY ON INTERNAL LABOUR MARKETS[2]

That the concept of efficient internal labour markets must be
espoused by managers and workers implies suggestions for policy.
It is an argument against an extremely closed internal labour market
illustrated by type 2 and approximated in practice by the civil and
military services. On the other hand, it is also an argument
against management's extreme indifference to workforce structure as
illustrated by type 1 and characterised in practice by higher turnover rates at all levels of the personnel. It should be possible

---

[1] Analytically, the rate or speed of growth is the function of
the distance between the equilibrium that a system could attain and
the disequilibrium in which the system actually finds itself at a
given time. In other words, growth is an alias for the adjustment
process when it pertains to aggregate output.

[2] On policy implications for external labour markets, see the
conclusion of Taira (1973). When the efficiency of the external
labour markets is improved as suggested there, the remaining policy
issue is how best to synchronise internal labour markets with external, which is suggested in this section.

therefore that some appropriate models of internal labour markets
can be constructed for several broad categories of firms differentiated by size and industry with due regard to the existing state
of relevant labour markets.   These models, if widely publicised by
responsible public agencies, are bound to have an "indicative"
impact on managers and workers.   These models can also be used for
estimating the economy-wide demands for labour of different grades
and skills, which can then be compared with the conditions of labour
supply determined in part by the demographic trends and the capacity
of educational and training facilities.   (For this kind of manpower planning, Lester (1966) is highly useful.)   This would be
the beginning of market-oriented, indicative planning for a fuller
utilisation of human capabilities overcoming the quantitative bias
in conventional concept of "manpower" with little regard to the
reality of differentiated human capabilities.   This kind of planning will centre around some generalised concept of employment service or labour market policy and will necessarily become a meeting
ground for all kinds of planners, consultants, economists, labour
market analysts, labour administrators, and representatives of
managers and workers.

REFERENCES

Becker, Gary S.: Human capital (New York, Columbia University
      Press, 1964).

Doeringer, Peter B. and Piore, Michael J.: Internal labour markets
      and manpower analysis (Lexington, Mass., Lexington Books, 1971).

Doeringer, Peter: "Low Pay, Labour Market Dualism and Industrial Re-
      lations Systems", in Wage Determination (ed. OECD (Paris), 1974).

Dore, Ronald: British factory/Japanese factory (Berkeley and Los
      Angeles, University of California Press, 1973).

Fisher, Malcolm R.: Wage determination in an integrating Europe
      (Leyden, A.W. Sijthoff, 1966).

Gregory, Peter and Reynolds, L.G.: Wages, productivity and
      industrialisation in Puerto Rico (Homewood, Ill., Irwin, 1965).

Howe, Christopher: Wage patterns and wage policy in modern China,
      1919-1972 (Cambridge, Eng., University Press, 1973).

Isarangkun, Chirayu N.: Manufacturing industries in Thailand
      (Ph.D. thesis, unpublished) (Australian National University,
      1969).

Kannappan, S.: "The economics of structuring an industrial labour
      force", in British Journal of Industrial Relations, Vol. 4
      (Nov. 1966), pp. 379-404.

Lester, Richard A.: Manpower planning in a free society (Princeton,
      Princeton University Press, 1966).

Menil, George de: Bargaining: monopoly power versus union power
      (Cambridge, Mass., MIT Press, 1971).

Mucia, Task Force on Urban Labour Markets: "An integrating theme for research" (mimeo), 1973.

Myrdal, G.: Asian drama (3 vols.) (New York, Random House, 1968).

Okochi, K., Karsh, B. and Levine, S.B., eds.: Workers and Employers in Japan (Tokyo and Princeton, University of Tokyo and Princeton University Presses, 1973).

Paveanbampen, Sumalee: "Internal labour market, industrialisation and developing economies", in Thai Journal of Development Administration (forthcoming) (1974).

Reder, M.W.: "The theory of occupational wage differentials", in American Economic Review, Vol. 45, 1955, pp. 833-852.

Scoville, James: "Interdependent labour markets: Afghanistan circa 1970", in Industrial Relations (forthcoming) (1974).

Standing, Guy and Taira, K.: "Labour market effects of multi-national enterprises in Latin America", in Nebraska Journal of Economics and Business, Vol. 12, No. 4, 1973, pp. 103-117.

Taira, Koji: Economic development and the labour market in Japan (New York, Columbia University Press, 1970).

_____, "Unemployment, labour markets and wage differentials in Asian countries", in Industrialisation and Manpower Policy in Asian Countries (ed. Japan Institute of Labour (Tokyo), 1973).

Urbanisation and employment: insights from a series of case studies of Third World metropolitan cities

by
Harold Lubell,
World Employment Programme,
International Labour Office

The rapid growth of large cities in many of the developing countries since 1950, primarily as a consequence of massive rural to urban migration, has brought on an urban crisis of unprecedented dimensions - a crisis of inadequate urban infrastructure and housing, of political and social organisation, and of employment - which is most apparent in these countries' metropolitan centres. An understanding of the urban employment problem of the Third World and efforts to seek solutions to it must therefore start with an analysis of the situation of specific big cities, a point of view adopted by the urbanisation and employment project of the ILO's World Employment Programme (WEP).[1] This paper is a report on some of the first findings of the project, the studies on Calcutta, Abidjan, Jakarta and Bogotá.

LINES OF INQUIRY

Data base

The approach followed by the WEP urbanisation and employment project in its series of urban case studies has been to evaluate the urban employment situation as a resultant of the interplay of demographic and social changes and the growth of the urban economy. The analysis has been "literary" rather than econometric: statistical data have been used to describe the existing situation, current relationships, and apparent trends, rather than to construct an econometric model. The primary focus has been on demographic and economic data complemented by some sociological information.

Demographic data from census returns and from sample surveys have been examined to determine trends in population and labour force growth, the relationships between migration and labour force status, the sectoral and occupational structure of employment, the extent of open unemployment and underemployment, and the relation of unemployment to two attributes which are of particular importance - age and education. The central set of economic data we have been looking at is value added by sector in the metropolitan area as compared with the provincial or regional or national figures, in order to understand the relationship between the metropolitan economy and its hinterland. (What we would also like to have in hand, but generally do not, is an input-output table for the metropolis showing

---

[1] The World Employment Programme (WEP), launched by the International Labour Organisation in 1969, constitutes the ILO's principal contribution to the International Development Strategy for the Second United Nations Development Decade (1970s). There are four major types of WEP action: comprehensive employment strategy missions and exploratory country employment missions; regional employment teams for Africa, for Asia and for Latin America and the Caribbean; country employment teams; and an action-oriented research programme. The last at this stage covers nine major project areas: technology and employment; income distribution and employment; population and employment; education and training and employment; rural employment promotion; urbanisation and employment; emergency employment schemes; internal and international migration; and the international division of labour.

inter-sectoral flows within the metropolis and inter-regional
sector flows between the metropolis and the rest of the national
economy.)   Comparison of the structure of production of goods and
and services indicates which are the relatively high labour absorbing (low labour productivity) sectors and which are the relatively
low labour absorbing (high labour productivity) sectors.   In the
typical developing country situation, manufacturing shows high
growth rates for output but lower growth rates for employment, and
even when the latter rates are high, manufacturing is such a small
part of the total urban economy that the total labour absorptive
capacity of manufacturing remains low.

Another set of data we have been working with relates to urban
infrastructure expenditures and employment, information that is
usually available if there exists a previous urban development plan
for the metropolitan area under study.

An important area of activity on which data are usually lacking
is the "informal sector" - the traditional or unorganised sector in
a dual economy.   In this field we are trying to generate our own
information by sponsoring field surveys carried out by local research
institutions, but the results have not yet begun to come in.

Questions to be answered

In carrying out these case studies, we have had in mind two
explicit sets of possible policies whose relevance and a priori
feasibility we have been trying to examine.   One set aims at the
increase in employment in the major urban centre or centres: the
use of urban infrastructure construction programmes as a device for
directly increasing employment of the urban labour force;   encouragement of productive employment opportunities in the informal sector,
hence outside of formal sector manufacturing, construction and
government services;   parallel to the latter, discouragement of in-
coherent slum clearance activities which destroy existing informal
sector economic activities;   and special measures to provide employment for the educated unemployed.   The other set of measures aims
at discouraging migration to the cities: increasing employment and
income-earning possibilities in the rural areas where most of the
migrants originate;   increasing employment possibilities in smaller
towns which the young people with some education tend to leave in a
search for jobs in the big city;   and, as a (usually ineffective)
last resort, police control measures to keep new migrants out of the
big city.

It is becoming increasingly clear from our case studies that one
of the fundamental issues facing urban employment policy is precisely
the main issue of economic development itself: can the national
economy generate the resources needed to sustain higher levels of
economic activity?   If effective demand rises in urban areas as a
result of the money incomes generated by programmes for urban employment creation, will the other productive agents be able to respond by
increasing their output of the goods (and services) demanded?   A
basic limitation on the expansion of urban employment and urban production in most of the developing countries still appears to be the
low supply elasticity of the rural economy, which leads to actual or
probable shortages of food to satisfy increased demand as urban and
rural incomes rise.   Any policy of urban economic expansion requires
easing of this supply constraint - as well as of a number of other
raw material shortages - in order to be feasible.   Only to the extent
that these basic supply constraints are either not binding in themselves or else can be eased is it possible to deal with urban employment creation primarily as an organisational and institutional problem.

URBAN SITUATIONS: SIMILARITIES AND DISSIMILARITIES

The background to the WEP series of urban case studies was set
by Paul Bairoch's monograph on Urban unemployment in developing
countries,[1] whose primary conclusion is a provocative and pessimistic one: that increased urban unemployment and underemployment are
inevitable unless rural to urban drift (the rural exodus) is slowed
down, that the only real choice is between rural underemployment and
urban hyper-unemployment. The obverse of this conclusion is that
any considerable increase in urban employment will inevitably pull
more members of the rural labour force into the cities in the search
for jobs in greater numbers than the number of employment opportunities created. One of the lines of inquiry of the case studies has
been to see how significant this basic paradox is in specific situations and to what extent it can be eluded by feasible policy measures.

Our Calcutta study[2] was designed in part to investigate the
extent to which the specific realities of the Calcutta situation fit
the general picture drawn by Bairoch, in part to examine the extent
to which an urban infrastructure development programme can serve to
absorb the urban unemployed. In the Calcutta case, the verdict is
far from clear. In the decade from 1960 to 1970, the population of
metropolitan Calcutta grew more slowly than that of all of West
Bengal and, by the same token, less than that of rural West Bengal,
perhaps because some degree of saturation occurs when an urban
agglomeration reaches Calcutta's size, perhaps because the degree of
political and economic chaos reached by Calcutta in the last years
of the 1960s discouraged immigration. A factor which quickly became
clear in the course of the study with respect to urban infrastructure
programmes was the importance of one particular aspect of the structure of the Calcutta labour market: construction work is carried out
by contractors who bring in unskilled rural labourers to carry out
specific jobs; the unemployed in Calcutta are not available for
construction jobs.

The fragmentation of the urban labour market goes beyond this
to what may be called an ethnic pattern of labour force participation
which is important for the policy question for whom jobs are to be
created. For example, of the two major industries in Calcutta, jute
manufacturing employs mostly "immigrants" from the neighbouring
Indian State of Bihar, while the engineering industries employ mostly
Bengalis. Development of the engineering industries will employ
more resident Bengalis; expansion of the jute industry (which is
unfortunately in a state of secular decline) will not. Furthermore,
the educational standards of resident Bengalis (including refugees
from former East Pakistan) are much higher than among the migrants
from Bihar and the other neighbouring Indian States, so that the
problems of the educated unemployed are felt most keenly by the resident Bengalis.

---

[1] Paul Bairoch: Urban unemployment in developing countries:
The nature of the problem and proposals for its solution (Geneva,
ILO, 1973).

[2] Harold Lubell: Calcutta: Its urban development and employment prospects. Foreword by J. Tinbergen (Geneva, ILO, 1974).

Our study on Abidjan[1] revealed at least one significant labour market phenomenon similar to that found in Calcutta. In Abidjan, unskilled jobs are filled mostly by immigrants: partly by immigrants from the savannah region in the north of the Ivory Coast (hence internal migrants) but primarily by immigrants from the further savannah region north of the frontier (hence international migrants). The educated unemployed are primarily Ivorians who are not interested in taking unskilled jobs; the unskilled who fill jobs which are available are immigrants from Upper Volta, Niger and Mali. The policy question - for whom do you want to create employment? - therefore becomes central to future employment policy for the Ivorian authorities. At present the Ivorian economy is short of manpower in the highest and lowest ranges of the occupation scale, so that most management positions are filled by non-Africans and a high proportion of the unskilled are filled by non-Ivorian Africans, in the latter case to a considerable extent because Ivorians are not available for such occupations. In the middle ranges of the occupational scale, including white-collar jobs, there are more Ivorians available than the economy demands. A policy concentrating on the absorption of Ivorians, for any given growth rate of the economy, would call for less reliance on unskilled labour and more on mechanisation and technical personnel - as well as on intensification of training of the Ivorians seeking such jobs. A manpower and employment policy conceived for a wider regional economic role of the Ivory Coast in francophone West Africa, as is implied by President Hophouët-Boigny's insistence on the "open door" for Voltaics, Nigerians and Malians, would favour more labour-intensive approaches to development.

There is considerable information available on the formal sector of the economies of the Ivory Coast and of Abidjan itself. The informal sector is, of course, harder to seize. Nevertheless, the mere recognition of the significance and the economic and employment potential of the informal sector leads to some immediate policy concerns in the Abidjan context which were not self-evident beforehand, among them: the anomaly of extending formal apprenticeship legislation to constituent elements of the informal sector; the implications for the informal urban economy of massive slum-clearance operations entailing the relocation of a significant proportion of the slum population of metropolitan Abidjan; the implications of the success of the informal sector, using a highly divisible unit of modern equipment - the sewing machine - as its main capital investment, in more than holding its own against formal sector factory production of ready-made clothing.

Our study on Jakarta[2] emphasises that the economy of Indonesia's largest city is dominated by small-scale private enterprises: over 90 per cent of registered enterprises in 1967 were privately owned, around two-thirds of them had less than four workers per establishment, and over 70 per cent were in the trade sector. In 1971, manufacturing employed only 10 per cent of the Jakarta workforce, as compared with close to 40 per cent in Calcutta - more or less the same share as agriculture. Indeed, employment in manufacturing fell

---

[1] Heather Joshi, Harold Lubell and Jean Mouly: Urban development and employment in Abidjan, WEP Research Working Paper (Geneva, ILO, Oct. 1974).

[2] S.V. Sethuraman: Urbanisation and employment in Jakarta, WEP Research Working Paper (Geneva, ILO, Oct. 1974).

in absolute terms from 1961 to 1971. Although the Jakarta regional
economy (as measured by regional gross domestic product) has been
expanding at a rate between 6 and 7 per cent per year in recent
years, employment increased at only 2.6 per cent per year from 1961
to 1971, as against a labour force growth rate of 3.2 per cent per
year and a population growth rate of over 4 per cent per year.
Open unemployment is, consequently, estimated to have increased from
7.4 per cent of the Jakarta labour force in 1961 to 12.8 per cent in
1971.

The bulk of the increase in the Jakarta labour force has been
absorbed into the informal sector: family-owned small farm enterprises, betjak drivers, hawkers, vendors and petty retail traders,
and the great majority of service workers. Of the employed population of over a million in Jakarta, almost half are apparently
engaged in the informal sector. Almost half of those in the informal sector are in trade and service activities, while another third
are in transport and construction. Lack of appropriate skills and
lack of adequate capital do not appear to have acted as a deterrent:
free, albeit illegal, entry and indigenous technology of production
of goods and services have been decisive to the vitality of the informal sector.

If migration continues at the same rate as in the recent past,
growth rates during the 1970s are likely to reach 5.5 per cent per
year for Jakarta's population and 4.8 per cent per year for the
labour force. Since the main cause for migration to Jakarta is the
even higher rates of unemployment in the neighbouring provinces than
in Jakarta and, since no major policy to reduce rural unemployment is
in sight, the migration flow is likely to continue.

The focus of our study on Bogotá[1] is on the implementation by the
Colombian Government of the promising policy prescription formulated
by Lauchlin Currie to use construction as a leading sector to break
out of the circle of economic underdevelopment and underemployment.
In Colombia, a change in the financial system - the introduction in
1972 of a new savings and loan system whose borrowing and lending
rates of interest are linked to the consumer price index - brought
about a construction boom in the country's urban centres and particularly in the capital which, by mid-1974, had created labour shortages in Bogotá and absorbed some of the country's backlog of unemployment. The resulting general increase in demand pushed other sectors to capacity production and increased further the rate of absorption of labour. So far, however, the effects of the boom have been
concentrated in the capital; furthermore, the increase in demand
has undoubtedly had an inflationary impact on prices. The great
uncertainty in the total situation is whether or not the rural sector will respond to increases in demand by increasing agricultural
output or whether the increase in money demand will simply be dissi-
pated in price rises.

---

[1] Harold Lubell, David McCallum and Ruben Talavera Goibura:
Urban development and employment in Bogotá (in preparation).

POLICY IMPLICATIONS

From the small number of case studies reported on here, it is not yet possible to derive general policy conclusions. We have, however, been trying to formulate specific policy suggestions for each of the situations examined.

In the Calcutta case, a fundamental improvement in the metropolis's employment situation depends on an easing of the material shortages which now block India's economic expansion in general. The potential for a partial local solution in the West Bengal context exists, however, in the short- to medium-term expansion in agricultural production promised by the inevitable extension of the Green Revolution to West Bengal and eventually to its even more backward neighbouring State, Bihar, as well. More specifically, Calcutta's engineering industry has an important potential role to play as supplier of inputs (tubewells, pumps and other agricultural equipment) to an expanding agricultural sector. Furthermore, since Calcutta's engineering industry contains a large informal sector, there also exists a potential for organising and integrating the urban informal sector's production into a wider development scheme. This potential is now being examined by the Calcutta authorities in the context of a follow-up study of the informal sector in the economy of metropolitan Calcutta[1] sponsored by the WEP urbanisation and employment project.

Among the specific policy lines recommended in the WEP monograph on Abidjan are the following: attempting to divert urban infrastructural and industrial investments away from Abidjan and towards Bouaké, the Ivory Coast's second city which lies inland from the coast, in the expectation that this will increase the role of Bouaké as an alternative point of attraction for migrants; reformulation of the concept of slum clearance in Abidjan to include the laying out of new zones for settlement by low-income households in such a way that the infrastructure of these areas can later be improved without destroying either the spontaneous investments made in them by their residents or the economic life and employment that are created in the slums themselves; giving greater consideration to the productive aspects of informal sector activity in Abidjan and avoiding unnecessary interference with and discouragement of such activity; inducing the modern sector - and the Public Works Department of the Government - to use more labour-intensive techniques where these are feasible; and formulating a concerted programme for systematic on-the-job training of Ivorian technicians and potential managers in existing enterprises.

The WEP monograph on Jakarta attempts to formulate a set of policy prescriptions which are consistent with the two aims of slowing down migration into Jakarta and of reducing unemployment while increasing labour productivity. In the area of urban services, efforts should be made to complement the present kampong infrastructure improvement programmes by using subsidies for investment

------

[1] Ajit N. Bose: The informal sector in the Calcutta metropolitan economy, WEP Research Working Paper (Geneva, ILO, Oct. 1974). Bose was a member of the West Bengal State Planning Board during the period 1972-74 and is currently executive director of the West Bengal Comprehensive Area Development Corporation.

in housing and by the removal of existing uncertainties associated with land ownership to encourage private investment in residential housing.   In order to promote investment in informal sector enterprises it may be necessary to experiment with lending procedures based on expected productivity instead of on existing collateral. In the area of public investment, efforts should be made to increase the financial resources available to the regional Government for development purposes by recovering the marginal cost of additional public services (e.g. electricity, water, roads) from their direct beneficiaries through betterment levies and more realistic property tax rates.   In the area of formation of human capital, efforts to develop vocational and management skills might be profitably focused on the informal sector - initially on the informal manufacturing sector, followed by other specific sectors such as construction and transportation.   Other policies to promote employment and productivity in the informal sector could include: review of current licensing and regulatory practices now designed to eliminate informal sector activity; efforts to upgrade the informal sector's technology and to integrate its output with the formal sector and Government by manipulating forward and backward linkages; and creation of appropriate market facilities.   Complementary policies suggested to contain the urbanisation process itself include: attempting to reduce unemployment, particularly seasonal unemployment, in rural West Java by a comprehensive rural works programme to create irrigation facilities independent of seasonal fluctuations in rainfall; development of other urban areas - for example, port towns - away from Jakarta; and development of a market for the educated labour force in regions other than Jakarta.

In the Bogotá case, there are several aspects of its urban situation which should favour the eventual success of an employment and development strategy based on urban construction.   One is the peculiarity that Colombia enjoys in having several large cities in the valleys separated by north-south mountain chains, so that the area from which each city draws its low-income rural to urban migrants is fairly circumscribed.   Furthermore, Bogotá is "protected" by its inclement climate from a mass in-migration from the overpopulated Caribbean coastal areas of the country.   At the same time, the country as a whole enjoys a respectable variety of natural resources and benefits from an easy balance of payments situation which is due in part to policies to encourage exports initiated in the late 1960s.   As a result, even if the strategy of using construction as a leading sector succeeds, these favourable factors special to the Colombian case will make it difficult to decide a priori the extent of its general applicability.   Success of the Colombia experiment would, nevertheless, demonstrate the potential advantages of opting for a bold policy of using the urbanisation process as an instrument of development and of employment creation - instead of clinging to a fearful policy of seeking to delay the inevitable tide of migration to cities.

Sectoral interdependence in urban labour markets and variations in the social and economic environment

by
James G. Scoville,
Institute of Labor and Industrial Relations,
University of Illinois;

Chairman, MUCIA Inter-University Task Force
on Urban Labour Markets

Advances in analyses of economic phenomena seem to progress from simplicity to complication, with false starts and mis-applications of effort strewn along the way. Compare the number of equations in the General Theory with those in the most recent post-Keynesian models of the economy. Consider the lengthy dis-cussion of user cost in the same volume in the light of its con-tribution to our thinking relative to that of the key idea of the General Theory. It should be a salve to us in our endeavours that even such a vital work by an immortal has been subject both to dramatic improvements and to the discarding of many pieces of its argument.

For, indeed, I would like to dwell on some areas in the study of urban labour markets in LDCs where: (1) we may profit from dis-carding some of our present notions and vehicles of analysis; (2) we will need to improve the sophistication of our conceptualisa-tions of labour markets; and (3) where we can seek vastly greater returns for our efforts through much more intensive comparative analysis. These three themes will appear interwoven throughout the following pages.

Let us begin with a rough appraisal of the state of the art on the model-building side. The writings of Lewis, Ranis and Fei, Todaro, Jorgenson and others have proposed or resuscitated a variety of dualities, some with roots deep in classical economics. What-ever you make of these models, their central feature is simply that of focusing on one or another duality: capitalist-noncapitalist, modern-traditional, urban-rural, self-employed-wage earning, and so on. Now, it seems unlikely that the world has ordered itself into tidy dualities to serve the analytical appetites of economists. No doubt simplification of reality is the key to any powerful idea or model whatsoever; but oversimplification would seem to lie at the root of the many criticisms and difficulties these models have encountered.

Thus, my first suggestion is that in the area of theory we must seek to disaggregate the dualities, to decompose some of the sectors into their smaller components. We must begin to incorporate the internal diversity of, for example, the modern and traditional sec-tors into our models of wage and employment determination. In my tiresome series of papers on Afghanistan, I have tried to take a closer look at one part of the traditional sector - that of tradi-tional industry. I have gathered some crude data, built the sub-sector into a model of labour market attraction and movement, and produced a considerable set of testable hypotheses.[1] (At this point, the process has stalled: truly appropriate data with which to implement the term "testable" for other markets have either not been collected or have escaped my search.) In a "related" effort, O.J. Scoville has argued the importance for the analysis of "rural" labour markets of identifying the functions and characteristics of the "agribusiness" sector.[2] The Kenya Report's emphasis on the

---

[1] "Afghan labour markets - a model of interdependence", in Industrial Relations, Oct. 1974. Joseph E. Stiglitz has adopted a similar model in "Wage determination and unemployment in LDCs", QJE, May 1974. For the detailed data, see James G. Scoville: "Incomes in traditional industry: Kabul. 1972", in Indian Journal of Industrial Relations, July 1974.

[2] "The agribusiness sector - an important link in economic growth models", American Journal of Agricultural Economics, 55:3, Aug. 1973.

"informal sector" reflects a concern with somewhat similar parts of the labour market.[1]   A brief look at some data substantiates the importance of non-modern employment.

EMPLOYMENT IN THE TRADITIONAL MANUFACTURING SECTOR

Traditional sector activities cover a wide range of goods pro-duced and services provided, with the nature of the crafts pursued varying from place to place and era to era.   For one example, even if not from a labour market perspective, a team of sociologists or anthropologists has done an extensive mapping of the level and pat-tern of activities in the old covered bazaar of Tashkurghan, Afghanistan.[2]   From their description, we get the impression of a great deal of full-time manufacturing activity which previous analy-ses of the workings of LDC labour markets have steadfastly ignored.

Another fairly exhaustive description of traditional industrial employments can be found in Hans E. Wulff's Traditional Crafts of Persia.[3]   Wulff, an engineer, has focused on the technological and historical sides of these activities, with the unfortunate concomitant exclusion of income and employment information.   However, the diver-sity and number of crafts and enterprises discussed would support the contention that these activities have important effects on income and employment.   The activities surveyed include metal refining and work-ing, tile and ceramic, clothing and leather, woodworking, carpets, jewellery and goldbeating, along with many others.   While some of these crafts are doubtless of declining importance, others are not. The scope of the book suggests the importance of getting the data that we want on this range of employment.

In the case of Iran, we are fortunate enough to have some esti-mates of the importance of small-scale (under ten employees) enter-prises in employment and value added by industry.   While "small-scale industry" and "traditional industry" are by no means synonymous, the data are at least suggestive, reinforcing the desirability of more detailed modelling and analysis of the industrial sector.   In 1967, 68 per cent of Iran's total industrial employment and 36 per cent of total value added came from the small-scale sector.   In terms of the importance of small-scale industry for employment, the following industries had very high proportions: apparel, 96 per cent; miscel-laneous manufacturing, 93 per cent; wood and wood products, 89 per cent.   As far as share of value added by small enterprises, the top three industries were non-electrical machinery, 77 per cent; miscel-laneous manufacturing, 74 per cent; and apparel, 71 per cent.[4]

---

[1] Employment, incomes and equality: a strategy for increasing productive employment in Kenya (Geneva, ILO, 1972).   The WEP mission to the Philippines has dealt with the topic at even greater length. See Sharing in Development (Geneva, ILO, 1974), special paper 9, "Medium-scale and small-scale industry", and Chapter 5 on the service sector.

[2] P. Centlivres: Un Bazar d'Asie Centrale.

[3] Cambridge, Mass.: MIT Press, 1966.

[4] Estimated by the Iranian Ministry of Economy and reproduced in Robert E. Looney: The Economic Development of Iran (N.Y., Praeger, 1973), p. 114.

For the Indian State of West Bengal, a similar conclusion about the analytical importance of small-scale (undefined, but anything not covered by its Factories Act) industry can be drawn from its recent rates of growth. Thus, while total employment in registered factories declined by 0.7 per cent per year from 1967 to 1971, the number of workers in small-scale enterprises grew approximately 4.2 per cent annually from 1965 to 1969-71.[1]

Much of the material discussed above has centred upon traditional sector employments which are fairly similar to the jobs which we talk about in the modern sector of industry. Familiar concepts like employer, worker, wages, hours of work, etc., seem to be applicable to these employments with little or no modification.[2] There is, of course, an enormous area of more "peripheral" employments which are less amenable to the usual Western concepts or modes of analysis. Moonlighting (as strictly defined), simultaneous multiple-job holding practices, and the less-visible income-producing activities pose greater problems for incorporation into our analysis of urban labour markets.

INCOMES: ALTERNATIVES TO THE MODERN SECTOR

The role which the newly differentiated sectors will play in models of the labour market will depend on the levels of income available in them, as well as the amount of employment they generate. Very little work appears to have been done so far on the subject of the alternative income opportunities offered in traditional industry. The table below shows the results of my rather crude survey of the Kabul labour market around 1970. As can be seen, traditional industrial opportunities compare favourably for all "occupations" with the incomes available in the modern sector and a fortiori with incomes in agriculture.[3]

----

[1] Government of West Bengal: West Bengal Economic Review, 1972/73, pp. 18, 80. The growth rate for small industry is calculated by centring employment on the year 1970.

[2] Thus, for example, of 1,673 small-scale industrial workers covered by a survey in Abeokuta, Western Nigeria, 94 per cent were full time. See Ministry of Economic Planning and Reconstruction: Interim Report on the Survey of Small-Scale Industries (Ibadan, 1971), p. 15.

[3] For a recent discussion of some problems regarding farm earnings, see Jacques Freyssinet and Alain Mounier: "Measuring the incomes of agricultural workers", International Labour Review, Sep. 1974.

Table 1. Incomes by sector and occupation: Kabul

Sector and occupation	Afghanis per year
1. Agriculture-income per adult male, 5 pro- vinces, 1970	4 800
2. Modern industry-average compensation: Kabul and vicinity, 1970:	
(a) Unskilled men, year round	9 600
(b) Power-loom weavers	16 400
(c) Mechanics	34 400
(d) Other operatives	16 300
3. Traditional sector trades - median labour income, Kabul, 1972:	
(a) Owner-operators of shops	40 000
(b) Adult male workers	36 000
(c) Boys, aged 12-18, excluding part-time workers and apprentices	14 500

Sources: Described in detail in my "Afghan labour markets - a model
of interdependence", in Industrial Relations, Oct. 1974,
p. 276.   Basic data for lines 3(a)-3(c) are found in my
"Incomes in traditional industry: Kabul, 1972", in Indian
Journal of Industrial Relations, July 1974.

Of course, it is not likely that traditional industry everywhere
occupies the same relative position on the income scale.   Indeed, it
is precisely the point of my Industrial Relations article that
countries and labour markets will vary in this respect, and with predictable impacts on the structure of modern sector wages.[1]   Some
evidence of a different situation, where traditional sector employment is less advantageous, is available for West Bengal - Banerjee
reports that income per family member in small industry stood at
609 rupees at the same time that hired labour was averaging Rs. 1,068.[2]

The other scattered data which I have encountered are less useful.   Data presented by Jennifer Bray indicate 1965-66 income per
man-hour for traditional cloth weavers in a pre-industrial town of

---

[1] "Afghan labour markets - a model of interdependence", pp. 285-6.

[2] R.M. Banerjee: "Employment in small industry in West Bengal",
in Manpower Journal (New Delhi, Apr.-June 1972), p. 116.

Nigeria to be between 1s. (wet season) and 3s. (dry season), with an annual average probably in excess of 2s.[1]   At the same time, in the capital city of Lagos (which would be expected to have a higher wage level), the following hourly rates were observed:

Bakers (ovenmen)	9.0 pence
Cabinetmakers	9.8 pence
Construction carpenters and painters	15.0 pence
Common labour, construction and municipal	11.5 pence[2]

Clearly, the traditional weavers are relatively high on the earnings scale, even if the comparisons we are forced to make are very crude.

Estimates of traditional industrial incomes in several trades in India have been developed by M.N. Upadhyay, and are shown in table 2.   The difference in traditional sector incomes among the various trades and labour markets is striking.   It would be valuable to know the causes of this diversity.

Table 2. Handicraft incomes, India (circa 1961)

Craft and occupation	Income
1. Government nirmal industry (toys), Ahmedabad:	
(a) Carpenters	150-180 Rs./month
(b) Average for all workers	126 Rs./month
2. Himroo (shawl) work, Hyderabad:	
(a) Skilled	1.50 to 3 Rs./day
(b) Unskilled	1 R. /day
3. Silver filigree, Karimnager (AP) average	2 Rs./day
4. Kondapally toys (AP) average	100 Rs./month

Sources: (by line of table 2) - M.N. Upadhyay, Economics of Handi-craft Industry (S. Chand and Co. (Pvt.) Ltd., New Delhi, 1973): line 1(a), pp. 51-2, 56; line 1(b), p. 58; line 2, p. 93; line 3, p. 101; line 4, p. 111.

---

[1] Jennifer M. Bray: "The economics of traditional cloth produc-tion in Iseyin, Nigeria", in Economic Development and Cultural Change, July 1969, pp. 550-1.   Her income estimates shown there are much lower, due to an arithmetic error.

[2] ILO: Bulletin of Labour Statistics, 1966:2, p. 101.   Data apply to October 1965.

At about the same time as the figures in table 2 were compiled, average monthly earnings in Indian manufacturing (including white-collar workers) stood at Rs.118.1.[1] Thus it would appear that some handicrafts offered attractive alternatives to modern sector jobs.

To be complete, one should note that a comprehensive labour market model should include not only alternative but supplementary sources of income. Keith Hart emphasises this subject by starting with one simple question: how does the worker deal with the gap between wages and the urban cost of living? His recent study summarises those prevalent in one West African city: they range from running a gin mill in one's flat, confidence activities, and prostitution (both male and female) to the more seemly traditional manufacturing and service trades.[2] The author's conclusion that these activities keep the blue-collar worker's life chancy but viable impels us to consider the inclusion of these income opportunities in our model.

THE INTERNAL TRAINING PROCESS OF THE MODERN SECTOR

An area of concern centres on the workings of the so-called "internal labour market". Despite its importance for the training, discipline and stability of the labour force, the range of employer (and worker) activities embraced by this concept has seldom been part of labour market models. Miller did some work with it,[3] as did Perrakis,[4] in an attempt to explain size of firm wage differentials on the basis of employer selectivity.

Clearly, the kinds and levels of disaggregations which are appropriate will depend both on the analytical purpose involved and on the countries under scrutiny. Nor, in some place, might any importance at all be attached to the traditional industrial sector, to the concept of wage earners, or many other otherwise useful categories. Nevertheless, in the general case, far more differentiation among sectors and more emphasis on their interrelationships are called for in our model-building exercises if we are to understand prevailing income/earnings differentials.

---

[1] ILO: Yearbook of Labour Statistics, 1967, table 19A.

[2] "Informal urban income opportunities in Ghana", Journal of Modern African Studies, 11:1, Mar. 1973.

[3] R.U. Miller: "The relevance of surplus labour theory to the urban labour markets of Latin America", Bulletin, IILS, Mar. 1971.

[4] Stylianos Perrakis: "The labour surplus model and wage behaviour in Mexico", Industrial Relations, Feb. 1972.

A SIMPLE MODEL: MODERN AND TRADITIONAL MARKETS

The way in which these sectors may be related in the Kabul labour market is shown in diagrams 1 to 4.[1]   Since the major use of the model should be for comparative analysis of the outcomes of labour markets, the primed curves (e.g., D') refer to some other labour market (West Bengal?) which offers less attractive incomes in traditional skills.   The other curves are assumed to be identical, begging questions of scaling, etc.

The market for traditional skills is represented in diagram 1, showing that Kabul has relatively high incomes in these employments. Diagram 2 shows the effect of this on the market for skilled workers in the modern sector - the high alternative incomes reduce the supply, leading to high modern sector skilled wages.

Diagram 3 shows a crude representation of the "internal" market processes of the modern sector: for every level of skilled wages, there is an optimal level of "promotion" of unskilled workers via on-the-job training, hiring upgradable workers away from other firms, etc.   The higher the skilled wage, the more unskilled industrial workers can be profitably promoted.[2]

This in turn leads to a reduction of supply in the unskilled modern sector market, which will push up unskilled wages in comparison with the Lewisian subsistence wage (W_o).   Let us note in passing why the modern sector unskilled supply curves (S_u and S_u') differ from the Lewis-type supply curve (S_L).   The reasons are many: even unskilled industrial workers possess more skills and other desirable traits than do truly common labourers, e.g. porters of firewood and water carriers in the Kabul market.   Further, there are alternative opportunities available here as well, such as apprenticeship or work in lesser skilled jobs in traditional industry.   Finally, unskilled workers receive some formal and informal training, which is of value to their employer and others, for which they must be compensated to avoid costs of turnover.

Thus, attractive opportunities in traditional skills may raise the whole modern sector wage structure.[3]   One other effect can be seen easily: if costs of promotion or technology hinder upgrading (so that the line in diagram 3 is steeper), then unskilled wages will be lower and skilled wages higher.

----

[1] This model is similar in spirit to the one presented in Scoville, op. cit., but contains fewer explicit variables.   Also, the labour flows (turnover and new hires) among the sectors are treated implicitly here, since this version is a stock model.   The notation, where possible, is the same.

[2] By author's licence, this effect has been "incorporated" in diagram 2.

[3] The algebraic model indicates that the modern sector skill differential ($W_s/(W_o+r)$) will also be wider.

Diagram 1. The market for traditional skills

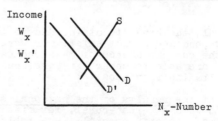

Diagram 2. The market for skilled
workers in the modern sector

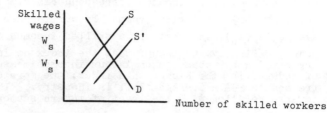

Diagram 3. Optimal level of promotion of
unskilled workers as function of skilled wages

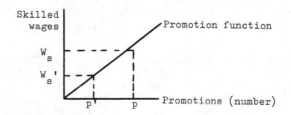

Diagram 4. The market for unskilled
labour in the modern sector

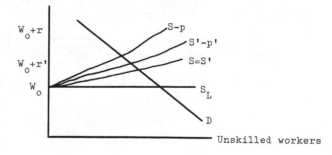

A CRUDE TEST OF THE MODEL

In general, the kind of data needed to test the basic model of market interdependence do not exist. However, with a few assumptions about the correspondence of measured categories to those of the model, we are able to undertake some analysis of the income structure of Iranian provinces.

A study of the results of the national survey for first quarter 1348[1] presents data by urban-rural, for five skills (farmers, common labour, skilled, masters, specialists - table 22:2-3) and three industries (agriculture, industry, services - table 21:2-3). Unfortunately, data are not available by skill and industry. We must assume that urban masters will reflect traditional sector opportunities (W_x), that urban common labour incomes correspond closely to those in the modern sector (W_o+r), that rural common labour incomes reflect the base level available (W_o), and that urban skilled incomes correspond to W_s in the model. Finally, we assume that the index of incomes in urban industry divided by urban common labour incomes measures the "skilledness" of industry:[2] the higher this index, the more common labour has to be trained to reach average skill in industry. The index should have an inverse relation with the level of modern sector unskilled wages.

For the 20 ostān of Iran,[3] equation (1) summarises the model's application to the urban-rural common labour differential. The significant first variable supports the contention that modern sector unskilled wages are pulled up by high "masters'" incomes. While not significant at 5 per cent, the sign on the "industrial skilledness" variable is correct and provides comfort, if not support, for that part of the model.

(1) $\dfrac{\text{Common labour urban income}}{\text{Common labour rural income}} = 1.20 + \underset{(.03)}{.19} \dfrac{\text{Urban master's income}}{\text{Common labour rural income}}$

$- \underset{(.44)}{.64} \dfrac{\text{Urban industry average income}}{\text{Common labour urban income}}$

$$R^2 = .83$$

---

[1] Ministry of Labour and Social Affairs, Publication No. 44, Tehran (Esfand 1349: Mar. 1971), in Persian.

[2] For a similar use of this index, see my Manpower and Occupational Analysis: Concepts and Measurements (D.C. Heath, 1972), pp. 83-86.

[3] Due to missing observations on some of the data, the sample is only 18 in each case.

Equation (2) is an attempt to explain the modern sector skill differential in the framework of our model. While less successful in terms of R^2, it conforms to the theoretical arguments that cause the traditional sector differential to be reflected in the width of modern sector differentials.

$$(2) \quad \frac{\text{Skilled urban income}}{\text{Common labour urban income}} = 1.62 + \underset{(.04)}{.18} \frac{\text{Urban masters' income}}{\text{Common labour rural income}}$$

$$R^2 = .58$$

Due to the paucity of observations, possible questions about the congruence of the data to the conceptualisations of the model, and statistical problems inherent in the use of ratio variables in regression equation (1), we claim very little for the strength of these results. Nevertheless, they are not inconsistent with the interdependency model.

BENEFITS OF SUCH MODELS

What have we gained from this exercise, and what would be the benefits of even more ambitious proliferation of sectors?

An immediate payoff of such amplification is to increase the number of subjects covered by our models. The constellation of wage differentials and the multi-faceted patterns of labour mobility are only two sets of variables which come to mind. Contrast this possibility with the single wage or income differential typical of current formulations, and with the single flow of labour (e.g. from rural to urban) that these models embrace. Furthermore, through analysis of the training time, cost and technological variables important in diagram 3, we can study the wage structure of different industries in markets of varying labour force "quality". In general, more detailed models with more variables should allow us to address ourselves to more interesting questions than the various dualities have afforded.

One might mention parenthetically the broad issue of how one goes about this modelling process. Are the kinds of market models so familiar to economists from the Western, developed areas suitable as a basic framework? Or do we need to make a list of modifications to "Western culturebound" theory? (If so, where?) This was a topic of rather heated dispute at the 1973 Asian Regional Conference on Industrial Relations sponsored by the Japan Institute of Labour.[1] A fellow contributor, Professor Taira, may have been surprised at the opposition to his defence of the market model as regards labour; all of us will have to confront this question. I suspect that the basic modifications to more appropriate, expanded models will be quite minimal.

---

[1] _Industrialisation and Manpower Policy in Asian Countries_ (Tokyo, Japan Institute of Labour, 1973), p. 318.

NOTES ON THE EMPIRICAL SIDE

If we turn our attention from the model building or theoretical side of our enterprise, I see a number of analogous difficulties in our past approaches on the empirical front. We are slowly getting a better base of information about urban labour markets in LDCs through the efforts of the ILO and many national economic or labour relations research units. Nevertheless, I remain troubled by the fashions in which these figures are arranged, particularly in terms of such organising devices as ISIC and ISCO. We have long ago reached consensus that unemployment, as measured by the United States definition (for one example), can give only a very partial and relatively unimportant piece of the labour market picture in an LDC. Why then can we not see that ISIC probably submerges as much information as it reveals about employment patterns and trends in LDCs? The traditional industrial activities to which I have referred would fall into a number of ISIC one-digit groups; the same for ISCO. With regard to analysis of wage structure, it is unlikely that average earnings by ISCO or ISIC groups will give us much of value; more useful by far are likely to be the wage or income levels for various key positions. Some of these have been suggested in the previous literature: common agricultural labour incomes, common "modern sector" labour wages, clerical earnings, to mention but three. Our future modelling, as well as data gathering, should focus more clearly on additional key rates both in the external labour market (for example, incomes of traditional craftsmen, artisans, traders, transporters, etc.) and in the modern sector enterprise (skilled craftsmen, key operators of equipment, etc.). I would expect the key external market jobs and occupations (to which those rates apply) to vary widely from place to place depending on custom and the relative importance of various activities, while key internal labour market jobs are more likely to be determined by the kind and level of modern technology prevalent in the given market. Out of the variety of studies and models will perhaps emerge an analogue to ISCO and ISIC which would more faithfully embrace the labour market patternings of the LDCs, indicate the crucial incomes in the wage structure, and provide a more fruitful means of organising information on incomes, employment, labour mobility and the like.

TOWARDS BETTER COMPARATIVE ANALYSIS OF LABOUR MARKETS

From the comments above, it should be clear that I do not see a single model of labour market segmentation or differentiation[1] nor a single set of income and employment indicators as having everywhere the same usefulness and generality. Indeed, many of the theoretically appropriate variables may have zero coefficients, and the empirical categories have zero observations, in many places. This does not disturb me. Rather, I would hope that such differences among labour markets would impel us to broaden the scope of our studies that we might get insights as to why they work differently.

---

[1] For an example of a model emphasising a different "non-modern" sector, see John F. Weeks: "Wage policy and the colonial legacy - a comparative study", in Journal of Modern African Studies, 9:3, Oct. 1971. Weeks suggests that planters' needs for cheap agricultural labour may (via government policies) be linked to wage and employment developments in the modern sector.

The fundamental research and analytical problem can be posed in the following way. The shapes and relative levels of the curves in diagrams 1 to 4 embody assumptions and perceptions about a specific labour market. What new diagrams - for new sectors - would have to be introduced in studying other labour markets, and which diagrams deleted or modified? What differences would exist in the shapes and levels of the curves? What factors would be behind the differences?

To get at these questions implies a need for larger, comparative studies of labour markets which (I hardly need to point out) are not much in evidence. We have or are getting a fair number of studies of individual or closely related labour markets; we lack the studies which allow us to discern the impacts of major environmental variations among labour markets which shape the way they function. An incomplete listing of the kinds of labour market environment variables which have, in all likelihood, major effects on the structure, the processes, and the outcomes of labour markets will make this need clearer.

1. Some labour markets are sharply segmented by race or ethnic groups; others are not. What effects does this variable have on labour market efficiency, level of employment, skill differentials, income distribution, and so on?

2. The same questions can be raised about the varying degrees of sexual segmentation of labour markets. Moreover, the effects of combined ethnic and sex barriers between sectors should be explored.

3. What effects does the presence of a substantial extractive sector make on the operations of the labour market? Does it make any difference whether this sector is "modern" (oil) or not (coal, perhaps)? The influences of this sector would be felt from the ratio of wages to output, and the frequent direct connections to international commodity markets in which prices are set.

4. What effects does the presence of a substantial foreign sector make? Are the effects different according to its field of enterprise? Taira and Standing have already established that this is an interesting area of inquiry.[1]

5. How do variations in the levels of literacy and education affect the operations of the labour market? Can it be that the neo-classical model is more appropriate the more "primitive" the labour market in terms of human resource development?

6. Can we contrast the workings of the labour markets between those situations where trade unions (supported by governments, no doubt) are important and where they are not?

7. How does the rate of growth (and the underlying development strategy as well) affect the workings, as well as the outcomes, of the labour market processes?

---

[1] Guy Standing and Koji Taira: "Labour market effects of multinational enterprises in Latin America", Nebraska Journal of Economics and Business, Aug. 1973.

8.   Can we differentiate among labour markets with differing
     customs and institutions in the field of skill development -
     markets with apprenticeship systems, with formal training sys-
     tems, or with little at all in this area?

9.   What predictable differences are there in the structure and
     processes of the labour market under the various régimes of
     governmental intervention in the fixing of wages and/or the
     conduct of industrial relations?   What happens in those cases
     where "the labour market" is (or is supposed to be) replaced by
     alternative allocative mechanisms?

     Although this is a partial list, it is obviously a tall order
and impossible to do all at once.   Nevertheless, it seems to underscore the important things which we as scholars or as policy makers
can learn from broader gauge comparative studies of a diversity of
labour markets.   Some of these areas of concern will be studied in
coming years by members of the MUCIA group.   Perhaps the arguments
above will serve as a useful catalyst for the contributors to this
volume and future research.

PART IV

COUNTRY EXPERIENCES

Urban labour market structure and employment issues in the Sudan

Subbiah Kannappan,
Department of Economics,
Michigan State University

I. SOME DIMENSIONS OF THE PROBLEM

Counting areas with over 20,000 inhabitants, we estimate the present urban population to be 1,894,100, or 13.4 per cent of a total population of 14.17 million in 1973.[1] Much of our information is confined to Khartoum, which is more complex and diversified than the other urban communities.

Alternative yardsticks of the urban economy

The share of national income accruing to the urban population certainly exceeds 13.4 per cent. Almost all of industrial investment and the bulk of employment in Government, modern commerce and industry are found in the larger urban centres. The concentration of industrial and commercial units with modern, capital-intensive processes, skilled technical and professional manpower, and health and educational services add qualitatively and quantitatively to the significance of urban areas.

Recent trends and prospects for the future

There has been an acceleration of urbanisation since 1955-56, during which the urban population rose from 6.4 per cent to 13.4 per cent in 1973. Migration has been the biggest factor in the growth of Khartoum.

The ILO Preparatory Team's Household Survey of Khartoum (Three Towns) in 1974 indicates a possible steadying of the rate of in-migration during the preceding five years.[2]

The accelerated urbanisation and migration have caused concern although in principle it is desirable to encourage migration from low- to high-income areas. A policy question focuses on whether existing practices, particularly government wage and employment policies and practices, encourage an "excessive" inflow into urban areas.

II. URBAN LABOUR MARKET MAGNITUDES AND CHARACTERISTICS

Since the bulk of the information pertains to Khartoum, our analysis will focus disproportionately on the city (Khartoum Province, the Three Towns, or Greater Khartoum, as the case may be). This is only a partial loss, as Khartoum constitutes the single most important urban concentration with three-quarters of all the urban inhabitants in the country (See table 1, p. 106). Further, the findings which stress flexible labour market adjustments are even more valid for the other urban centres.

---

[1] Taken from MEFIT, SPA, consulting engineers: Regional Plan of Khartoum and Master Plan for the Three Towns, Vol. I, phase 1 (Rome, MEFIT, Sep. 1974).

[2] Referred to hereafter as the ILO Survey of 1974. The computations have been worked out by Mr. A. Oberai of the ILO. The fall in the last two years should be disregarded as due to the characteristics of the sample.

Employment participation and
organisation in Greater Khartoum

The majority of Greater Khartoum's labour force is employed in small establishments outside of government and organised manufacture and commerce.   Wage earners in the larger industrial and parastatal enterprises and in the civil service probably account for under 30 per cent of the Khartoum urban labour force, perhaps less than 20 per cent of the labour force of the entire Khartoum Province (metropolitan area).   This may be estimated at between 280,000 to 400,000.[1]

Working with a 1967-68 distribution of the urban working population, this gives us an estimate of 145,000 to 200,000 wage earners for 1973.   A March 1973 survey of Sudan placed employment in establishments employing over 100 workers at about 44,000 (of which 35,000 were production process workers).[2]   In view of incomplete returns and under-enumeration, we will rely on a later survey which places "manufacturing" employment in Khartoum at around 33,000.[3] Adding government employment of 40,000 to 60,000 gives a modern sector total of between 20 and 30 per cent of the labour force of Khartoum.   This percentage is clearly smaller if we are concerned only with employment in the high-wage firms and units.

These are average employment figures, but there are fluctuations due to the employment of casual and seasonal labour.   There are no reliable figures of the resultant "swell" or "contraction" and we can only speculate on the extent to which they are due to demand as opposed to supply forces.   In self-employment, the slack season in agriculture provides the motive force for the entry of labour into the urban sector.   It is not clear if, and the extent to which, such seasonal inflows affect the scheduling of work in the modern sector. There is an obvious relationship in such large-scale modern sector operations as the Gezira schemes which depend upon seasonal labour. Elsewhere our knowledge is limited as to how the forces of demand and supply adjust themselves.

Outside of the high-wage formal sector - and even in it - it may be difficult to define the employment relationship with precision. Much employment, especially of physical labour, is casual employment with no identifiable single employer.   Much economic activity also may involve switching between wage employment and other kinds of economic activity as well as within wage employment.

Governments and modern sector employers - especially the high-paying variety - are the most concerned to develop a durable employment relationship.   However, a "permanent" job status is not easily granted.   Apart from customary rules of thumb governing recruitment and advancement, formal criteria also play an important role.   "Wage leaders" insist on elementary education as an entrance requirement

---

[1] See Appendix 1.

[2] Statistical Abstract, 1973 and Establishments Survey, 1973, Ministry of Public Service, Government of Sudan.

[3] Regional Plan of Khartoum, op. cit., Vol. II (MEFIT, 1974), XII, pp. 53 and 55.   In addition, they estimated some 31,000 temporary workers in manufacturing.

for the lowest category employment; additional educational and
technical qualifications may command entry but only at discrete
higher intervals in the job hierarchy. Prevailing personnel and
wage administration practices thus limit the channels and stages
of entry into "permanent" employment.

This leads to an "insulated" labour market somewhat immune to
influences from the rest of the economy. Relatively low rates of
absenteeism among "permanent" workers in the Sudan textiles and
the absence of seasonal fluctuations suggest some such "insulation".
However, turnover rates are relatively high and this may be due to
the practice of hiring casual and temporary workers.[1] Data for
public industrial concerns in 1973 indicate that 8,791 out of
21,967 workers were "temporary", or about 40 per cent (higher if we
exclude the white-collar workers).[2] Similarly, the Ministry of
Construction frequently adds to its demand for labour by hiring
additional workers on a casual or temporary basis or by engaging
contractors who provide employment on a non-permanent basis. The
same survey which estimated "manufacturing" employment at 33,000
placed "temporary" manufacturing employment at 31,000.[3]

The reliance on casual and temporary staff would fit in well
with variations in production schedules. It would also avoid the
more expensive "permanent" job commitments, particularly if associations with the non-permanent workforce can be stabilised. The law
requires that a permanent post be created if continuous employment
is offered for more than 182 days. Subcontracting is also a means
of supplementing available skills in permanent cadres and, more
important, deviating from the fixed wage schedules in government or
organised industry. The flexibility with which contractors can
hire scarce skills and other workers at higher or lower than the
institutionally determined wage rates is in fact a reason for contracts being awarded to them. Government contracts, for instance,
do not attempt to enforce any complement of fair wages, labour standards, etc.

---

[1] In 1967 and 1968 the average monthly turnover rate for unskilled and semi-skilled workers ranged between 2 and 4 per cent for
one mill and 3.5 and 21 per cent for the other. Ali Ahmed Suliman:
"The effect of labour turnover and absenteeism on the cost of production of the Sudan textile industry", Eastern African Economic Review,
Dec. 1971. In Bombay, by contrast, separation rates for establishments employing over 2,000 were 1.16 and 1.30 per cent in 1967 and
1968: Indian Labour Statistics (Simla, 1974), p. 129.

[2] In some public concerns in 1973, the following pattern was
obtained:

	Number	Percentages
Skilled	3 554	16
Not skilled	7 003	32
Temporary	8 791	40
White collar	2 616	-

Source: Statistical Abstract, 1973.

[3] Regional Plan of Khartoum, op. cit., Vol. II, pp, 53, 55 et
passim.

The hazy borderline surrounding permanent employment due to the "cushion" or elasticity provided by the hiring of casual and temporary workers emphasises the possibility of greater wage flexibility and weaker job commitments as well as greater ease of entry in the rest of the urban labour market. However, it may be helpful to note some complicating details.

Treating the formal as the "high-wage" sector leaves us with a large number outside in wage and self-employment. In Greater Khartoum, this would include the fringe of urban-based farmers with secondary involvement in non-farm wage or self-employment. There are also several own-account workers, including some who hire labour. The latter would include, but by no means be identical to, the self-employed and successful entrepreneurs who have generated much of the hope concerning the dynamism of the informal sector.

This category would also include the poor and illiterate over-lapping confused territories involving low-paid wage employment, petty vending, and others among the least-successful own-account activities. These diverse possibilities can be entertained - despite lack of skills and of capital - only because entry is easy and alternatives are limited.

But barriers and more or less demanding expectations also con-dition participation in the urban labour market. The educated worker, say one with a high-school education, is not a ready and willing candidate for the low-paying jobs mentioned above, for the rewards are low and it may pay to wait (a point discussed later). Even a transient involvement in low-wage employment may be shunned if it should impede the search for, or prejudice the chances of, a better paying job later. Nor can it be readily assumed that he is a potential "informal" sector entrepreneur. Not everyone can do well in business or self-employment. Even a small-scale entre-preneur needs contacts, a helpful base, requisite ability and some credit. He may get his start from surplus from the sale of agri-cultural output, accumulated personal savings, a helpful relative, a government loan or licence, and so forth. The data on the sociological composition of the urban labour force emphasise the importance of tribal affiliations and ethnic clusters in occupa-tional affiliation and in conditioning access to jobs and educa-tional and income opportunities.[1]

To sum up this discussion, the main point is that the urban labour market is more complicated than the simpler models which have been floating around. The high-wage sector is relatively thin, even more so in the newly developing urban areas than Khartoum. There is a hazy area around modern sector employment and several overlapping segments of the urban labour market beyond, which are characterised by flexible wage and labour market practices and pro-vide scope for the forces of supply and demand to work themselves out. The bulk of the labour force - low-income wage earners and self-employed - are to be found here. They are poorly equipped for successful entrepreneurship. And for the educated, the prospects may be better in formal sector wage employment.

---

[1] See Appendix 2: Sociological composition of urban occupa-tional categories.

The urban wage structure and earnings

In the Sudan, formal wage structures cover only Government and the larger employers, and only a minority of the labour force. Variations in wages or earnings are much greater elsewhere.

Wage rates in Government are higher than in private employment. A survey of establishments employing five or more workers in 1974 indicated this to be true for virtually every size class. Within Government, established state enterprises like the Sudan Railways pay better than other branches of Government. However, one must note the practice of employing casual and temporary staff and of contracting out work through others. State enterprises are being encouraged to rationalise their pay structure and personnel adminis- tration according to established government practice.

The position as regards private employment is more complex because of greater variation in size, activities undertaken, skills employed, the influence of government regulations, the pressures of unionisation, and so on.

The small number of foreign firms are at the top of the wage hierarchy, even topping the Government. A few of the larger Sudanese firms, including public enterprises, appear to be in this category[1], carried over from the days prior to nationalisation, and the rest, although among the better paying employers, perhaps trail the government scales of pay. Our information is rather scanty on the smaller enterprises[2].

But it is widely believed that the numerous smaller private firms pay wages well below the government level[3]. It is interesting to note that this variability is mainly in the private sector. It is indicative of the limited scope of regulation and the relatively free play of market forces in the urban labour market as a whole[4].

A comparison of monthly earnings from a 1971 survey of migrants, non-migrants and returned Khartoumites with 1971 wage figures from a leading nationalised firm proved illustrative[5]. In the latter, the

---

[1] See Table 1, p. 106.

[2] In 1974, of 949 units surveyed in the private sector, 829 were in the "individual business" and "partnership" categories; 677 of these employed less than 10. The public and private companies which may be expected to provide some "wage leadership", 29. Establishments survey, Ministry of Public Service and Administrative Reform, July 1974.

[3] Abdel-Rahman El Tayib Ali Taha: The Sudanese Labour Movement: A Study of Labour Unionism in a Developing Society (unpublished doctoral dissertation), (UCLA, 1970), pp. 215 and ff.

[4] The public sector plays a small role in the smaller size cate- gories. The actual variability in private employment is likely to be greater than recorded here for such reasons as exclusion of self- employment earnings, respondent bias, etc.

[5] Mohamed El-Awad Galal-el-Din: Internal Migration in the Sudan since World War II, with special reference to Migration to Greater Khartoum (unpublished doctoral dissertation), (London School of Economics, 1973), table 7.12 for the 1971 survey data. For 1971 wage figures, see this as a comparison among gross categories which obscures the influence of many factors such as skill, literacy, educa- tion attainment, work experience, etc., which we will take up later.

lowest category operative probably earned around ₤S20 (the
incentive and monthly attendance bonus have been included as
scheduled maxima rather than as actual payments).   Assuming that
the survey respondents were equally distributed around the mean of
the size class ₤S16-25, some 18 per cent of returned Khartoumites,
32 per cent of non-migrants, and 41 per cent of migrants were earning an income below the lowest wage in a wage-leader firm.   The
percentage was higher for a recent migrant.

Wages paid include a cost-of-living allowance (called COLA).
Across-the-board increments take place only at infrequent intervals
and the most recent revisions affected only the COLA, which is not
tied to any price index.   In government and parastatal enterprises there are seven, partly overlapping, grades below and special
grades above for supervisory or managerial personnel.[1]   The pattern
in leading private enterprises is similar for manual operatives.
Workers are started at the lowest step in each group and there are
annual increments until they reach the top.   The bulk of employment
is at the bottom two or three groups and it appears that there may
be some "bunching" at the top of each.

It is also customary to make additional payments, in kind or
in cash.   These may include attendance and incentive bonuses, an
annual bonus of one month's wage (not tied to productivity or performance), and various fringe benefits such as subsidised lunch and
medical care (sometimes for the whole family), free transport or
transport allowance, housing loans, provident fund, social security,
recreational facilities, and so forth.   In comparing urban earnings,
it must be kept in mind that the typical industrial establishment
does not work more than 250 days or 42 weeks of 6 days each.   Many
workers work less for such reasons as absenteeism and there is provision for authorised absences for sickness, etc.

A discussion of formal or high-wage sector practices naturally
raises the question of how important unions and collective bargaining are in wage determination.   Units in public employment appear
to be strongly unionised and, in the private sector, the percentage
unionised declines with size.   In units below 30, and in establishments outside manufacturing and Government, unionisation is
generally rare.   At the same time, percentage unionisation figures
can give only an incomplete picture of union effectiveness as union
leaders rely also on political action.   Union militancy and
rhetoric are centred around the practices of the better-paying firms.
Public regulation has also focused on employment in Government and
in the larger private units.   But a line of causation should not be
readily inferred, for the wage leadership of these firms is also
attributable to efficiency and production requirements rather than
collective bargaining or regulatory pressures.   Elsewhere, such
institutional pressures and efficiency considerations are not
strong.[2]

---

[1] For more details see Mohamed Murtada Mustafa and others:
"The labour market: efficiency problems in spatial, seasonal and
skills allocation", preparatory conference paper, Khartoum, 1975,
pp. 9-10.

[2] In fact, a leading Sudanese academic authority and former
member of government wage commissions indicated that the net result
of any wage increase in the formal or high-wage sector would be to
widen the differentials as this will have little effect on the urban
floor.

III. THE URBAN PULL: SOME POLICY ISSUES

The relative prosperity of the urban economy, the accelerating migration and the surfacing of problems of urban squalor direct attention to organised sector wage pressures in limiting employment generation and inducing excessive inflows.

Migration important for growth and equity

Migration to urban areas, and more generally from low- to high-income areas, is in principle desirable: it encourages resource mobility to high productivity areas and, in so doing, enhances national income.

There are numerous examples of tribal and family work-sharing arrangements in areas of out-migration which imply a maximisation of family income from migration.[1] Prevailing geographical and rural-urban differentials also emphasise the gains from migration. Available data, though fragmentary, suggest that this is exactly what is taking place: there is movement - to Khartoum from the south and west to the north and east, to several small towns (the rate of growth is even more impressive for the other urban areas in the south, Nyala, etc.), and also of course from Khartoum to Gezira, Red Sea areas, etc. Indeed, it is only recently that Khartoum emerged as a net importer of labour, obscuring its historical and indeed continuing role as a supplier of labour[2] to various development and agricultural projects in the country. Recent data on in-migration to Khartoum from the 1974 ILO Survey indicates that it comes principally from the following provinces: Northern (37.4 per cent); Kordofan (17.1 per cent); Blue Nile (17.7 per cent); Darfur (9.1 per cent); and Kassala (4.8 per cent), these being the last place of residence. Migration from the south, the country's poorest areas, is limited. It comes almost equally from the urban and rural areas (52 and 48 per cent respectively), but about 8 per cent of the former had originally moved from their rural birthplaces.

If migration were to be stopped overnight, what would be the consequence? A lot of the menial labour, particularly in the service sector, is done by such migrants and there will be consequent shortages.[3] Even in a well-established and well-paying factory, such as the Sudan textiles, results may be serious as production depends a good deal on non-Khartoum labour.[4] And it will of course

---

[1] United Nations Economic Commission for Africa: Employment of Women in the Sudan, Jan. 1975. This was reissued as a preparatory conference (6-8 Feb. 1975) task-force paper: Women and Development (Khartoum, Economic and Social Research Council, 1975).

[2] P.F.M. McLoughlin: "Labour market conditions and wages in the Three Towns, 1900-1950", Sudan Notes and Records, Vol. LI, 1970, pp. 105-118.

[3] The tendency for migrants to perform the menial and lower-paying jobs is not unique to Khartoum and may be found in many other metropolitan areas in both developed and underdeveloped nations.

[4] A.A. Suliman, op. cit., p. 52. Khartoum contributes only 5 per cent of the workforce. Migrant percentages from other regions are as follows: south 25, west 55, north 13, and east 2.

do nothing to relieve the pressures of those who come to Khartoum
for study, for work, or just for alms because the opportunities [1]
are either non-existent or meagre in the areas of out-migration.
The inducement to migrate will remain as long as certain areas
remain underdeveloped and have large human factor endowments relative to complementary inputs.

Are urban wages too high?

Nevertheless, the issue remains whether prevailing rural-urban
differentials are too large and any special characteristics of the
urban labour market encourage excessive migration.

An interesting problem is the impact of the Minimum Wage Law.
In 1974, the Government adopted £S16.50 as a minimum wage for the
lowest category employee in public services and enterprises, and
allowed private firms until 1976 to catch up in three annual increments. Already, in 1974, the lowest category group I employee in
the Sudan Railways was earning more than this sum. All but the
lowest two steps of group I employees in the public services were
also better paid. A 1974 Survey of Establishments employing five
or more indicated that, in the public sector as a whole, average
weekly earnings in all size categories were well in excess of the
pro-rated monthly minimum. Among the private firms surveyed, with
a lower monthly minimum, only those likely to have been clearly
affected were those employing less than ten workers, or slightly
under 7 per cent of private employment (or 5.6 per cent of all
employment). Allowing for the fact that the dispersion might cast
some well below the average earnings for the firms surveyed, we may
seek a higher cut-off point and include firms whose average weekly
earnings were £S4. The likely beneficiaries of the Minimum Wage
Law move up to only about 14.5 per cent of employment in private
firms surveyed (or 11.1 per cent of all employment).[2] These are
upper estimates of likely beneficiaries among firms covered by the
Law, which is largely inapplicable in other wage and self-employment.
When one adds to this the problems of enforcement in the smaller
units, precisely where earnings may fall below the legal minimum, it
seems likely that its coverage of the urban low-income population
was negligible.

Whether in general the urban wage is too large relative to
rural wages is difficult to answer because of the differences in cost
of living, requirements of living (such as transport to work), the
cost of moving to urban areas, the time spent in looking for a suitable job, the possibilities of failure in this search, and so on.
Cultural factors are also relevant and affect both the pecuniary and
non-pecuniary calculus of migration. The presence of relatives in

---

[1] Galal-el-Din, op. cit., table 10.3, indicating migrant moti-
vations in coming to Khartoum. Frivolous reasons play a negligible
role, including the oft-cited attractions of city life.

[2] Assuming that the Minimum Wage Law was applicable to the 1973
situation, and ignoring the higher rates prevailing in public sector
firms, gives us again an upper estimate of only 11,700 likely beneficiaries in firms employing 30 or over. It works out to slightly
over 20 per cent of the employment in firms covered by the 1973
Establishment Survey but a significantly smaller percentage of urban
wage employment or the labour force.

the urban area may aid in both respects and, of course, provide
visible proof of successful migration.   Undoubtedly this is one
reason why migration is limited from the southern provinces and
more pronounced among the ethnic communities well established in
Khartoum.   Observers also indicated that even £S300 per year would
not be attractive to a nomad with cattle wealth earning yearly
around £S104 in the Qoz and that a Gezira resident would need about
three times the money income to live in equivalent comfort in
Khartoum.

Labour force participation rates in Khartoum and the social
and familial structure of the rural and nomadic communities suggest
another consideration.   The over-all labour force participation rate
at 30 per cent is low due mainly to the negligible participation of
women.   It is thus important that the potential migrant, particularly one seeking a permanent job in the formal sector, earns
enough in the area of migration to compensate for his earnings and
that of his wife or family help.   Available evidence suggests that
women are an active part of the family workforce in rural areas.[1]

A detailed recent study indicates that migrants were satisfied
that they bettered themselves.[2]   The male-female ratio has been
declining, also indicative of such satisfaction.   Government
policies favouring the acquisition of low-cost land, and the location of educational and training institutions in Khartoum, are also
features attractive to the migrant.   However, there is a residency
requirement of five years for eligibility to acquire low-cost land.
Also the focus is on those who succeed as migrants.   We know little
about those who came and returned or left.

A third interesting aspect of the rural-urban wage differential
concerns the possibility that the institutional determination of the
urban wage rate at an unrealistically high level encourages excessive
migration.   Migrants come pouring in because of prevailing rural-
urban differentials, modified by the probability of finding employment.   However, these large differentials encourage a greater inflow
than can be absorbed under current demand conditions.   Increased
urban wages only worsen the problem by encouraging a stronger inflow.
The result is growing urban unemployment.

Such formulations rely unduly on the attractive pull of high
wages in formal, modern sector employment.   It is important to
identify which of the various wages in the urban labour market provide the typical migrant with the best picture of his alternatives.
Neither the industrial (modern sector) nor government wage rate nor
any composite (given the wide variation in urban earnings) will be
a satisfactory yardstick for comparison.   There are few openings in
the modern sector and entry is governed by requirements of literacy
and education so that jobs here cannot provide promising "ports of

---

[1] Employment of Women in the Sudan, op. cit.   Interviews and
related readings indicate that tribal arrangements may also imply a
definite but shared responsibility for cultivation, living expenditures, and cash needs.   A migrant to the city cannot just assume
that his work will be done during his absence; his share of benefits
is contingent upon his continued contribution, especially as regards
the last item.

[2] Galal-el-Din, op. cit., Chapters 7, 10 and 11.

entry" for the majority of migrants.   Prevailing urban institutional
wages, even when modified by the urban unemployment rate, provide for
a rough measure of the probability of landing such high-paying jobs,
or of the gains from migration.

But the difficulties of entry into high-paying jobs would set up
more specific queues - at employment exchanges, factory gates and
government offices or with friends or relatives - wherever there
appear to be persons who control the doors to opportunity.   However,
these rational responses do not necessarily imply excessive urban
migration or unemployment.   People search for better jobs while
being employed or accept casual or temporary employment if the
experience would increase the chances of subsequent absorption.   Or
they form queues before schools and training institutes.

There is nothing unusual about such queues.   They make sense
when the jobseeker is as good as those employed in the high-wage
sector or can become as good by training or experience.   Certain
circumstances may swell the queues unduly.   Widespread ignorance as
to the conditions of entry, hiring criteria which turn out to be more
rationing devices than functional requirements, and the possibility
of weakening these by say, political pressure, are some of these.
It is not that these conditions do not exist in the Sudan, but their
over-all impact on urban unemployment as a whole must be judged to
be small.   For the majority, remaining in the queue is an expensive
luxury compared to returning to their homes or accepting lesser-
paying alternatives in the city itself.

An examination of the unemployment figures will be appropriate
at this stage.

IV.   URBAN UNEMPLOYMENT AND THE JOB SEARCH PROCESS

We have three successive moment-of-time estimates of the urban
unemployment rate for Khartoum, all of them around 5 per cent.[1]
Although there are variations in coverage and definitions, and problems of response bias, etc., they yield a consistent picture of a low
over-all rate of unemployment.

But for some groups, more than others, it may be necessary to
search longer (for such reasons as lack of knowledge as to alternatives or preferences as to specific jobs) or it may pay to wait for

---

[1] The 1964-66 Population and Housing Survey estimates unemployment at around 5 per cent for Khartoum and Omdurman; the migration
survey of Dr. Galal-el-Din for 1971 estimates male (15 years and
over) unemployment rate at 5.6 per cent; and the ILO Survey,
October 1974, yields a 5.2 per cent unemployment rate for the Three
Towns.   (See W. Keddeman: An Introduction to the Employment Situation in the Sudan, Mar. 1975, D.62, pp. 9-10.)   Of the other surveys, only the MEFIT 1974 Survey gives a higher estimate but details
of coverage are lacking.   Other sources which may be mentioned
include the 1955-56 Census which provided an "unemployment" estimate
for the nation as a whole (1.2 to 1.7 per cent), and the 1973 Census.

appropriate opportunities to open up.   Those in this category
include new entrants into the labour market, young persons or others
without prior work experience, women and the educated.   The 1967-68
Household Budget Survey revealed disproportionately high unemployment
rates among urban females (over four times the comparable rate for
males) and among those never employed before (over three times the
comparable rate for those previously employed and over 20 times the
rate for females never employed compared to females employed before).[1]
The 1973 Census (provisional tabulations) indicate similar strikingly
higher rates for male youth (15-19 years old) in the northern provinces, Red Sea and Equatoria, although, in the last area, female
unemployment rates are lower.[2]

What about the registrants on the employment exchanges?   The
figures of registrants include those beyond the urban area (even
though a local address may be given) and persons who have been
"hired" but seek subsequently to satisfy the legal requirements of
registration.[3]   The law now forbids employers even to advertise
their requirements except with prior permission from the concerned
labour office.

The employment exchanges in the Sudan are a poor gauge of the
general employment situation as they service only a small proportion
of jobseekers.   During the last quarter of 1973, registrations and
placements totalled only 12,019 and 1,015 respectively for the
country as a whole.   In Khartoum Province during the same period
registrations totalled 6,395 and placements 485.

To assess the effectiveness of the exchanges we need data on
placements related to referrals in response to employer requests
and some breakdowns by skills, educational attainments, period of
waiting and so on.   One would also like to know what the registrants
do while waiting to be notified by the employment office.   Information on the type of job being sought would also help.

A visit to the Khartoum Employment Office, the most developed in
the country, and discussions with government officials, employers and
jobseekers indicate limited development.   Employers indicated that
their experience with the referral mechanism had not been encouraging,
even for casual workers.   The employment exchanges undertake almost
no trade testing or field work involving contacts with potential
employers, training institutes, schools, etc.   The exchanges experience difficulty even in meeting employer requests for casual or
temporary workers as applicants appear primarily interested in longer
duration employment.   The few notices on the bulletin boards did not
provide adequate particulars about the employer, the job, the number
of vacancies, remuneration and service conditions, and the qualifications required.   Added to this was the waiting and the low rate of

---

[1] W. Keddeman, op. cit., p. 9.

[2] W. Keddeman, Note on 1973 Census (11 Mar. 1973), pp. 2-3.

[3] This latter is believed small, however, but may grow if the
recent law requiring registration is enforced strictly, swelling both
registrations and placements.

placements as a percentage of outstanding registrations.   An
unspecified proportion of registrants take on casual or temporary
jobs while waiting for a more desirable opening.   However, there
may be a reluctance to declare oneself to be employed for fear
that this would merit less attention from the employment offices.[1]

Adequate information is of particular relevance for migrants
and first-time entrants and hence the importance of friends, relatives, etc., in guiding migratory and job search behaviour.   Such
"informal" channels are important in the urban labour market, even
for the well-organised sectors.

In the last quarter of 1973, about 40 per cent of the
registered, classified as unemployed, had no prior work experience
in the Khartoum area, the proportion being about 80 per cent for
technical workers.[2]   Figures for the first quarter of 1973 indicate that, among those classified as registered unemployed, 52.3
per cent of the unskilled, 22.5 per cent of the skilled, and 87.8
per cent of those educated up to the second level were seeking work
for the first time.[3]   The 1967-68 Survey also indicated, as mentioned earlier, that two-thirds or more of the unemployed were
first-time entrants into the labour market.   Migrants from the
Southern, Darfur and Kordofan Provinces had substantially fewer
relatives in Khartoum than other migrants and this may be an important explanation of the more limited migration from these areas.[4]

Data concerning educated workers emphasise, however, the
advantages of waiting (idleness or unemployment) for better jobs.
Those entering Government and education had to wait the longest
compared to shorter periods (six months or less) for agriculture,
transport and industry (96.72, 92.95 and 84.85 obtaining jobs in
less than six months).[5]   Periods of waiting were longer for younger
employed graduates below 30, social science majors and lawyers, but
favourable for medicine, engineering and scientific fields.   The
"labour department", "personal contacts" and the "university authorities" emerged as the major sources of information (48.85, 22.46
and 16.58 per cent respectively).[6]   However, the 1971 sample of
migrants indicated that, at lower levels of education, those with
only limited education experienced greater difficulty and had to
wait for longer periods than those with higher levels of educational
attainment.   The position reversed itself and waiting was longer
for those with the highest levels of education.[7]

---

[1] Thus attempts to estimate unemployment in Atbara on the basis
of registration figures yielded a figure several times the estimate
provided by the 1973 Census.

[2] Statistical Abstract, 1973.

[3] B.C. Sanyal and El Sammani A. Yacoub: Higher Education and
Employment of Graduates: The Case of the Sudan (Paris, IIED, 1975),
draft, p. 42.

[4] Galal-el-Din, op. cit., p. 219.

[5] Sanyal and Yacoub, op. cit., pp. 172-175.

[6] ibid., pp. 168-170.   Incidentally, the Labour Department had
a unique position in assigning scarce jobs in public employment.

[7] Galal-el-Din, op. cit., table 11.3.

Employment prospects in government and modern industry
influence this behaviour.   Accordingly, we will examine the practices of the modern sector in some detail.

IV.   MODERN SECTOR EMPLOYMENT PRACTICES

Fundamental to the analysis of the modern sector is the concept of permanent employment.   It is the durable link between
employer and employee - at a relatively high wage and level of
productivity - that endows this sector with its distinctive character in the labour market.

The high wage rates in the modern sector reflect the importance attached to a stable association.   Such stability appears to
command a premium even in apparently favourable conditions of
labour supply.   In part this may reflect the dependence of modern
sector employers in Khartoum or the Gezira borad on imported
labour, sometimes from great distances.   Partly, this may reflect
the special requirements of employment and efficiency in the modern
sector - the requirements of regularity, the care of expensive
machinery or the execution of complex tasks, the potential for
learning by doing, and the need for a trained labour force.   The
relatively high turnover rates in the well-established textile
industry and practices to ensure stabilisation as in the railways
attest stability in modern industry as well as the potential costs
of seeking greater stabilisation.   Not only are wages already
higher in modern industry, but many components - attendance bonuses,
transport and travel allowances, housing loans or subsidies - are
specifically geared to the factor of stability.   The hiring preferences of modern sector employers are tied to this consideration,
although there is no simple line of causation, desired workers
being given stable employment and stable workers being given
desired employment.   But there is one governing thread: the
employer in Government or industry intends to stay in operation for
some time and conceives as a necessary complement a cadre of
employees who would operate at untypical levels of efficiency.

The criteria for entry into permanent employment in the modern
sector include various rules of thumb (in Atbara, the railway
authorities favour first preference to the offspring of employees),[1]
prior experience, and of course various kinds of certificates concerning formal preparation.   Many of the well-established and
prestigious employers insist on elementary education for new recruitment to the permanent payroll even for the lowest category manual
jobs.   They defend the practice on the ground that literate workers
adapted better to modern employment, literacy helped workers to read
elementary instructions, improved their chances of being upgraded,
etc.

Advances or new recruitment to higher grades or groups in the
wage hierarchy are also contingent upon successively higher levels
of educational attainment: intermediate education with some technical training was required for middle-level skilled manual jobs,

---

[1] The Sudan railway authorities actually moved to seek exemp-
tion from the provision to recruit through the employment exchange
on a first-come first-hired basis.

secondary education with technical training for the intermediate technical cadres, and college degrees in arts or the sciences, the former for administrative jobs and the latter for employment as engineers, scientists, etc. In the blue-collar ranks, trade union pressure has reinforced the tendency to limit direct recruitment from outside to persons with higher formal qualifications. Among a few élite employers there is a preference for graduates in business administration and some new specialities for executive and staff positions. Although employers are critical about the quality of technical training or general education, one sees no interest in modifying these requirements. The better technical school trainees have no problem finding jobs (the pressure for admission being in fact related to this factor); also some of the established employers provide their own training and insist upon prior formal education for admission. Employers of university graduates - some 75 per cent - similarly give first place to "academic records" among a list of desirable attributes.[1]

Are these modern sector practices leading to the creation of small numbers of more-productive and better-paid employees, a rationing mechanism, or are they functionally necessary? What is their significance in a strategy of employment promotion for the nation as a whole?

The first is a difficult question to answer. Despite the rhetoric, there is no question but that individual employers are profit maximisers who relate higher costs to increased productivity. Also they have the best experience as to the attributes which are most useful in getting tasks done. However, employers, like others, work within a framework of technology and knowledge that society possesses. It is important to explore the possibility of changing this framework by such means as research, innovation, substitution with alternative hiring criteria, and so forth. There is also the likelihood that the calculations of individual employers are biased in the existing direction by national policies and subsidies concerning the profitability of modern sector skills and economic activity.

Assuming that employers choose the attributes which best predict desired productivity or performance, one may still be concerned that opportunities are rationed to too few. This arises when the suspicion exists that those excluded from permanent employment are as good as those recruited or as likely to improve their performance after being hired if given comparable wages, bonuses, housing, etc.

This practice of paying those employed a higher wage than those available for work emphasises the paradox of shortages in the midst of a surplus. Where wages are pushed up by union or regulatory action, the employers' interest in raising productivity at the margin is easy enough to understand. For other, and possibly more significant, situations, two alternative explanations rule the field: that there is in fact not a true surplus when employer requirements are compared in finer detail with the attributes of those available; and that higher wages result in higher productivity, without time lags in some kind of a proportionate relationship,

---

[1] Sanyal and Yacoub, op. cit., p. 190.

a minimum standard of efficiency being decreed by operational
considerations (much like the relationship of lead-free gasoline to
recent automobiles). It is only when the latter is combined with
some kind of a "learning" effect, a focus on a minimum standard of
efficiency over time, that it becomes relevant to an analysis of
permanent employment. The relative importance of these sources of
wage pressures needs further investigation, and cannot be inferred
from superficial generalisations of a labour surplus alone.[1]

It can be said of employers and jobs paying more than the prevailing hiring-in wages that they are likely to emphasise tasks
only peripherally related to existing traditions or standards of
efficiency and to stress performance specific to that category of
firms. It is for this reason that the practices of the large
employers - Government, private or foreign - however satisfactory
they may be from a management or industrial relations point of
view cannot be made the general norm.[2]

However, given a conflict between this mode of organisation
and the relative factor endowments of a nation - limited capital
and abundant labour - one must expect strong pressure upon the
modern sector to enlarge its rolls of permanent employment. This
will be accommodated to some extent, employers, workers and governments collaborating in relieving these pressures. Naturally some
firms are more likely to yield to these pressures and some employment situations will be more vulnerable than others. The organisations and managerial practices which adapt to the "redundant"
labour will in time get institutionalised at a lower level of firm
efficiency. The "redundant" labour is no longer surplus, for it
cannot be withdrawn except at a cost in terms of lost output.

In one of the largest public sector companies, careful and
elaborate calculations were made as to the required labour force,
and something like 15 per cent of the permanent workers were determined to be "surplus". The company, however, went out of the way
to control absenteeism (which was running at a rate considerably
less than the presumed surplus) by such means as free transport to
workers and attendance bonuses. Questioned why the management did
not carry on with a reduced complement, the existing practice was
defended on the ground that workers were trained to carry out only
a limited number of machine-tending assignments and few operators
could handle the work of absentees.

---

[1] In the Sudan, the turnover rates faced by some modern sector
firms suggest a possible shortage; the availability of casual and
temporary workers suggests a surplus. The Bombay textile industry
experience, one well analysed from this perspective, indicated a
historical shortage of stable family migrant workers at the prevailing wages. See Dipak Mazumdar: "Labour supply in early industrialisation: the case of the Bombay textile industry", Economic
History Review, Aug. 1973.

[2] Subbiah Kannappan: "The economics of structuring an industrial labour force: Some reflections on the commitment problem",
The British Journal of Industrial Relations, Nov. 1966, pp. 379-404.

Comparable questions are raised as regards the employment policies of the Sudan Railways, whose payroll "surplus" is stressed by top management and has been a matter of concern for some time. However, this has not stopped the growth of employment. At the beginning of fiscal year 1961-62 (1 July 1961) employment stood at 29,299, and at the end of fiscal year 1971-72 (30 June 1972) it was 40,000. During the 11 years, recruitment exceeded discharges eight times. For railway employment proper (as Sudan Railways manage other activities also), the corresponding totals are 19,754 and 25,184 respectively. Again recruitment exceeded discharges in 8 out of 11 years. Employment in 1975 was more than in 1971-72.

Field visits and interviews confirmed management's interest in being a model employer in terms of wages and fringe benefits. Community and housing development policies had made Atbara, the railway headquarters, among the more attractive towns of the Sudan. But there were also problems of inefficiency, poor maintenance and indiscipline. Deiselisation had brought in the need for new workers, and the old ones were rendered surplus but could not be removed or easily shifted to other assignments. Union and political pressures led to the upgrading of some categories of workers but the work they formerly handled suffered in consequence. These were only the peaks of an iceberg indicating a more general condition of administrative rigidities, labour surpluses and neglected work which have made the performance of the entire industry a matter of national concern.

Increased worker efficiency and labour productivity is more easily stipulated than realised. It is probably the dream of every works or personnel manager to realise a higher average output and save on the wage bill. But almost invariably these involve greater flexibility in work assignments, a better-trained or adaptable labour force, and some sharing of the gains. One should not forget the equally important imperative of managerial efficiency. External conditions also play a part, such as machine breakdowns, irregularity in the supply of raw materials, etc., as, with given work rules, workers will be idle (and estimated to be in surplus) if production schedules cannot be maintained (this was certainly the case with a packaging factory where one or more complements of workers were standing idle by machine units because of the erratic supply of raw materials through Port Sudan). Estimates of surplus are thus contingent upon hypothesised alternative conditions. These conditions do not now exist and cannot be realised with the facility with which the relevant calculations can be made.

How important are policies aimed at reducing this labour surplus? If the surplus is largely a work-sharing arrangement which does not affect the employers' wage bill and output for a given plant capacity and organisation, attempts to reduce it would only swell the ranks of the unemployed with problematic gains in unit costs. Actually, however, this is unlikely and the redundancy would lead to two difficult problems. It would add to the complexities and complications of work organisation, discipline and productivity. Across-the-board increases, whether of fringe benefits or wages, may favour disproportionately the employed with no commensurate increase in productivity and make the task of employment generation more difficult.

The above analysis raises the disturbing possibility not merely of the difficulty of reducing redundancies in high-wage modern employment but of success in this respect leading to even more exclusive islands of select employment characterised by high wages and productivity. The fundamental problem is that generating employment in the modern sector must contend with the relatively higher factor cost (wage and fringe benefits as well as non-wage costs of employment) and the capital needed for each additional unit of employment. The basic issue is not that wages are high or unwarranted in this sector (although this may be the case) but that developing additional employment is expensive. The criteria for entry are likely to exclude the vast bulk of the nation's human resources, including many segments of the urban poor. At the same time, the pressures for entry into this sector will make it difficult to keep numbers down to the optimal level.

But this would be an inefficient method of generating employment. This is one of the reasons why modern sector employers rely on many forms of non-permanent employment. There is a real need for experimentation and innovation in this area. There is also a need for research into different modes of organising and planning the demand for labour, especially the urban poor. Also important are alternative investment priorities, judged in terms of the yields and employment generated. The possibility of modifying existing hiring and employment criteria has already been discussed. There is probably less promise in this last than in the other steps.

VI. CONCLUDING OBSERVATIONS

The urban labour market comprises a small proportion of the nation's labour force, but it is a significant component of the national economy. It is not a homogeneous whole but consists of distinct and overlapping segments. Close to the Government and modern industry there is a high-wage sector of permanent employment. The distinction between this high-wage modern sector, often called the formal sector, and the rest of the economy, called the informal sector, is by no means clear cut. One reason for this is the considerable reliance on temporary and casual employment by modern sector employers which would imply that some modern sector employees have alternatives in the rest of the economy. The informal sector is also by no means homogeneous. It consists of successful entrepreneurs as well as the self-employed professionals; it also consists of the unskilled with limited means and contacts engaged in types of activity which overlap wage earning, casual services and petty hawking. There are also an undefined number in the category of the urban poor earning incomes which are at the barest margin of subsistence. These include those with impaired physical capacity of varying severity.

This chapter points out that the modern sector embraces at most 30 per cent of the urban labour force. Trade union activity and government wage regulation are limited to the larger employers in industrial and commercial establishments. However, requirements of literacy, training and prior work experience limit opportunities in this sector to a few. As such, modern sector wages are of marginal relevance to the typical migrant.

Available unemployment data confirm this point in another way. The unemployment rate is around 5 per cent, a plausible and not unreasonable figure. Urban workers, after a period of search and waiting, take on whatever jobs are available. These are poor jobs but they are taken because there are few better alternatives. It is mainly those who have some means such as the educated, or have special preferences such as the women, who wait longer, although the job search process implies greater difficulties for the migrants and new entrants. Those with special problems include migrants without relatives, first-time entrants, females and youth. In the bulk of the cases, the search is active and expectations are adjusted fairly quickly, so that even they too find jobs within a few months after looking for work. This is the reason for the low unemployment rate despite the fact that a substantial proportion of migrants are first-time jobseekers and the problems of credentials, virtual absence of organised labour market intelligence, etc.

We conclude that the functioning of the urban labour market indicates a rather rational process. People come into the urban areas looking for jobs because they are better here than any opportunities available to them elsewhere. When they look for jobs in the modern sector it is again because these are more remunerative. Urban residents (migrants and non-migrants) also seek additional training or schooling because prevailing hiring criteria emphasise the desirability of these qualifications.

To say that the labour market works reasonably well means only that it works along predictable directions and that individuals are responding to the structure of opportunities in the best way they can. People find jobs, not necessarily well-paying jobs. Most work, in wage or self-employment, at low levels of productivity. The exception is the relatively higher-paying modern sector and a measure of the shortfall between aspiration and realisation is the numbers, employed or unemployed, who would like a secure job here. The registrants in employment exchanges include an undefined proportion who are already employed but seek better employment in the modern sector. The slow rates of advancement according to prevailing wage structure and the absence of direct recruitment to higher positions also place premiums on further training. As of now, then, these hiring criteria (rather than actual performance) limit access to different ports of entry with their fairly rigid channels for advancement. Instead of waiting for jobs, people begin waiting in line for the certificates which lead to jobs.

This raises the question of the possibility of modifying the criteria for employment in the urban areas, especially in the modern sector. It would be useful to experiment with alternative hiring criteria, if more workers can qualify, and where the existing ones serve no clear functional purpose. The criteria for acceptance into permanent modern sector employment are the most exacting. Employers defend these, even the insistence on elementary education for unskilled employees. Even where internal requirements of efficiency give these criteria a functional justification, it may be worth while to try alternative entry qualifications.

At the same time, the modern sector cannot be a major instrument of employment expansion. The emphasis is not on the "excessive" wages paid but on the requirements of operational efficiency which make it more expensive to provide employment here. Also, the lure of modern sector employment encourages strong pressure for this sector to provide employment to more than it can absorb, leading to inefficiencies and redundancy. In addition, modern sector employment requires scarce capital to generate employment.

For a number in the urban labour market, and for those who seek to enter it, the means at their disposal are, however, severely limited. This is particularly true of the urban poor without skills and without the potential for acquiring skills. The poorer areas where the low-income workers live have scant transport and educational facilities. This is also true for many potential migrants from the south where incomes are very low as compared to Khartoum, but whose migration to this urban area is also limited. The poor, whether they are within Khartoum or beyond, have dismal prospects in wage or self-employment.

It is for these reasons that an employment strategy in relationship to the urban labour market must aim at doing more than improving the labour market processes as they now take place. An equitable system must also aim at extending the opportunities for the poor to improve their skills and human capital: too many have nothing but their brawn to offer and some do not have even that. At the same time a priority should be given to innovations which increase the demand for labour of the variety untouched by the modern sector and for underutilised labour outside the developed urban areas.

APPENDIX 1

Provisional population estimates for 1973 place Khartoum Province's urban population at 876,000.[1] This includes 492,000 males and 384,000 females. A lower estimate of urban Khartoum's labour force, based on male-female participation rates obtained from a 1964-66 Population and Housing Survey, would amount to 280,000.[2] The actual total may be considerably larger because of increased participation rates, particularly among women. Thus, the recent ILO 1974 Household Survey suggests that the over-all total is more likely to be around 370,000.[3] If the entire Khartoum Province. were to be included (rural Khartoum's residents being treated as part of the metropolitan labour market), the relevant total will be well in excess of 400,000.

---

[1] Provisional estimate, Department of Statistics, National Planning Commission, the Sudan. Khartoum Province's population was estimated at 1.11 million in 1973. The urban population was thus about 78.6 per cent of the provincial total. This compares with 60 per cent in 1964-65 and 49 per cent in 1955-56. Earlier figures were obtained from Statistical Yearbook, 1973, National Planning Commission, Department of Statistics. This is the source of most of the data cited in this chapter unless otherwise indicated.

[2] The male participation rate in that survey was 52.5 per cent and the female participation 5.3 per cent.

[3] The 1974 ILO Survey gives an over-all labour force participation rate of 42.47 per cent. Male participation rates for natives are 54.5 per cent, for migrants of over five years' standing 82.8 per cent, and for migrants of less than five years' standing 80.4; corresponding percentages for females are 8.2, 10.0 and 7.0 respectively.

APPENDIX 2

Sociological composition of urban occupational categories

A 1971 survey of Greater Khartoum indicated the dominance of
the following tribal and ethnic groups: Ja'aliyin, Juhayna,
Nubians and possibly Egyptians in the more lucrative occupational
categories, namely "professional", "semi-professional", and
"managerial and administrative". (Galal-el-Din, op. cit.,
table 8.6.) But relative to their strength among those sampled,
the Nubians and Egyptians were better represented in these occupations, especially the latter in management and administration.
The Ja'aliyin, the largest ethnic group in Khartoum, were disproportionately represented in the "trades", while the Juhayna
seemed under-represented in most fields except "domestic" and
"other" services, agriculture, etc. The Nubians, Darfurians and
Southerners seemed to be disproportionately concentrated in the
"domestic" services, while the Darfurians and West Africans seemed
to be doing a little better as "craftsmen and production process"
workers. The implicit ethnic preferences and opportunities are
underlined when we look at the disposition of each of these ethnic
groups among the different occupations. (Galal-el-Din, op. cit.,
table 8.7.)

About 70 per cent or over of the West Africans, Darfurians,
Nubians and Southerners are in the following occupations:
"domestic" and "other" services and "craftsmen and production process" workers. With the exception of the Southerners, only a
negligible fraction enters the "clerical" category. There is no
representation of the Southerners and Nubians in the professional
category, and of Darfurians and West Africans in the managerial.
Needless to say, these categories are themselves too broad and
mask the placement of these four communities in the lower paying
ranks of each of the occupations in which they are represented.

TABLE 1

Resident Population. 1955 to 1973 in Urban Centres
which by 1973 surpassed 20 000 inhabitants

Provinces & urban centres	Resident Pop. ('000)			Percentage on total population of provinces		
	1955-56	1964-66	1973-74	1955-56	1964-66	1973-74
Khartoum	253.6	438.9	799.8	50.2	57.4	71.9
Khartoum	93.1	173.5	349.1	18.4	22.6	31.4
Omdurman	113.6	185.4	300.5	22.5	24.3	27.0
Khartoum North	46.9	80.0	150.2	9.3	10.5	13.5
Kassala	114.4	204.2	326.1	12.1	14.5	21.6
Port Sudan	47.6	78.9	135.1	5.1	5.6	8.9
Kassala	40.6	68.1	100.5	4.2	4.8	6.6
Gedaref	17.5	45.1	66.2	1.9	3.2	4.5
Halfa El Gadida	8.7	12.1	24.3	0.9	0.9	1.6
Blue Nile	102.2	151.8	260.3	5.0	5.7	7.1
Wad Medani	47.7	63.7	118.0	2.3	2.4	3.1
Kosti	22.7	37.9	60.6	1.1	1.4	1.8
Duiem	12.3	15.9	26.8	0.6	0.6	0.7
Sennar El Medina	8.1	17.6	32.6	0.4	0.7	0.9
El Gezira Aba	11.4	16.7	22.3	0.6	0.6	0.6
Kordofan	68.9	82.4	119.8	3.9	3.4	5.7
El Obeid	52.4	62.6	92.2	3.0	2.6	4.4
El Nahud	16.5	19.8	27.6	0.9	0.8	1.3
Northern	36.3	48.3	64.3	4.2	4.9	6.9
Atbara	36.3	48.3	64.3	4.2	4.9	6.9
Darfur	56.6	96.3	176.6	4.3	6.5	8.5
Nyala	12.3	26.2	62.8	0.9	1.8	3.0
El Fashir	26.2	40.5	54.5	2.0	2.7	2.6
El Genaina	11.8	20.7	38.6	0.9	1.4	1.9
El Deain	6.3	8.9	20.7	0.5	0.6	1.0
Equatoria	10.7	19.8	56.7	1.2	1.7	7.9
Juba	10.7	19.8	56.7	1.2	1.7	7.9
Bahr El Ghazal	8.0	14.8	53.4	0.8	1.2	4.0
Wau	8.0	14.8	53.4	0.8	1.2	4.0
Upper Nile	9.7	17.9	37.1	1.1	1.6	4.9
Malakal	9.7	17.9	37.1	1.1	1.6	4.9
Total	660.4	1 074.4	1 894.1	6.4	8.3	13.4

Source: MEFIT S.P.A., Consulting Engineers, Regional Plan of Khartoum
and Master Plan for the Three Towns, Vol. I, Phase 1, Rome,
September 1974.

Labour Market Segmentation
in the Economic Development of Japan

by
Solomon B. Levine,
Professor of Business and Economics,
University of Wisconsin

Modern economic growth, even of the command variety, appears to require the creation and elaboration of markets as efficient and equitable institutions for allocating resources. However, it is widely recognised that markets do not spring forth full-blown in the form long idealised by classical and neo-classical economics. Rather, their development often requires conscious planning and monitoring with appropriate institutions for actual effectiveness. While sluggishness and imperfections tend to characterise the emergence of almost all markets - for capital, land, raw materials, goods and labour - most intractable among them is the market for labour[1] - services bought and sold for wages and/or salaries.

This seems to be so for at least two basic reasons. One is that participation in and utilisation of labour markets involves behavioural choices for potential labour force members and employees about which initially they usually have little knowledge or understanding and which therefore entail high risks. The second is that, even with concerted efforts to learn how to utilise labour markets effectively, workers and managers tend to structure such markets into fragmented segments which, once established, can harden and persist to the detriment of "open" labour market elaboration.

This essay focuses on the latter phenomenon by taking up the Japanese experience with labour market segmentation in the period Japan made her transition from backward agrarianism to full-blown industrialisation, roughly the 1870s to the 1930s. Space limitations, however, allow only a rough sketch of this history, but a volume of this kind should recognise the need to examine historical experiences at the national level for insights into current problems and policies.

It may be argued that the labour market histories of countries which have already reached an advanced stage of industrialisation have little relevance to the process of labour market formation now occurring in less-developed economies. However, there actually have not been any systematic tests of this assumption with respect to the aspect of labour market segmentation. Indeed, the question of labour market segmentation received relatively little systematic attention in the body of economic theorising and conceptualisation that grew up in the West while modern economic growth was under way. In general, the supposition was that labour market formation was practically effortless and that labour market fragmentation, if it existed, was highly transitory. However, whether or not those suppositions are correct remains to be analysed in the light of historical facts.

The case of Japan with respect to labour market development has recently had extensive review, and it is clear that many decades and several generations came and went before the Japanese economy could

---

[1] See Bert F. Hoselitz: "The development of a labour market in the process of economic growth", in The international labour movement in transition: essays on Africa, Asia, Europe, and South America, edited by Adolf Sturmthal and James G. Scoville (Urbana, Illinois, University of Illinois Press, 1973), pp. 34-57.

claim to have generated ubiquitous labour market structures as
usually assumed in classical and neo-classical economics.[1] Indeed,
it was not until the First World War - at least 50 years after industrialisation began - that a majority of the Japanese labour force
became engaged in non-agricultural occupations and not until the
1930s that males, presumably more fully committed to industry as a
permanent means for earning income, became a majority of the non-
agricultural labour force. It took another 20 to 30 years before
Japan's total labour force was predominantly engaged in employment
for wages and salaries rather than as self-employed or at work as
unpaid family members. The case of Japan, of course, is especially
pertinent for present-day LDCs as the only non-Western nation to
have joined the ranks of the advanced industrial economies.

While wage and salary employment certainly indicates the creation
and existence of labour markets, it tells very little about the way
in which the labour markets work - that is, whether they are open or
closed. This paper would argue, however, that over the long run the
more extensive wage and salary employment becomes in an economy, the
more open will be the labour markets and the less will segmentation
of labour markets continue. The early stages of modern economic
development are likely to demand some limited amount of labour market
formation, but for the purposes of economic growth, labour market
segmentation may well be long tolerated even as the paid labour force
continues to expand. It may not be until much later stages - when
further industrialisation presses up against the limits of labour
supply - that sustained growth will require a breakdown of barriers
between labour market segments.

The above process appears to describe the general labour market
experience of Japan. There is the implication in this that, had the
Japanese succeeded earlier than they did both to expand labour markets
and break down accompanying segmentation, the social and economic consequences would have been different. The growth rate of Japan's
modern economy may have been higher than it was and the social and
political tensions, domestic and international, associated with the
growth which actually occurred in Japan, may have been relieved by
higher and more equitably distributed incomes.[2]

---

[1] Koji Taira: Economic development and the labour market in
Japan (New York, Columbia University Press, 1970). See also
Mikio Sumiya: Social impact of industrialisation in Japan (Japan,
Japanese National Commission for UNESCO, 1963). The data about labour
market history in Japan in this paper relies heavily upon these two
sources and upon Kazuo Okochi, Bernard Karsh and Solomon B. Levine,
eds.: Workers and employers in Japan: the Japanese employment relations system (Princeton, Princeton University Press, 1974).

[2] As Taira points out, there has been considerable dispute over
just how high Japan's growth rate was from 1870 to 1940. His own
conclusion, with which I agree, is that miscalculations, based on poor
or suspect data, led to exaggerated estimations and that, in fact,
once these are reasonably corrected, Japan's pre-1940 growth was not
especially remarkable but rather ordinary compared to other industrialising nations in that period. (See Taira, op. cit., pp. 5-7.)
Moreover, there is reason to suspect that Japan "suffered" inordin-
ately high social costs in the course of industrialising, which in
real terms probably warrants a reduction in the growth rate, whether
remarkably high or just ordinary. On this point, see John W. Bennett
and Solomon B. Levine: "Industrialisation and social deprivation:
welfare, environment, and the post-industrial society in Japan",
forthcoming.

Of crucial importance in this approach is to get away from
high-level abstractions such as changes in cultural values toward
"rationality" and to investigate, as Hoselitz urges, "the more
proximate institutions".[1]   Among the most important of these
institutions appear to be the formal education system and industrial
training programmes, management organisation and policy, family and
community structure, and labour unionism.   In these respects, all
cases of modern industrialisation display common tendencies, although
their forms vary significantly from one national setting to another.
In the paper that follows, each of these institutions is assessed
for their impact on labour market segmentation in the case of Japan
only.   Before proceeding to that task, the history of Japan's
labour market segmentation should be summarised.

HISTORY OF JAPANESE LABOUR
MARKET SEGMENTATION: 1870-1940

Even in the early decades following the Meiji Restoration
(1868) when despite leadership determination "to catch up with the
West", Japan hesitatingly initiated modern industrial operations,
the labour markets formed during that era were fragmented geographically and by status and occupational sector.   Although the
new Meiji Government took as one of its first steps the encouragement of geographic and social mobility as part of its bold plan to
extirpate feudalism, the response of the Japanese in terms of
expanding the use of open labour markets was not notable - at least
not immediately.   Hanging over from the pre-Restoration days were
wage and salary worker divisions such as the ex-samurai administrators, merchant house masters and apprenticeships, seasonal rural
wage labour, unskilled city dayworkers (often vagrants and vaga-
bonds), and artisan and craftsmen patron-client (oyakata-kokata)
groupings.   In view of inadequate modern communications and transportation, these groups were highly regional, each typically confined to a city, town or rural village.   Not only was access to
most of these groups extremely limited (and, in the case of dayworkers, undesirable except for social "deviants"), but also they
tended to contain closed subgroupings and certainly to offer little
opportunity to move from one category to another.   While the Meiji
Government officially abolished craft guilds and the samurai class
and outlawed discrimination against outcastes, the new policy could
not break down more finely drawn boundaries between non-competing
groups.

As is well known, the Government of Japan itself first launched
and operated most of the major industrial undertakings in the
initial 15 years after the Restoration - infrastructure as well as
direct manufacturing activities.   For these, "instant" workforces
were required, and the Government took direct responsibility for
their creation.   Interestingly, in attempting to man these various
operations - which included shipyards, arsenals, mines, factories,
railways, telegraph, and so forth - the Government itself had little
choice but to call upon recruits to serve as wage and salary earners

---

[1] Hoselitz, op. cit., p. 57.

from the various separated labour market groups already in
existence. Except in a few instances where the Government attempted to attract boys from the farms to work in these new operations,
the Government made little attempt to create labour markets through
wage offers attractive enough to lure and hold workers in sufficiently large numbers to break down the existing segments. Many
of the government operations indeed proved financial failures if
not well below expected standards of efficiency so that, when
economic panic hit Japan in the late 1870s, the Government began to
divest itself of most of its industrial undertakings in hopes that
the private sector, especially if offered incentives and safeguards
against risk, would perform better. No doubt, part of the reason
for failure was the inability to develop labour markets which would
bring to the government enterprises skilled and committed administrators and employees. Perhaps, indeed, few would have been
forthcoming under the existing conditions, but one may suspect that
sources of appropriate labour not only were unexplored but also
little was done to assure acquisition of efficient and reliable
workforces in competition with the established groupings in the
labour markets at that time. It should be noted that Government
itself created even new segments for some of its operations.
Notable among these were the highly selective groups, recruited and
trained specifically for such operations as the government-owned
telegraph and railways, which quickly developed their own closed
entities.

By the 1880s Japan had opted for a system of private enterprise to carry forward the drive for economic development. With
political favours, concentration of capital and advantageous taxes
and subsidies, this led to the emergence of a "dualistic" industrial structure by the time of the period between the Sino-Japanese
war (1894-95) and the Russo-Japanese war (1904-05). A handful of
highly profitable mammoth conglomerates known as the Zaibatsu,
devoted to the introduction and expansion of the most advanced
technologies and processes, ranged alongside thousands and thousands
of small shops and petty enterprise (as well as farms) which were
admixtures of traditional and new industrial and commercial activities, for the most part barely above subsistence levels.

Despite this great expansion of both large and small industrialisation efforts, which were to have another, even bigger,
boost during the First World War, dualism not only blunted the
generation of labour markets but also segmented what labour markets
were coming into existence. Many of the large firms - notably in
cotton textiles and metal manufacturing - were reluctant to employ
rising wage rates and improved working conditions as the means for
attracting labour into their operations, but instead proceeded on
the belief that non-economic "incentives", including physical co-
ercion in some instances, would accomplish this purpose. Most
small firms avoided the use of wage labour entirely by drawing
heavily upon family members and near kin, often from the overpopulated farms and villages. An important aspect of segmentation,
then, lay in the very divisions between wage and non-wage labour,
although there was probably some growing interchange between the
two groups.

Within the wage labour sector, moreover, sharp separations continued. A most notable grouping were the patron-client entities,
which particularly abounded in the small-scale metal and machinery
industry. These were utilised to a major extent for furnishing
manpower needed in large-scale undertakings - in iron and steel,

shipbuilding and heavy machinery, mining and the like.   Typically,
the patron-client arrangement was a semi-closed clustering of
learners (<u>kokata</u>) around a master or boss (<u>oyakata</u>), which would
either engage in business on their own or contract to provide services to the highest bidder on a short-term basis.   Out of this
grew the labour-boss system for which, down to the Second World War
era, Japan was well known.   The typical patron-client structure
was an admixture of both wage and non-wage elements in a sense akin
to a family enterprise.   These were used to hold the entity
together and regulate entry and exit of members and establishment
of new related patron-client branches.

     Such industries as large-scale textile manufacturing attempted
to avoid the use of open labour markets by developing exclusive
geographical jurisdictions over labour supplies as a means, it was
hoped, to avoid wage bidding and reduce labour turnover costs.
When this approach failed in the urban areas around the mills, the
companies just tried harder by reaching out to the remote overpopulated farm villages where, they believed, would be the weakest
resistance to offers of low wages and benefits.   The target, of
course, was the young uneducated female, whose marginal contribution to farm and village was close to zero.   Again, this strategy
represented an attempt to minimise labour market development and
substitute non-economic incentives, particularly the use of affec-
tive paternalism, for attracting and holding workforces.   How
successful the approach actually was is open to serious question,
for turnover among these workers remained very high down to the
1930s.   It served the purpose of sharply dividing the female from
the male labour force in modern industry and, for several decades,
until the 1930s, there were more female industrial workers than
male, largely in short-term employment.   This segmentation,
although no longer predominant, has continued to the present in
several Japanes industries, notably electronics as well as cotton
textile manufacturing.

     The startling, rapid expansion of industry during the First
World War, when Japan was suddenly called upon to become a major
supply base for the Allied Powers, quickly ran into labour shortages and wage rates began to soar.   The short-lived nature of
this prosperity and the ensuing sharp depression and a recessed
period that lasted until 1931 discouraged the widespread emergence
of open labour markets.   Rather, there was not only a reversion
to the pre-existing divisions, but also a new form of segmentation
began to emerge in large-scale industry.   The latter resulted from
the attempt, which proved largely successful, of big enterprise
management to wrest control over labour skills and skill training
away from the patron-client retinues.   Although this movement had
already begun in some major enterprises as early as the 1890s, it
only became widespread by the 1920s when, in the light of economically depressed conditions and the first imposition of government-
required labour standards, management felt compelled to "rationalise" and to eliminate any independent control over wages and working conditions by workers.   Coupled with this were fears of
radicalism on the part of newly formed labour organisations,
inspired, many managers believed, by the triumph of Bolshevism in
Russia and labour unrest in Western Europe.   The new management
policy saw the beginnings of practices in large-scale Japanese
enterprises which today are identified with "lifetime employment"
and "length-of-service" wage payment.   It may be argued that this
new approach actually was an attempt to broaden the labour market
by offering improved terms of employment to attract and hold
potentially higher quality workers than could be supplied to the

companies through the <u>oyakata-kokata</u> entities.   On the other hand,
it seemed clearly a strategy to substitute one segregated workers'
group for another and thus introduce an additional element of
labour market segmentation.   Only a certain class of labour force
entrants was deemed eligible to enter the new workforces of these
enterprises, mainly young males directly from school graduation.
By carefully controlling the size of this "permanent" workforce,
an enterprise built its own "internal" labour market rather than
being forced to depend upon "outside" closed groups for skills and
skill development.   Needless to say, internal labour markets could
not be built overnight; and when Japan turned in the 1930s under
the prodding and then direction of the militarists to a rapid step-
up of heavy industry, most of the large enterprises buffered their
permanent core worker groups by employing considerable portions of
their workforces on a "temporary" basis.   This, in turn, further
segmented the labour market into non-competing sectors.   It would
not be until the 1960s that labour market segmentation in Japan
would show signs of dissolution following successive attempts to
freeze workforces in place during wartime, unemployment and underemployment following the surrender, the rise of labour unionism to
demand and obtain employment security within enterprises, and,
after 15 years of recovery and high-speed growth, the emergence of
labour shortages, particularly among young workers.   In the meantime, vestiges of labour market segmentation stubbornly continued.

THE PROXIMATE INSTITUTIONS

     It should be clear from this brief history of labour market
segmentation during Japan's transformation from agrarianism to
industrialism that the institutions which could contribute to the
development of open labour markets either worked in the opposite
direction or only slowly exerted their effects.

     Turning first to modern education and industrial skill train-
ing, it can be observed that the new Meiji Government early took
steps to prepare the next generations for non-agricultural employment.   The most important of these was the launching, as early as
1872, of universal compulsory elementary education.   Another was
universal military conscription.   Yet it took 30 years to reach
the goal of virtually all children completing six years of primary
schooling, and during that period less than 5 per cent of the
appropriate age group went on to secondary schools and less than
1 per cent to the university-level institutions.   This meant, of
course, that for the ensuing 20 to 30 years, much of the adult
labour force did not have educational backgrounds beyond the three
Rs and "morals" indoctrination.   It also meant that relatively
tiny élitist groups were equipped through formal schooling to enter
the more sophisticated types of employment and professions.   While
steadfastly attempting to raise general education levels for the
whole population, by the early 1900s the Government in effect opted
for a system of selective educational "tracking" which, wittingly
or not, served to fortify the tendency toward labour market segmentation.   This came in the form of a complex structuring of school
levels and institutions beyond compulsory elementary education that
would allocate the potential labour force on a selective basis among
the different sectors of the emerging "dualistic" economy.   By
1940, close to half of the appropriate age group was completing at
least nine years of schooling, but of significantly different types

depending on the likely employment available. It is significant, too, that higher education remained a privilege of a small group of barely 4 per cent of the relevant age group up to that time.

Employees, moreover, could not rely upon formal schooling alone to prepare labour force members adequately for the new jobs in an industrialising Japan. School level and type served merely to certify a graduate's ability and willingness to learn and to accept the discipline of modern work in a general sense. Accordingly, there began numerous private and semi-private efforts to provide more specific training, particularly for those who, having passed initial screening, were employed in the large enterprises. Such "quasi-secondary" education further added to the segmentation induced by the dualistic economic structure. There was a notable step-up in these programmes, also beginning with the Russo-Japanese war, and by the 1920s it assured that over half the appropriate age group had education and training beyond the elementary level. By 1940, the figure reached 90 per cent. But most of the supplementary or quasi-secondary training was carried on within enterprises to meet their specific technical needs rather than to provide labour flexibility and versatility across industries. This meant that the skills learned were not easily transferred from one enterprise to another, further compartmentalising workforces. It was not until the 1960s, close to two decades after the initiation of the education reforms by the Allied Occupation, that such separate tracking was virtually eliminated and comprehensive schooling was achieved, and that Japan actually began to possess a highly versatile labour force through the institution of formal schooling.

Japanese management organisation and policy, as already noted, were generally slow in recognising the value of open labour markets for efficient allocation of labour. It is not clear why this was so, but except in isolated instances it was not until the 1920s that management made conscious efforts to utilise labour markets more in the style of classical economics. Probably this was the result of the rapid emergence of modern industrial operations and management's long preoccupation with the immediate technical aspects of plant, machinery and raw materials, rather than with planning long-term manpower requirements. Managerial talent itself was in short supply. Accordingly, there was a greater willingness to rely upon established institutions for providing labour skills, particularly, as noted, the patron-client entities, rather than developing new ones. Still another factor actively affecting management was the development of the school tracking policy of the Government that fortified segmentation, and the management attitudes of noblesse oblige carried over from the feudal period by ex-samurai administrators and then by the select group of new élitist university graduates who filled many of the managerial positions in modern industry. When management seriously turned to manpower controls on a large scale in the 1920s, the long absence of experience with open labour markets led management to substitute one type of segmentation for another by developing risk-minimising "internal" labour markets.

Both the educational and managerial policies, of course, were immersed in a stubborn matrix of family and community institutions which did not lend themselves readily to the generation of open labour markets. Most of Japan's labour supply for the new industrial jobs came from rural backgrounds where, for centuries, there was a strong institutionalisation of tight-knit family and community structures in which rewards (and punishments) were not geared to the economic contribution of the individual member. As a result, there

was a widespread assumption, conscious and unconscious, that such
modes of organisation could readily be transferred to modern
economic enterprises. The rapid spread of small undertakings
which utilised family members as workers, throughout a large portion of the "dualistic" economy, also affected the outlook of
large-scale firms as well. Familism also permeated the oyakata-
kokata entities upon which the large enterprises heavily depended
for their workforces over several decades. The appeal of open
labour markets, based on impersonal transactions expressed in wages
and other material benefits for the individual, was found to be
weak compared to the psychological security and personalism of the
family and community structures. It took unfolding experience and
rising education over a long period to shake the hold of these
institutions, which diluted only gradually and then on a segmented
basis.

Finally, broad-based organised labour institutions did not
become powerful enough to break down labour market segmentation
during the pre-Second World War era. Efforts to organise labour
unions appeared as early as the 1870s, although not seriously
until the late 1890s, but almost immediately they were crushed by
govermnent and employer opposition or fell apart from financial
weakness. Far more successful was the spread of unionism during
the First World War, as severe labour shortages mounted, which
actually continued into the 1930s before final obliteration by
government policy under the militarists. Yet the labour movement
for the time it thrived made little impact on labour market arrangements, as neither the Government nor large-scale employers granted
it little legitimation. For the most part, unions managed to survive either in small-scale industrial sectors or among the patron-
client retinues which served the large enterprises, but they threat-
ened the rationalisation plans of management, who themselves used
the appeal of reviving "traditional" familism in controlling the
"radicalism" of unions. Indeed, organised labour by the mid-1920s
split into rival ideological groupings and was unable after that
to present a unified front for widespread and open labour markets
in which they might bargain collectively.

Thus, on all these institutional scores, labour markets did
not rate high as a major means for the efficient and equitable
allocation of labour in the economic development of Japan prior to
1940. The way in which the institutions themselves evolved in
Japan gave support to the tendency of labour markets to segment even
as they grew.

Employment and wages in the Ethiopian manufacturing sector

by
Teshome Mulat,
(formerly) Haile Selassie University, Addis Ababa;
International Institute for Labour Studies, Geneva

I. INTRODUCTION

The relationship between wages and employment in the manufacturing (or modern) sector of LDCs has drawn the attention of labour market researchers for some time now. Despite increases in the number and diversity of reported writings on the topic, however, the use of results for developing labour market policies has not been particularly encouraging. Even on the analytical plane, definition of a relationship between wages and employment for a given labour market often generates controversy.

Some writings about the manufacturing sector in LDCs emphasise the negative employment effect of relatively high wage levels and wage increases. Some of these studies base their case on the familiar competitive labour market models with normally sloped labour supply and demand curves which show that wage rates above equilibrium rates directly reduce the level of employment. In recent years a reinforcing argument is provided by some migration studies, where it is argued that rural-urban income differentials in LDCs, widened by high urban (manufacturing) wage rates, have only helped accelerated urban ward migration.[1] Together with downward rigidity of urban wages, such migrations imply a rightward shift of labour supply curves in urban centres with depressing effects on relative employment levels.

Another explanation for negative employment effects of modern sector wages lies in the argument that relative factor costs in LDCs encourage shifts in factor use away from labour. As interest payments are lower than wages, a firm aiming at cost minimisation would substitute capital for labour subject to the limits of technology. Thus we have the importance attached in recent literature to "factor price distortions".[2]

In line with these arguments many economists have been critical of politics which render capital relatively "cheap" (e.g., zero or only nominal duties on capital imports, low interest payments on capital borrowings, tax holidays on investments, etc.). Accordingly, governments have often been advised to practise "wage restraint".

---

[1] See, for example, R.G. Ridker and H. Lubell (eds.): Employment and unemployment problems of the Near East and South Asia - Volumes 1 and 2 (Vikas Publications, 1971); M.P. Todaro: "Income expectations, rural-urban migration and employment in Africa", in International Labour Review, Nov. 1971; D. Turnham assisted by I. Jaeger: The employment problem in developed countries: a review of evidence (Paris, OECD, 1971). See also in P. Bairoch: Urban unemployment in developing countries (Geneva, International Labour Office, 1971).

[2] See, for example, A.D. Witte: "Employment in the manufacturing sectors of developing economies: a study of Mexico and Peru", The Journal of Development Studies, Oct. 1973. For other sources see in D. Morawetz: "Employment implications of industrialisation in developing countries: a survey", The Economic Journal, Sep. 1974. See also P. Bairoch: Urban unemployment in developing countries - the nature of the problem and proposals for its solution (Geneva, International Labour Organisation, 1973).

The recent ILO employment mission's policy recommendations to the Ethiopian Government[1] run along similar lines. The mission, basing its case primarily on an earlier document produced by the Planning Commission Office,[2] strongly advised the Government to adopt a statutory wage policy which would freeze for years wages earned in public employment and in the manufacturing sector of the economy. But recent developments in the country have forced wages in an opposite direction.[3] Neither the attempts at restraining wage increases nor the recent claims by work groups for improvements in earnings come out of any knowledge of the complex relationships between wages and employment in industry. Such studies are non-existent.

The primary aim of this note is to bring together some of the evidence bearing on the relationship between wages and employment in the Ethiopian manufacturing sector.

II. INDUSTRY EMPLOYMENT IN ETHIOPIA

Actual employment (and wage) levels in the Ethiopian manufac-turing industry remain unknown quantities. No comprehensive census was ever taken and a few estimates made show considerable variations in results attained. In table 1, an attempt is made to bring together some of these estimates for comparison. Employment levels in industry are expressed as percentages of labour force estimates. The observed variations in those ratios reflect differences in labour force estimates in various sources. They are also due to differences in definition and coverage of industry employment. Des-pite considerable variations in employment estimates, all sources show that the manufacturing sector employs less than 1 per cent of the country's labour force. Using cross-country data it is demon-strated elsewhere that the proportion of the labour force employed by the manufacturing sector is a rising function of time for any economy, i.e., the proportion increases with industrialisation.[4] Appendix I gives industry employment estimates for some countries for purposes of comparison. These evidences reveal the unsatis-factory performance of the Ethiopian manufacturing industry, despite an industrialisation strategy adopted as early as the 1950s.[5]

----

[1] For the report summary see M. Blaug: "Employment and unemployment in Ethiopia", International Labour Review, Aug. 1972.

[2] Planning Commission Office: The employment problem of Ethiopia (Addis Ababa, 1972) (mimeo.).

[3] Following the disturbances in March 1974, the last Government accepted to consider union requests for minimum wages, increased pay for the armed forces and, in its bid to get public support, raised incomes of some underpaid public employees.

[4] See, for example, Teshome Mulat: Changes in the level and structure of employment in developing countries (University of Manchester, an unpublished Ph.D. thesis, 1971).

[5] See M. Blaug, op. cit.

Table 1. Some estimates of manufacturing industry employment in Ethiopia

(Employment levels expressed as percentages of labour force estimates)

	MNCD report[1]		MNCD estimate[2]		CSO estimate[3]	PCO estimate[4]	Iwuji estimate[5]
	Modern manufacturing	All manufacturing	Modern manufacturing	All manufacturing			
1965							
1967					0.29	0.52	
1968			0.53	0.32	0.30		
1970	0.46	0.60			0.40		0.40

1 See Ministry of National Community Development and Social Affairs (MNCD): Survey of the occupational pattern of employment in Ethiopia (Addis Ababa, 1962 EC, Feb. 1971 (EC means Ethiopian calendar)). In this source only employment in manufacturing industries is reported. The percentages are computed by dividing these reported employment levels by corresponding labour force estimates from the Central Statistical Office (CSO).

2 The estimates for industry employment were made by the MNCD in 1968 and are contained in the report above. The percentages are computed by dividing these estimates by corresponding labour force estimates from CSO source.

3 Reported employment in manufacturing industry is expressed as percentages of labour force estimates. For both variables the source used is Central Statistical Office (CSO), Statistical abstract (Addis Ababa), an annual report.

4 See Planning Commission Office: The employment problem of Ethiopia (Addis Ababa, 1972), mimeo.

5 Dr. Iwuji's estimates reported here refer to wage employment in manufacturing industry. See E.C. Iwuji: Report on wage/salary structures in English-speaking Africa (Geneva, ILO, 1974), mimeo.

Another characteristic of industry employment in Ethiopia is that the structure of industry employment has changed little over the years. The employment distribution by major industrial groups for the past decade is computed from CSO sources and given in table 2 below. Food and textiles account for 60 per cent or more of industry employment and the relative position of industries (in terms of employment creation) has not changed over the years.

Table 2. Employment distribution by major industrial groups
(percentages)

	1962	1964-65	1965-66	1966-67	1968-69	1970-71
Food	32	39	24	18	15	16
Beverages	5	5	6	6	7	6
Tobacco	1	1	3	1	1	1
Textiles	37	33	40	43	45	44
Leather and shoe	3	4	5	5	4	4
Wood	4	5	5	7	7	7
Non-metallic minerals	5	7	8	9	8	9
Printing	1	2	3	3	3	3
Chemical	2	3	4	5	5	3
Steel, metal and electrical	-	2	2	2	3	2

Source: Computed from CSO data.

III. WAGES IN THE MANUFACTURING SECTOR

Wage level estimates for the manufacturing sector of Ethiopia also show considerable variations. Three different estimates are shown in table 3. The Central Personnel Agency Scale refers to wages in public sector employment and an abridged version of the scale is included here for comparison. The MNCD study of 1969 covers industry wages in Addis Ababa. Since most of the manufacturing industries are in and around Addis Ababa, the estimate on wage level given by this source may be considered representative.

The main source for wage data in this study is the CSO's Statistical abstract. This source contains aggregate wage data by industrial branches. The computations given here are arrived at by dividing reported wage bill by reported employment. It is assumed that these computations give indications as to the general level of earning in industry.

Table 3. Some wage level estimates in the Ethiopian manufacturing industries

CSO estimate[1] (Eth.$ per annum)

Wage variable	1962	1964-65	1965-66	1966-67	1968-69	1969-70	1970-71
Average industry wage ($\bar{W}r$)	736	879	984	1 144	1 302	1 445*	1 500*
Standard deviation (S)	254.1	325.4	324.34	324.75	444.61	459.09*	449.3*
Coefficient of variation (S/$\bar{W}r$)	0.345	0.370	0.329	0.284	0.341	0.318	0.299

CPA scale[2] (Eth.$ per month)

	Administrative services (AD)	Sub-professional services (SP)	Clerical and fiscal services (CF)	Trades and crafts services (TC)	Custodial and manual services (CM)	Professional and scientific services (PS)
Minimum	230	50	50	30	25	500
Maximum	1 440	1 035	1 035	636	230	2 000

MNCD study, 1969[3] (Eth.$ per month): Ethiopians 82.7; non-Ethiopians 1 070.4.

[1] Central Statistical Office: Statistical abstract. The computations given here are derived from data in this source.

[2] Negarit Gazetta, No. 15, 1 June 1972.

[3] MNCD: "Wage study" (Addis Ababa, Dec. 1970), mimeo.

* Do not include petroleum refinery.

Many researchers believe that industry wage levels are too high in Ethiopia.[1]   They are high relative to earnings in the rural sector for the economy and are estimated to be contributive factors to large immigrations to the cities.   High wage levels in industry are partially explained by the "excessive wages" paid to public employees,[2] the argument being that private industry is forced to raise wages to get the requisite labour supply in competition against the public sector.

But the high wage level in industry shown by the CSO source does not reveal the state of well-being of industrial workers.   A major shortcoming of the wage data from this source is that it does not reveal earning differentials within an industry.   Whatever fragmentary evidences exist show that low skill category workers (who constitute the greatest majority of industrial employment) earn very low incomes.   The recent request by the Confederation of Ethiopian Labour Unions (CELU) for minimum wage legislation is based on the argument that existing wages in industry are too low.[3]   The MNCD estimate (see table 4) also shows that earnings by Ethiopians in private industry are very low.[4]   These observations cast doubts about the strength of the ILO mission's report recommendations for wage restraint (unless such proposals are made more specific to highly paid workers in managerial and professional grades).

The industry wage structure can be studied from many angles. The earning differential between Ethiopians and non-Ethiopians is very high.[5]   This is mainly due to the fact that non-Ethiopians occupy managerial and professional positions in industry.   The CPA scale (which covers public sector employment) shows that occupational differentials are very large.   Some studies relating to private industry show that pay differentials between skilled and unskilled workers are too large.[6]   According to the ILO report pay levels in industry as well as in public employment are influenced more by educational levels attained than by productivity.[7]

---

[1] ibid.   See also E.C. Iwuji, op. cit.

[2] ibid.

[3] Reported in Ethiopian Herald, 1 Mar. 1974.

[4] Estimates on cost of living and recommendations on minimum pay rates are also available in ILO/UNDP: Report to the Government of Ethiopia on minimum wage fixing (Geneva, ILO/TAP/Ethiopia/R.10, 1970).   The cost of living has increased considerably since then whereas appreciable changes in pay for low-income earners have been considered only during the disturbances in March 1974.

[5] See in E.C. Iwuji, op. cit.

[6] ibid.

[7] M. Blaug, op. cit.

Another way of looking at industry wage structure would be to consider inter-industry wage differentials. Using the wage and employment distributions by major industrial groups given in the CSO source we have computed average wages for all industries and coefficients of variations (see table 3). It is clear that, for any one year, the computations show considerable differentials in inter-industry wages.

IV. EMPLOYMENT AND WAGE TRENDS IN INDUSTRY

Available estimates show that both wages and employment had an upward trend during the past decade. The Morawetz estimate gives a 6.4 per cent per annum employment growth rate for the period 1963-69. This is close to the results obtained from CSO data which show that reported employment has been growing at the annual average growth rate of 7.8 per cent over the period 1955-71 (see table 4). However, the observed high growth rate has not been distributed evenly throughout the period. In fact the calculations show that employment growth rates were falling in the late 1960s compared to previous periods (such declines being noted in the ILO report and the PCO study also). We have also shown (see table 2) that the distribution of employment by major industrial groups has not changed significantly in the past decade.

Table 4. Growth rates of selected variables
(average annual)

Variable	CSO source[1]		Projection[2]	Morawetz estimate[3]
	1955-71	1965-71	1970-90	1963-69
Industry employment (L)	7.8	2	4.6	6.4
Average wage (W/L)	5.9	12		
Average productivity (Y/L)	8.2	17	4.3	

[1] Computed from CSO: Statistical abstract.

[2] See PCO, op. cit.

[3] See, for details, D. Morawetz, op. cit.

As regards wage trends in the manufacturing sector of the Ethiopian economy, two points can be made: (a) the money wage rate, computed for the whole manufacturing sector at about 6 per cent per annum over the 1955-71 period. The rate of growth of average wages during the 1965-72 period, however, has been much higher than the employment growth rate observed for the same period; (b) the inter-industry wage structure appears to have changed little over the years, as can be shown by the constancy of the coefficient of variation of average wages (see table 3) but inter-industry wage differentials remained large. These results (i.e. constancy of coefficient of variation and relatively high inter-industry wage differentials) do not show for Ethiopia the expected decline in measured coefficient of variation with time.

Other related variables, in particular investment and labour productivity, have also shown increases during the 1955-72 period. Of particular interest would be to compare the growth rates of wages and labour productivity. The CSO data yield results that suggest that, both during the 1955-72 and 1965-72 periods, wage rates have been growing much slower than the rate of growth of (gross) labour productivity. The wage restraint proposal advanced by the ILO report is not apparently supported by this piece of evidence. The doubt over the accuracy of the wage restraint proposal remains, as will be shown in the next few pages, even if both wages and labour productivity are measured in real terms.

V. THE WAGE EMPLOYMENT FUNCTION

Some simple but relatively effective models have been used for purposes of estimating the effects of wage changes on employment levels in industry in LDCs.[1] The general approach is to employ multiple regression analyses where employment is hypothesised as a function of variables such as capital, productivity, and wages. The variables can be measured as levels, gross changes, percentage changes, etc. In the Ethiopian case an attempt is made to employ CSO data to see if such a wage employment function can be established for the Ethiopian manufacturing sector. After trying a number of multiple regression models and employing various measurements (specifications) of variables, the best result obtained is:[2]

$$\log L = 1.9331 + 0.8933 \log (Wr) \qquad \ldots\ldots (1)$$
$$(18.959)^{**}$$
$$R^2 = 0.5583$$

where L and (Wr) are respectively employment and the (unweighted) average wage estimate for Ethiopian manufacturing sector.

---

[1] See, for example, J. Isbester: "Urban employment and wages in a developing economy. The case of Mexico", Economic development and cultural change, Oct. 1971; L.G. Reynolds and P. Gregory: Wages, productivity and industrialisation in Puerto Rico (Homewood, III, Richard D. Irwin, 1965). See also studies by Bacha et al for Brazil and by Roemer for Ghana reviewed in D. Morawetz, op. cit.

[2] The numbers in brackets are F statistics. Two asterisks represent significance at the per cent level.

In equation (1), times series data are used covering the period
1955-71. The productivity and capital intensity measures are left
out as explanatory variables because of statistical insigificance
(even at a 5 per cent level) of the relevant coefficients.

Both Reynolds (Puerto Rico) and Isbester (Mexico) used cross-
section data for their studies of employment and wage relationships
in industry.[1] Cross-sectional data (i.e. data breakdowns by major
industrial subgroups) are available from the CSO sources beginning
1966-67. However, comparable cross-section data over the period
1966-71 can yield only limited sample size and strictly comparable
data are available only for the period 1968-71. Using these data
the following results are obtained:[2]

$$\bar{L} = 1.12247 + 0.40784\ \bar{W} \qquad \ldots\ldots (2)$$

$$(2.99278)$$

$$R^2 = 0.16633$$

$$\bar{L} = 19.67495 - 0.06467\ \bar{W} \qquad \ldots\ldots (3)$$

$$(0.095)$$

$$R^2 = 0.029$$

$\bar{L}$ and $\bar{W}$ are percentage changes in employment and average wage
rates respectively. Equation (2) results are obtained from the
1966-71 data, and equation (3) from the 1968-71 data (for which the
number of observations are much larger).

Any interpretation of these statistical computations must be
highly qualified and requires caution. The cross-section evidence
has failed to establish any stable association between wage rate and
employment. Even the time series result, although statistically
significant, raises a number of doubts.

The coefficient of employment elasticity (of 0.8) calculated
from the times series data contrasts with results obtained from similar equations obtained for Puerto Rico, Mexico and Ghana.[3] But the
positive coefficient in the Ethiopian case raises doubts about the
causation implied in the equation.

_____

[1] L.G. Reynolds and P. Gregory, op. cit.; J. Isbester, op. cit.

[2] The numbers in brackets in equations (2) and (3) are F
statistics.

[3] L.G. Reynolds and P. Gregory, op. cit., have found that a
1 per cent change in wage rate in Puerto Rico was associated with a
1 per cent change of employment in the opposite direction.
M. Roemer's study (reported in D. Morawetz, op. cit.) on Ghanaian
manufacturing industry also gives an employment elasticity coefficient with respect to change in wages of about 1.2. For Mexico,
see J. Isbester, op. cit.

However, such a result is consistent with the adjustment behaviour of firms operating under conditions of excess capacity and disguised unemployment. With profits (and sales) rising, manufacturing firms may choose to raise wages and not adopt a policy of increasing employment significantly by keeping wages at their previous levels.

Crude estimates of output elasticities of employment emphasise this point further. For six years, 1965-71, the elasticity of employment with respect to output is fairly low.[1] It appears that manufacturing firms in Ethiopia meet additional demand for output by exploiting excess capacity and paying higher wages with as little addition to employment as is necessary.

Another factor that complicates the wage employment relationship interpretation is the relevance of the possible employment effects of increases in capital costs and relative declines in investment rates observed for the 1965-71 period. The incremental capital/labour ratio has been rising steadily over the past few years. This rise in the "cost of creating a job" plus the observed

---

[1] Although it has not been possible to retain the output and capital intensity variables in the multiple regression models used, simple calculations using CSO data yield the estimates below.

Method	1965-71	
	Wage elasticity of employment	Output elasticity of employment
Wage employment equation	0.893 (1955-71)	
Elasticity is calculated for each year between 1965 and 1971. The arithmetic mean of these six coefficients is given here	0.738	0.054

Note that the elasticities given here on the second row are not the same as would be obtained by dividing estimates of employment growth rates by corresponding percentage changes in wages and gross productivity in table 4. The computations given here are averages of elasticities (computed for each year) over the 1965-71 period.

relative declines in the percentage growth rates of capital stocks in industry contribute to the relative slackening rate of employment growth in the latter years.[1]

CONCLUDING REMARKS

From the point of view of developing appropriate wage policies for industry the estimation of the extent to which wage rates have influenced employment growth patterns is important.   Even here not all questions are answered.   The slackening in the rate of growth of employment in Ethiopian industry during the 1965-71 period is due to a number of other factors including relative declines in investment rates and the limited size of markets for manufacturing outputs.   There is little basis for pinpointing high wage rates for the poor performance of industry in the employment field.

However, another important consideration for a wage policy is income distribution.   Is labour paid the value of its marginal product?   The argument in support of increased profits rests, among other things, on the notion of increased investable funds. But in many LDCs increased profits are not necessarily ploughed back into these economies as much as they are distributed to share-holders abroad.[2]   The question of labour sharing of profits becomes an important wage policy consideration in such cases.

---

[1] The following table may shed some light on the possible employment effects of investment and capital intensity factors over the years.

Period	Average annual growth rate of capital stock (K) (percentages)	Average incremental capital-labour ratios ($\Delta K/\Delta L$)
1955-71	13	14.887
1965-71	9	27.217
1955-64	16	7.489

Source: Computed from CSO, Statistical abstract, op. cit.

Because of lack of appropriate capital cost deflators (for purposes of calculations in real terms), the computations here show only the money changes in the incremental ratio $\left(\dfrac{\Delta K}{\Delta L}\right)$.

[2] In Ethiopia, L. Bondestam's study (CSO, mimeo.) on the sugar industry reveals the uncontrolled flight of profits (as proceeds to foreign investors) out of the country.   This may be a more general phenomenon in all manufacturing.

An attempt is made here using the CSO data to compute wage
and labour productivity in Ethiopian industry in real terms.[1]
The use of two different deflators in the calculation of real
wages did not yield significantly different results (see diagram
below).   It appears that real wages have been lagging behind
(gross) productivity.   The differential between computed real
wage and productivity indexes is also widening in recent years.
These computations suggest that, judged by income distribution
criteria, the case made in support of a policy of wage restraint
in industry may prove untenable.

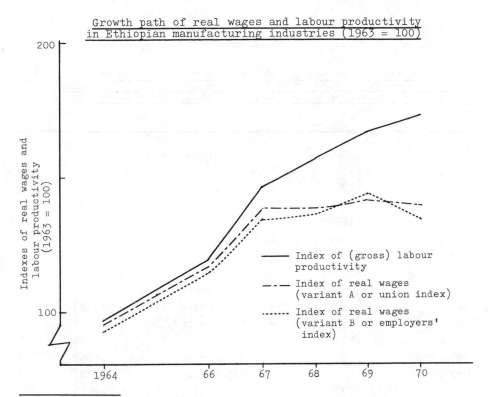

Growth path of real wages and labour productivity
in Ethiopian manufacturing industries (1963 = 100)

Indexes of real wages and labour productivity (1963 = 100)

—————— Index of (gross) labour
productivity

— ·· — Index of real wages
(variant A or union index)

·········· Index of real wages
(variant B or employers'
index)

---

[1] Consumer price indices (1963 = 100) are used for the calculation of real wages variant A.   These series represent the pur-
chasing power of workers' incomes.   Producers (employers), on the
other hand, would like such indices to reflect costs of production.
Variant B is such index where the deflators used are from index
members of GDP at constant prices (1963 = 100).   These latter
series are also used in the computation of gross labour productivity indices.

Note that one shortcoming of the productivity index in the
diagram is that it measures gross labour productivity and not net.
Net productivity indices are best worked out from production functions for industry in which other explanatory variables such as
capital, skill factors, etc., are used together with labour inputs.

Finally, our investigations, tentative though they may be, imply that wage regulation or supply-side questions may not constitute the critical issues for labour market policies (given the institutional arrangements). What we have found is that the rate of growth of investment in industry is slackening in recent years and that employment is both output and wage inelastic. Wages also appear less significant given that real wages have lagged behind productivity. Demand-side considerations may perhaps explain better the unsatisfactory performance of industry in the employment field. Further investigation is certainly in order before making a policy of wage restraint such a crucial aspect of employment strategy.

APPENDIX

Estimates of manufacturing sector employment for some countries (wage employment in manufacturing industries expressed as percentages of total labour force)

Algeria	(1966)	5	Argentina	(1960)	19
Egypt	(1966)	9	Canada	(1961)	22
Ghana	(1970)*	1.6	Colombia	(1964)	8
Ivory Coast	(1964)	0.8	Chile	(1970)	12
Kenya	(1970)*	2	Guyana	(1965)	10
Liberia	(1962)	0.8	Jamaica	(1960)	6
Nigeria	(1970)*	0.6	USA	(1971)	25
Tanzania	(1970)	0.7	France	(1968)	24
Bangladesh	(1961)	1.5	Germany	(1971)	37
India	(1971)	4	Greece	(1971)	11
Indonesia	(1971)	4	Ireland	(1966)	17
Japan	(1970)	22	Italy	(1972)	26
Pakistan	(1971)	4	Portugal	(1960)	17
Sri Lanka	(1963)	6	Spain	(1970)	23
Thailand	(1970)	2	UK	(1966)	33
New Zealand	(1966)	24			

Source: ILO Yearbook of Labour Statistics (Geneva, 1973).

* Government reports in E.C. Iwuji, op. cit.

Wage aspirations, urban unemployment and labour market structures

by
Pang Eng Fong
Economic Research Centre,
University of Singapore

The dimensions of urban unemployment observed so far in South-east Asia seem quite clear.[1] Firstly, it is structural in nature resulting from an imbalance between job opportunities and aspirations and between the rate of employment creation and the rate of labour force increase. Secondly, the conventionally measured joblessness rate is typically a two-digit figure. Thirdly, it afflicts those in the age group 15-24 more severely than other age groups, females more than males. Fourthly, the average level of schooling among young jobseekers, the majority of whom are adolescent first-timers, tends to be somewhat higher than that for the labour force as a whole. Fifthly, its intensity is aggravated by the massive inflow of migrants from the rural areas.

There is also general agreement that the problem of urban unemployment, threatening though it may be in its political and social implications, represents but one aspect of the total picture of human resource underutilisation in urban South-east Asia. The central problem is mass poverty. Indeed, some commentators (e.g., Myrdal) have argued that the urban unemployment problem is essentially a bourgeois problem as it occurs primarily among young adolescents from households with better than average incomes.

In this paper we will not grapple with the entire problem of unemployment and underemployment in urban cities in South-east Asia, but rather present some fragmentary evidence on the gap between wage aspirations and the type of employment desired by job-seekers and the available opportunities. The various ILO mission reports, particularly the Sri Lanka (Ceylon) volume, have emphasised the mismatch between job aspirations of the unemployed and the available supply of jobs. The Ceylon report, for example, indicated that over three-quarters of young school leavers with four years of secondary education were looking for white-collar employment in the public sector. From a private perspective their aspirations are perfectly rational: the public sector offers higher wages and greater job security than either estate employment or self-employment.[2]

The imbalance between job aspirations and employment opportunities is, of course, not peculiar to developing countries; it occurs also in the developed world. The difference lies in the pressures for adjustments among jobseekers and the speed at which expectations are brought into line with reality.

---

[1] For details see Paul Bairoch: Urban unemployment in developing countries (Geneva, International Labour Office, 1973); and David Turnham: The employment problem in less-developed countries: a review of evidence (Paris, Development Centre, OECD, 1971).

[2] In a survey of the attitudes of undergraduates, the report noted the response of an architecture student who elaborated on why he preferred a public sector job. His reasons were: "(i) pensionable; foreign scholarships; (ii) no housing problems, quarters provided; (iii) travelling facilities in government vehicles; (iv) job is permanent, no matter what happens; (v) holidays; (vi) government servants are very free when compared with the private sector". International Labour Office: Matching employment opportunities and expectations: a programme of action for Ceylon (Geneva, ILO, 1971), technical papers, p. 148.

In developed countries, a much greater proportion of the unemployed are household heads who cannot rely on the support of relatives and friends for any extended period of time. For developing countries, a number of reasons are commonly cited for the relatively slow adjustment of expectations to opportunities; one reason may be the relative inefficiency of labour market institutions in signalling reliable information swiftly to jobseekers. Another is that, among the better-educated unemployed, there is a distinct taste for modern sector employment, a taste inculcated in them by an educational system geared to producing white-collar workers for the public sector. As a consequence, they are unwilling to adjust their sights downwards rapidly for the payoffs from securing a suitable job far exceed the costs of a long spell of worklessness. Yet another reason may be the fear on the part of the educated unemployed that, if he lowers his aspirations and accepts a less well-paid, lower-status job, his future chances of obtaining employment appropriate to his perceived station may be irrevocably jeopardised. It is hard to judge the importance of this last reason among the unemployed in urban South-east Asia, but its incidence among Indian matriculates and college graduates is sufficiently well documented.[1]

Clearly, job aspiration embodies a complex set of considerations of which wage aspiration is but one. Our knowledge of the wage and non-wage job aspirations of the unemployed in LDCs is inadequate. We do not know in any detail their determinants and their rate of change with unemployment. Here, only the relationship between wage aspiration and unemployment is examined. Studies on the developed countries suggest that wage aspiration levels tend to decline with the length of unemployment and that workers are more prepared to accept lower-paid less-desirable jobs as their period of unemployment increases.[2] Another study indicates that almost seven out of ten workers had a minimum wage below which they would not accept a job.[3]

It is likely that the relationship between wage aspiration levels and unemployment is not a simple or stable one. Aspiration levels and their rate of downward adjustment are influenced by such factors as the status of the worker, resources, age, sex, education, work experience, etc. We should note here also that not all jobseekers will necessarily have wage expectations above the rates prevailing in the labour market. Some, motivated by fear of failure or a lack of self-esteem, may well have unrealistically low aspirations.

---

[1] See Mark Blaug, P.R.G. Layard, M. Woodland: The causes of graduate unemployment in India (Allen Lane, Penguin Press, 1969); and Stewart F. Richards: "Geographic mobility of industrial workers in India", in D.J. Dwyer (ed.), The city as a centre of change in Asia (Hong Kong, Hong Kong University Press, 1972), p. 89.

[2] Hirschel Kasper: "The asking price of labour and the duration of unemployment", in Review of Economics and Statistics, May 1967; Irvin Sobel and Hugh Folk: "Labour market adjustments by unemployed workers", in Employment, policy and the labour market, A.M. Ross (ed.) (Berkeley, University of California Press, 1965), pp. 333-357.

[3] H.L. Sheppard and A.H. Belitsky: Job hunt (Baltimore, Johns Hopkins University Press, 1966).

Surveys on aspiration levels usually contain a question on the reservation wage. The question is usually phrased thus: What is the minimum wage you must have before you accept a job? This interview approach to the determination of reservation wages runs the obvious risk of interviewer bias, as it does not focus on the decision behaviour of the jobseeker, that is, the actual wage at which he is prepared to work. Furthermore, the question on reservation wage does not relate the expected wage to the amount of work that a person is willing to offer, a matter which will be influenced by such variables as age and sex. Females, for instance, will probably offer a smaller number of hours.

STRUCTURE OF WAGE ASPIRATIONS IN SINGAPORE

In June 1973 the Economic Research Centre conducted a small national sample survey of 719 households, admittedly a very small fraction of the total universe of some 380,000 households.[1] The aim of the survey was to determine among other things the job-seeking behaviour and labour supply elasticity among the unemployed. Before we present the results of the survey, it may be useful to summarise the employment promotion record of the city-state, one of whose special characteristics is the absence of a large rural population. Since Singapore became a republic in 1965, the economy has progressed swiftly. In recent years, the annual GDP growth rate has averaged about 14 per cent. Unemployment levels, which stood at 9.2 per cent in 1966, fell to less than 5 per cent in 1973. Some 100,000 migrant workers have been imported to meet manpower shortages in the rapidly expanding manufacturing and construction sectors, the two leading growth sectors in the economy. The success of Singapore at generating employment has been attributed to the following factors: political and social stability, pragmatic political leadership, tough-minded labour laws enacted in 1968 to restrict the negotiating powers of trade unions, a battery of investment incentives and a disciplined labour force.[2]

One hundred and fourteen persons were identified as job-seekers in the survey, i.e. as persons who have taken active steps to look for work. Each jobseeker was asked four questions designed to relate his offer of hours of work to the expected wage. These questions, although subject to the usual interview bias, give a sharper definition of the minimum reservation wage which can be taken as the minimum wage expected for the minimum hours of work a person must have for a job. The four questions are:

---

[1] The survey was part of an ILO-sponsored study on the determinants of labour force participation in Singapore.

[2] For a detailed analysis of employment promotion in Singapore, see David H. Clark: Employment promotion in Singapore, unpublished paper, Apr. 1974.

(i) What is the most number of hours you are prepared to work each week?

(ii) If offered a job, what is the least number of hours a week the job must have before you accept it?

(iii) What monthly pay would you expect for the <u>most</u> number of hours you are prepared to work a week?

(iv) What monthly pay would you expect for the <u>least</u> number of hours you are prepared to work each week?

The results on the minimum and maximum hours of work are not surprising. Females offer less minimum and maximum hours of work. Prime-age males offer maximum hours which are not too different from that worked by most employees in the country.[1] Minimum hours supplied by females over 30 years of age averaged 30 hours, indicating that they are only looking for part-time jobs.

The results on wage expectations are more interesting. Table 1 presents the mean wage aspirations as they relate to the minimum and maximum hours of work that jobseekers are willing to supply. A number of observations may be made about table 1. For males, both mean "maximum" and "minimum" expected wages decline with the period of unemployment. But for females (15-19), the relationship does not hold, probably because of the influences of intervening factors such as relationship to household head, household income, educational level, etc. Further, the gap between the "minimum" and "maximum" wage aspirations is much smaller among older jobseekers, which indicates that wage aspirations of the latter are much more elastic and their adaptation to market realities is more likely to be speedier. One explanation is that teenagers are usually dependants and thus are able to endure a longer spell of unemployment without being compelled to lower their wage aspirations significantly.

The relationship between schooling and wage aspirations is in line with <u>a priori</u> reasoning. Individuals with completed secondary education expect more by way of minimum and maximum wages than those with lower levels of schooling. Incidentally, it is interesting to note here that the expected minimum wage of males with primary schooling ($137) is about the same as that for an entry job such as office attendant in the public sector. Public sector jobs requiring a completed secondary education pay about $200, somewhat similar to the "maximum" wage aspirations of females with similar schooling. (See also Appendix table 1.) It would appear that the aspiration structure of the unemployed in Singapore is not terribly out of line with employment opportunities.

The results on the effect of language of education on wage aspirations are difficult to interpret. It is well known in Singapore, where the language of Government, commerce and industry is English, that an English-language education commands higher pay in the labour market. Therefore, one would expect English-language educated jobseekers to anticipate higher wages than their

---

[1] Ministry of Labour: <u>1972 Annual Report</u>, p. 110, gives the average weekly hours worked by males as 49.3 hours and females as 47.0 hours.

Table 1. Minimum and maximum monthly mean income expectations of jobseekers, Singapore, 1973 (by sex and age group)

(Singapore dollars)

	Male						Female			
	15-19		20-29		30+		15-19		20-29	
	Minimum	Maximum	Minimum	Maximum	Minimum	Maximum	Minimum	Maximum	Minimum	Maximum
Length of unemployment										
Less than 6 months	162	208	313	503	285	395	127	146	195	235
More than 6 months	158	190	275	363	250	336	145	175	138	156
Level of education										
Primary or less	137	164	300	...	175	272	110	135	132	150
Some secondary	128	151	263	408	390	500	165	185	157	188
Completed secondary	...	...	367	533	...	...	155	200	225	300
Language of education										
English	163	200	225	367	316	403	140	173	132	158
Chinese	...	...	385	600	225	281	126	150	216	278
Working experience										
None	137	165	...	...	...	...	138	173	188	263
Less than 1 year	159	201	250	...	...	...	133	154	...	192
More than 1 year	...	...	319	472	263	357	143	177	156	185
Household income										
Less than $500	136	162	175	242	294	392	129	158	137	158
More than $500	200	256	344	559	225	321	145	180	198	258

Source: ERC labour force participation survey, 1973, unpublished tabulations.

... Less than 4 observations.

counterparts from Chinese-medium schools. Instead the contrary
result is indicated for both males and females in the age group
20-29. To be sure, part of this may be due to the higher average
level of schooling among the Chinese educated. But this fact
fails to explain fully the considerable gap in the mean "maximum"
and "minimum" income expectations of the Chinese educated and
English educated. One may note also that the results for males
over 30 and for female teenagers are consistent with the hypothesis of higher wage aspiration levels among the English educated.

Work experience has a positive effect on the wage aspiration
level for males, the reservation wage rising with the amount of
work experience. But for females the reservation wage of the
inexperienced is as high or higher than for those with work
experience.

Yet another issue is the relationship between household income
and wage aspirations. One would hypothesise that those persons
coming from high-income households would anticipate higher minimum
income because of what sociologists call the need to maintain
status consistency and what economists term the negative income
effect. Generally, both males and females coming from households
with more than $500 monthly income have higher wage aspirations.

To sum up, the above analysis suggests that wage aspiration is
not a simple function of the length of unemployment, age, sex or
other socio-economic variables. The analysis also implies that
attempts to influence the structure of aspirations among the
unemployed must necessarily be disaggregative in its focus.
Furthermore, the data suggest that the structural aspects of the
unemployment question are relatively unimportant in Singapore, in
contrast to the pattern observed elsewhere in South-east Asia.

The adjustment of aspirations and
urban labour market sectors

Even if, however, there is significant disparity between wage
aspirations and job opportunities, would a speedier alignment of
the two reduce the period of unemployment and, more importantly,
increase the volume of employment? Obviously the provision of
more and better labour market information could help bring worker
aspirations more in line with the realities of the marketplace.
But are labour market institutions, as they are presently constitu-
ted, conducive to a swift adjustment of the demand and supply of
labour? Clearly, this would depend on the hiring practices and
preferences of employers. For a more useful and detailed analysis
of these questions, we need to look at the various employment sectors in the urban economy. The urban economic structure is typically divided into a modern and traditional sector; the modern
sector being relatively high wage, capital intensive and having
better access to credit facilities, while the traditional sector is
generally small scale, domestically oriented and lower in productivity. Yet others have divided the modern or capitalist sector
into two sub-markets, namely a market for entry jobs and non-entry
jobs.[1] These divisions illuminate aspects of employer behaviour,

---

[1] See Richard U. Miller: "The relevance of surplus labour
theory to the urban labour markets in Latin America", in International Labour Studies, Bulletin 8, 1971, pp. 220-246.

but do not go quite far enough, nor do they yield specific policies
for development planning. A more useful perspective might be to
treat the urban employment structure as consisting of four inter-
linked sub-markets.

The first is an individual enterprise sector or the street/
bazaar sector. The most visible face of the urban economy, this
sector consists largely of individuals working long hours at marginal jobs for a subsistence income. The pool of workers in this sector is continually replenished and augmented by the influx of
persons from the countryside and by urban-born who lack the
requisite credentials or are otherwise "inappropriately" socialised.
Self-created employment and underemployment, rather than open
unemployment, characterise this sector. Self-employment in margin-
ally productive activities is open to all with the minimum amount
of resourcefulness and ingenuity. For many members, it is a
temporary stopping point before they secure more productive employment in the family enterprise, government or modern sectors. We
would not find in this sector too many highly educated persons, for
these people are likely to come from better-income households and
may not be willing or may not have to work at a subsistence job.
Shared poverty is a common phenomenon, and income inequality among
participants is small.

The second employment market is the small or family enterprise
sector. This is a relatively more productive sector, more predominant in middle-sized and small towns and a potential source of
labour absorption. Its expansion is, however, limited by the fact
that the demand for workers is not purely based on economic considerations. Jobs are frequently allocated on the basis of kinship, clan or tribal connections. In urban South-east Asia, for
example, there is a considerable degree of occupational specialisation along racial and linguistic lines which limits the job
creation potential. Labour supply to this sector is not as elastic as in the individual enterprise sector. Individuals who lack
the connections will circle the outside of the market hoping to
gain entry by building up friendship ties. Income distribution is
likely to be more unequal than in the individual enterprise sector.
Many who find work in this sector are also exploring for jobs in
the modern or government sectors, a move facilitated by skill or
credential acquisition. In the early stages of industrialisation,
the family enterprise sector is a key supplier of skilled and
experienced workers to the corporate firms. This supply is
quickly exhausted and the modern firm must begin training and upgrading incumbent workers to meet its expansion needs. Thus, a
series of internal labour markets gradually evolves. Employers'
hiring requirements in the family enterprise sector are flexible.
The stress is on connections rather than on credentials. Individuals who are willing to lower their wage aspirations may not be
able to find jobs because of the particularistic patterns of hiring.
Other policies, such as the provision of easier access to credit
and technical and marketing assistance, are probably needed to make
the sector more productive.

The third sector is the government sector, which typically
employs about 10-15 per cent of the workforce in urban areas. It
is singled out because of its importance in influencing workers'
aspirations and the private sector pay structure. This sector
stipulates rather rigid requirements, particularly in terms of education for entry jobs. Preferences for workers are explicitly stated
and frequently not amenable to change in the short term. Rules and

regulations governing the allocation of workers are voluminous.
The internal labour market is most developed in this sector, and the
focal point of change is not particular wage rates but the entire
wage structure. Individuals seeking work in this sector are
usually socialised by the educational system, attracted to it by the
relatively high wages and job security it offers. In many LDCs,
particularly ex-colonial ones, the sector is organised and legislation on minimum wages, statutory minimum fringe benefits, etc., are
extensive. Partly because of this, the level of benefits is difficult to reduce. However, the Government may use this sector to
alter the racial distribution of jobs as, for example, in the case
of Malaysia which has positive discriminatory rules to encourage a
larger flow of Malays (Bumiputras) into the towns. Labour supply
to this sector is elastic for entry jobs because of the vast output
of the school system.

The fourth sector is the modern firm sector. Here hiring
standards are not quite as rigid as those in the government sector.
Expanding firms are quite willing to hire skilled and experienced
workers from the family enterprise sector. Partly because of
government incentives and the under-pricing of capital, this sector
tends to be capital intensive and to operate with inappropriate
technologies. It has been frequently suggested that the pricing of
capital and labour should be more in line with the resource endowments of the country. But this is not easy to do. Many modern
multinational firms are more concerned with product quality than
with wage saving. Managers prefer to deal with machines rather
than men from widely divergent social and cultural environments.
Furthermore, lack of supervisory manpower further compounds the
difficulties of training and retaining a large workforce. In the
initial stages of the firm's life history, its internal labour
market is likely to be underdeveloped, so that most jobs are open to
the outsider. Employers are not likely to advertise except as a
last resort, preferring to recruit friends and relatives of existing
employees. When there is a shortage, the firm is quite adaptable
and willing to adjust its hiring standards downwards. The supply
of labour to entry jobs in this sector is probably quite elastic.
Wages are likely to be sticky downwards because of social legislation and minimum statutory fringe benefits. Further, since its
pay levels - particularly for entry jobs - are quite closely
patterned after that of the government sector, tinkering with the
pay structure will not increase the number of jobs.

The different sectors of the urban employment market can be
placed on a continuum based on the degree of rigidity in entry
qualifications into the sector, with the street/bazaar sector at one
end and the family enterprise and government sectors at the other.
Both the family enterprise and government sectors are encircled by
rigid barriers to entry, but of diametrically opposed nature. The
particularistic orientation of the family enterprise sector, with
hiring based frequently on ascriptive characteristics like race or
language, poses a formidable obstacle to the individual outsider who
hopes to get in and to governmental hopes that it will be an employment generating sector. The government sector, on the other hand,
employs the universalistic criterion of credentialism, but that, too,
is an extremely rigid criterion and has pernicious effects,
especially the production of an excess supply of accredited jobseekers who cannot possibly be absorbed by the sector.

The results of our analysis are pessimistic as far as the use of
the wage instrument for promoting employment creation is concerned.
A more rapid adjustment of wage aspirations to market realities may
not help to expand the volume of employment, although it may help to

shorten the period of unemployment for some individuals. Because of the way the urban employment market is stratified, capital, connections and credentials are probably more important in determining success in finding a job than the ability of a person to adjust his wage aspirations speedily.

APPENDIX TABLE 1

Mean individual income by selected
characteristics, Singapore, 1973
(Singapore dollars)

Characteristic	Mean income	Standard deviation
1. Age		
15-19	133	59
20-29	285	213
30-39	342	267
40-49	290	216
50-59	337	276
60 or more	251	189
2. Race of household head		
Malay	208	123
Chinese	285	227
Indian/Pakistani	247	225
Other	444	399
3. Household type		
Single person	212	74
One nuclear family	387	242
One extended family	276	218
Multi-family	192	138
4. Highest level of education		
No formal schooling	168	105
Some primary	221	118
Completed primary	209	109
Some secondary	289	205
Completed secondary	348	263
Pre-university/college/university	642	391
5. Hours spent at all jobs		
Less than 20	148	90
20-34	251	185
35-44	298	243
45-54	273	213
55 and more	274	236
6. Intention to look for more work		
Yes	240	168
No	285	236

Source: Economic Research Centre, Labour force participation survey, June 1973, unpublished tabulations.

Mobility and wage structure in an urban labour market: a study in Ahmedabad (India)

by

T.S. Papola,

University of Bombay

The present paper reports on the functioning of an urban labour market in the traditional set-up in the context of rapid industrialisation.

I. SCOPE AND LOCALE OF STUDY

The labour market of an urban area in an underdeveloped economy could be classified into three segments: one, consisting of casual workers or independent wage earners with no regular attachment with any establishment; two, the employees of small establishments not within the purview of any statutory measures for regulation of work and payment; and three, the employees of larger establishments such as "factories" (so defined under the law) where the contract is formal, job security is assured, and the hours of work and mode of payment are regulated.

The Ahmedabad labour force is broadly distributed into these segments as follows: 50 per cent in large establishments divided almost equally between regular factory employment and public services; 35 per cent in the small establishments in manufacturing, trade and commerce, construction, transport and other services; and 15 per cent as independent and casual wage earners with no regular attachment to a small or large establishment. The factory sector, the focus of the present study, accounts for only 25 per cent of the labour force numbering about 150,000 workers in 1971.

The factory sector has some special characteristics with its distinctive implications for the labour market. Textiles, mainly cotton, have a predominant place in the city's industrial structure, employing around 120,000 factory workers. Over the last two decades, employment in this industry has hardly increased, while new industries in the engineering group (metal products, machinery, transport equipment and chemicals) have grown rapidly. However, the over-all increase in the demand for labour has been small and the annual rate of increase in employment has been between 3 and 4 per cent. Given the over-all surplus situation in the labour market (unemployment being estimated at around 3 per cent of the labour force), it should have been relatively easy to get adequate supplies of labour. But the skill requirements of the new industries have been significantly different, and shortages have been reported for several skilled categories.

The factory labour force of Ahmedabad has always been of a predominantly local and regional origin. In the 1940s, the Labour Investigation Committee found that around 60 per cent of the workers came from within a vicinity of 100 miles. Today, this highly local character seems to have given way to a regional one: the city contributes only 15 per cent of the labour force while the rest of the area of the district contributes another 4 per cent; but the Gujarat State (of which Ahmedabad is the capital and the major city) accounts for 73 per cent of the city factory workforce. Another 20 per cent is contributed by two other States, the neighbouring States of Rajasthan (13 per cent) and Uttar Pradesh (7 per cent), both relatively poorer States; 43 per cent of the workers reported urban origin and the rest rural.

The labour force is stabilised to a greater extent than it might first appear. Many of the workers have ceased to have any interest or economic stake in their reported place of origin. Although 85 per cent do not report Ahmedabad city as the place of their origin, they are not necessarily "foreigners". About 63 per cent of the workers have been in the city for over 10 years and 51 per cent for 20 years or more. The proposition is further strengthened by the fact that 85 per cent of the workers live in the city with their families - usually large with an average size of 6 persons and a dependency ratio of 2.25. Over time, the contribution of the fresh migrants to the factory workforce has been on the decline. Of the 10,000 vacancies filled in during the two years preceding the study, fresh migrants got into only 1,500.

II. MOBILITY

Before we turn to the question of mobility, let us state the major socio-economic characteristics of the factory workers in Ahmedabad as revealed in our study. A typical factory worker in Ahmedabad is relatively young, about 32 years of age, is not necessarily an Ahmedabadi, but a Gujarati in most cases. Even if he belongs to some other State he has stayed in Ahmedabad quite long, say for about 15 years. He has been to school for about 7 years but has not undergone any formal training in his occupation prior to employment. He lives with his family of about 6 persons, but there is another earner in his family. On an average he earns a monthly wage of around Rs.200 and this has to support 2 persons besides himself. Living with his family, with not too low an income and with a permanent job, he finds himself "well settled". The preferred method of increasing family income is not by frequent job changes but by finding an additional job for another family member in the city.

Given these characteristics and the over-all labour surplus, one would expect a low degree of mobility. The majority of factory workers (60 per cent) in Ahmedabad have, however, made at least one job change. Of these, 40 per cent of the mobile workers have had only one change, 12 per cent two, and the rest three or more. The average worker has changed jobs once during his work career, the change being involuntary (dismissal, retrenchment, etc.) in only 6 per cent of the cases (table 1). This measure of change, however, does not take into account the period of the working life. The measure of per worker per year change is 0.126, implying that an average worker changes jobs once every 8 years. These job changes involved complex mobility - inter-plant, inter-occupation, inter-industry and geographical - in a single change. The changes more often involved inter-occupation and inter-industry mobility than inter-plant or geographical. This appears to imply the lack of a high degree of industry and occupation specificity of skills. In printing and machinery plants, however, job changes more often involve inter-plant than occupational shifts.

To examine differential mobility by occupations, we focused on the following four groups: (i) occupations common to several industries and not in short supply; (ii) occupations common to several industries but in short supply; (iii) occupations specific to one industry and not in short supply; and (iv) specific and shortage occupations (table 2). We do not get a clear idea of the

Table 1. Mobility - per worker changes

Industry	No. of workers (sample)	Inter-firm changes	Inter-industry changes	Occupational changes	Geographical changes	Involuntary changes	Voluntary changes	Total (voluntary + involuntary)	Mobility measure: per worker per year job changes
Food manufacturing	76	0.394	0.513	0.828	0.2500	-	0.6184	0.6184	0.102
Textiles	380	0.381	0.373	0.450	0.2894	0.0553	0.6737	0.7289	0.084
Wood and cork	63	0.015	0.253	0.126	0.1904	0.0635	0.3174	0.3809	0.062
Printing, publishing, etc.	48	0.875	0.562	0.583	0.5000	0.0833	1.3958	1.4791	0.023
Rubber products	27	0.147	0.703	0.518	0.3703	0.00741	0.7407	0.8148	0.218
Chemicals and chemical products	13	0.230	0.692	0.538	0.4615	0.1538	0.7692	0.9230	0.115
Non-metallic mineral products	24	0.375	0.791	0.500	0.6290	-	1.4166	1.4166	0.196
Basic metal	15	0.266	0.733	0.466	0.333	-	1.1333	1.1333	0.150
Metal products	100	0.070	0.960	0.640	0.3400	-	1.2100	1.2100	0.191
Machinery	197	0.604	0.634	0.573	0.3959	0.0406	1.4517	1.4923	0.164
Transport equipment	108	0.407	0.787	0.953	0.3148	0.2037	0.9259	1.1296	0.124
Miscellaneous manufacturing	15	0.400	0.600	0.960	0.9333	-	0.9333	0.9333	0.192
Total	1 066	0.388	0.560	0.568	0.3367	0.05909	0.9305	0.9896	0.126

determinants of occupational mobility.   The occupations common to
several industries, in general, show an above average degree of
mobility, and the tendency is strengthened by excess demand and
large deviations in wage rates.   Workers in industry-specific
occupations also appear mobile, even though across plants, for
relatively small wage gains, but only when their skills are in
short supply.

Table 2. Mobility and wage deviations

Occupations	Mobility index	Inter-industry deviations (%)	Inter-plant wage deviations (%)
Group (i)			
Clerk	0.18	38.50	20.00
Unskilled labour	0.29	22.00	40.00
Peon	0.17	25.00	45.00
Group (ii)			
Fitter	0.12	35.00	28.00
Turner	0.17	20.00	18.00
Moulder	0.15	30.00	20.00
Machineman	0.11	15.00	33.00
Group (iii)			
Spinner	0.07	-	7.00
Weaver	0.03	-	14.00
Driver	0.08	-	28.00
Group (iv)			
Compositor	0.27	-	15.00
Chemist	0.18	-	11.00

As for potential mobility, about 56 per cent expressed a
desire for change but only 48 per cent could be considered as
serious.   The rest have made no efforts whatsoever to effect a
change - not even inquiries among other workers.   Those not desirous of change predominate in industries with better promotion prospects, in the over-35 age groups, among those with ten years or
more in the current job, and in the higher ranges (above Rs.300
per month).   The main reason mentioned for not desiring a change
is that they are "well settled" in life (reported by 35 per cent
of them) followed by "no better job available" (given by 18 per
cent of the workers).   "Too old", "children studying", "nearer
home" and "other family members working here" are among the other
reasons given.   Thus, those not desiring change may be grouped

into two main categories: those who are satisfied with the present
job (82 per cent) and those who feel that better jobs are not
available (18 per cent).   Among those desirous of change 65 per
cent are willing to move out of Ahmedabad.   Such willingness is
inversely related to age and family size.   Among single workers
66 per cent are willing to go out of Ahmedabad but among those
with one family member only 40 per cent.   With five or more in the
family the geographically mobile decline to 29 per cent.   There is
also an association between the desire to change and the earnings
level.   Persons desirous of change are dominant among those earning Rs.100 or less and the situation is reversed among those earning Rs.400 and over.   But in the middle ranges of earnings, which
incidentally correspond with the middle range of family size, an
increase in earnings does not necessarily lead to an increase in
immobile workers, the percentage of workers wanting a change being
lower among those earning below Rs.100 than among those earning
between Rs.100 to Rs.249 monthly.   The family sizes are substantially different between these two groups, the average for the
former being three and for the latter seven.   Even with another
earner, the latter family is not compensated for the increase in
family size.

     In analysing the worker's interest _ changing jobs, the key
variables are: (i) the income and the size of family rather than
the individual worker's earnings; and (ii) the influence of family
size in lowering the per capita income levels.

     The last aspect of mobility is an examination of the relation-
ship between education and potential mobility.   Does education
make a worker more mobile?   What are the effects of education and
training on different types of mobility?   Does training make a
worker's skill specific to an industry and thus limit his movements
across industries?   The evidence we have here (table 3) suggests
that having gone to school does not make a worker more mobile.   It
is only at the post-matriculation level that the percentage of
workers desiring change becomes significantly higher than among the
uneducated.   The percentage of geographically mobile workers
increases with the years of schooling, although this percentage is
higher among the uneducated than any educated category except the
graduates.   The same is true regarding the "freely" mobile workers,
i.e. those who are willing to move across industries as well as
outside Ahmedabad.   However, workers' mobility across industries
does not seem to be significantly affected by education.   On the
other hand, increased training may limit potential inter-industry
mobility.   Training, however, does not seem to have a discernible
effect on geographical mobility.   Although increased training may
tend to make a worker's skill industry specific, the over-all
specificity is low: 67 per cent of the workers with as much as
five years' training are willing to move across industries.

The efforts to secure job changes

     As stated earlier, 16 per cent of those desiring change made
no efforts to secure job changes.   The intensity as well as the
desire for change appear to decline with age.   Thus, among those
wanting a change in the age group 19-25, 90 per cent are making
efforts in that direction; in the age group 25-45 the percentage
is around 70; and among those above 45 years it is only 40 per
cent.   The same is true for the workers who have stayed longer
with their plants.   More interesting, however, is the relationship

Table 3. Education and mobility

Education (years of schooling and training)	Total workers (percentages to total sample)	Non-changers (%)	Changers (%)	Geographically mobile (% of changers)	Industrially mobile (% of changers)	Geographically and industrially mobile (% of changers)
0	19.23	48.29	51.71	49.10	84.90	41.51
1-3	6.94	37.83	62.17	17.39	80.43	8.69
4-6	22.42	51.03	48.97	28.20	72.65	21.36
7-9	27.96	50.67	49.33	27.21	77.55	17.00
10-14	19.32	31.55	68.45	36.45	86.52	29.06
15 and above	4.13	13.63	84.37	60.52	78.94	52.63
Total	100.00	44.18	55.82	34.79	80.33	26.72

Technical training

Training (number of years)

				Geographically mobile (% of changers)	Industrially mobile (% of changers)	Geographically and industrially mobile (% of changers)
0				42.24	82.35	33.30
1				21.42	86.66	20.00
2				19.58	72.22	12.50
3				18.91	70.27	11.00
4				57.14	70.00	28.00
5				60.00	67.00	20.00

between the level of education and efforts towards job change.
Less than half of the illiterate workers desirous of change made
corresponding efforts, and around 75, 92 and 100 per cent among
those with primary, secondary and college education respectively.

What is the nature of these efforts?   The most often
mentioned is "looking into advertisements", closely followed by
"inquiries from other workers" (table 4).   Only 8 per cent of
them have actually applied for a job and only 15 per cent have
registered their names with the employment exchange.   Comparing
these with the earlier efforts which secured them their jobs, it
appears that the reliance on informal channels like "approach to
other worker" declines, while reliance on formal channels like
employment exchange and advertisements increases.   Among illiter-
ates and primary and secondary education holders the most common
means is inquiries of other workers, and among those with higher
education the "advertisement hunt" is the most prevalent.
Registration with employment exchanges is more popular among the
college educated: 1 of every 6 tries relied on this method, while
among those with lower education it is only 1 in 28.

To sum up, since potential mobility is less than actual past
mobility, it appears that the workforce has a tendency to
stabilise further.   The low extent of their past and potential
mobility suggests that the labour market has a tendency towards a
stable equilibrium.   It is found that, after accounting for age
and years of service, a mobile worker on an average had an advantage of about 10 per cent in earnings, but a larger number of job
changes did not necessarily bring higher advantage.   The absence
of any substantial advantage following from mobility suggests the
existence of a wage structure which does not allow any significant
differentials which could be wiped out by sheer movements of
workers from one job to another.

III. WAGE STRUCTURE

The above labour mobility confirms the hypothesis that wage
differentials in a local labour market are generally at a minimum
because of the greater effectiveness of competition.   This does
not mean that all differentials are at equilibrium and are based
on rational grounds.   Even in a well-integrated competitive local
labour market the differentials among non-competing groups would
be relatively higher and more persistent.   Assuming a low degree
of substitutability and significant differences in skills, different occupations may belong to non-competing groups.   As industries differ in their occupation mix, the respective workforces
also fall in different competing groups.   Workers in different
plants of the same industry or even in different industries belonging to similar occupations may, however, constitute competing
groups.   Even in competitive markets without restraints on mobility
and knowledge, the wage variations among the former would be
larger than among the latter.

Table 4. Efforts made for job changes and the level of education

Education (number of years)	Efforts					
	Making no efforts	Registration in employment exchange	Application to some employer	Inquiries from other worker	Looking into advertisement	Total
0	45	2	1	20	14	82
1- 3	18	4	2	24	21	69
4- 6	15	4	2	49	24	94
7-10	12	10	9	82	113	226
11-14	6	43	21	78	125	273
15 and above	0	11	6	13	17	47
Total	96	74	41	266	314	791
	(12.14)	(9.35)	(5.18)	(33.63)	(39.70)	(100.00)
Successful efforts for the past jobs		(1.87)	(9.36)	(68.87)	(19.90)	(100.00)

Occupational differentials

The industries selected in our sample employ workers from several occupations. In textiles and printing, the occupational composition seems to differ significantly among units. The range of wage rates is, therefore, wide in each unit and industry. The units in machinery manufacturing and chemical industries show the highest degree of occupational wage differentials, the co-efficient of variation in most of these units being higher than 40 per cent. A textile unit shows a smaller occupational wage dispersion, 14 of 23 units have a coefficient of variation less than 40 per cent and 9 less than 20 per cent. The pattern is similar in printing, non-metallic mineral products and basic metals. It appears as if the range of sophistication among skills in an industry increases the dispersion in occupational wage rates. A look at the list of occupations in chemicals and machinery reveals a wide array of occupations with varying degrees of skill of unskilled, semi-skilled and skilled groups. In textiles, non-metallic mineral, basic metals and food manufacturing, the occupations vary more horizontally than vertically and the distance between the highest and the lowest in terms of skills is not as high.

Another interesting feature is the similarity in the rank order of the occupational wage rates among plants, particularly in printing and textile units. This suggests that the occupational differentials have some basis in job characteristics such as skill, education, training, workload, etc. We do not have any basis to assess the workload of jobs. The years of education and training are significantly related with the occupational wage rates in most of the industries. In textiles, wage rates of occupations appear to be positively correlated with open market hiring (as opposed to from within the industry). In printing the only variable explaining around 60 per cent of the occupational wage variation is the relative abundance of jobseekers in an occupation (as indicated by the percentage of those with qualifications higher than the required minimum among the fresh recruits of the preceding two years). This variable is significantly inversely correlated with occupational wage rates.

Inter-plant differentials

For the analysis of inter-plant wage structure, the wage rates of the common occupations are appropriate for comparison. In most of the industries, inter-unit comparisons of average wage rates yielded a coefficient of variation between 10 to 30 per cent. The average size of the units combined with profitability explained a large part of these differentials among units, the major exception being the textile industry.

The inter-plant deviations in the textile industry eluded explanation even when the wage rates in similar occupations were considered. As the occupational wage rates are standardised for all units, the differentials probably reflect the composition of workers in terms of years of service (due to the system of annual increments). Assuming that the older units employ workers with greater years of service, the positive correlation coefficient between age of the units and their wage rates (+ 0.565) may be quite meaningful in textiles. The coefficients were, however, insignificant in other industries.

The influence of economic variables is evident in wage rate variations among units in the machinery manufacturing industry, an industry relatively free of institutional rigidities of the textile type. In four out of five occupations (machineman, moulder, fitter and clerk, the fifth being coolie), the one variable which is found to be significant is the rate of return on capital.

Inter-industry wage differentials

Among the 12 selected industry groups the absolute variation in average wage rates turns out to be Rs.40.43 and relative variation 25.01 per cent (around the average of Rs.194.67). The importance of variations among occupations is brought out in table 5, which indicates these to be significant for 8 occupations in 8 of 12 industries studied.

Table 5.   Inter-industry wage deviation: selected occupations

	Average wage rate (Rs.)	Absolute variation (Rs.)	Relative variation (%)
Office staff	301.99	116.27	38.50
Fitter	246.92	86.44	35.00
Technical assistant	365.25	51.74	14.16
Supervisor	296.65	92.77	21.17
Machineman	158.13	23.16	14.64
Watchman	155.50	27.55	17.71
Peon	178.80	43.89	24.54
Coolie	115.60	25.28	21.86

However, wage rate variation among occupations is less than that among the average wage rates of individual industries. The exception is the category office staff and fitters, which is not a homogeneous group and for which qualifications vary widely among industries. The labour markets tend to be occupational rather than industrial, and the evidence is consistent with the operation of "wage contours" across the industries in the local labour market, particularly when one considers the low variation among such categories as watchmen and technical assistants.

Among industry influences on occupational wage rate variation, it may be noted that industries which pay a high wage rate to one occupation tend to do the same for other occupations. The coefficients of correlation among the ranks of industries by wage rates in certain pairs of common occupation are found to be generally significant. For example, ranks of industries by their wage rates for office staff, fitter, technical assistant, moulder, supervisor, machineman and watchman. The coefficient of concordance among the series of industry wage ranks for the eight occupations (0.6706 significant at 95 per cent level of confidence) suggests that the industries can be easily identifiable as high wage or low wage ones even when many occupations are considered.

A further analysis was attempted to assess the influence of key economic factors: growth rate, average unit size, output per worker, profitability, and capital intensity. Average unit size emerged as the one variable which was found to be most commonly significant for six selected occupations. Although not surprising, it does not fit in well with the logic of competitive economic theory. Why should a plant or industry pay a high wage simply because it is large sized? What market or institutional forces compel this result?

IV. LABOUR MARKETING PROCESSES

Let us now turn to the operational aspects of the labour market to examine how far the labour marketing processes have been able to achieve efficiency and equity in the allocation of labour.

Quantitatively, the Ahmedabad labour market did not experience any severe strains and stresses in getting an adequate number of people for the filling of vacancies and new jobs during the last decade or so. But the changes in industrial structure led to a change in the occupational pattern of the demand for labour and, therefore, shortages in certain occupations were noticed. According to the Employment Market Information Report of Ahmedabad, the occupations in which shortages were experienced include chemist, fitter, turner, moulder, shaper, grinder, machineman, plate toucher, compositor, proofreader, and mechanic. Surpluses were noted among the unskilled, and persons without any vocational training or job experience and seeking white-collar jobs. Employers in metal products and machinery groups of industry faced with the inability of the market to fulfil their requirements, even at relatively high rates, have resorted increasingly to in-plant training.

The wage increases in these industries have led to an increase in inter-industry and inter-plant mobility, as registered by an increase in the extent of quits and entries in these shortage occupations. In the shortage occupations, the quits have been consistently from low-wage units and industries and entries into the high-wage ones. Phenomena to note include:

Fitters, for example, have a high degree of wage variation among industries (from Rs.158 in non-metallic mineral products to Rs.307 in food manufacturing) as well as among units in the same industry (Rs.165 to Rs.315 in the machinery group). There have been quits but not entries in the industries and units with low wages and no quits and few entries in those with high wages. The picture is similar for moulders.

Machinery manufacturing is the single industry in which voluntary separations are absent in most of the occupations. Its wage rates are not necessarily higher in each of these occupations as compared to other industries; but it alone has a significantly large contribution to the employment opportunities in these occupations. For fitters and turners, two important occupations in this industry, voluntary separations are negligible; although quits from individual plants are high, they are still fewer than the total entries.

Voluntary quits in case of occupations which are not in short supply are generally low and entries are not necessarily more to the high-wage units and industries. However, here entries are primarily determined by job opportunities rather than by relative wage rates.

Job information

It is not easy to ascertain the extent to an individual worker's knowledge about job availabilities. This was done on the basis of a conversation with them, and even then the assessment could only be qualitative and subjective. The degree of knowledge and information possessed by a worker was classified as "good", "fair", "poor" and "nil" on the basis of a standardised set of questions. Over two-thirds of the workers had some information on job availability and earnings, and their knowledge could be regarded as "fair" or "good" in around 42-43 per cent and poor in only 27 per cent of the cases. The characterisation of the mass of Indian factory workers as predominantly uninformed and indifferent to market prospects is not sustained by the evidence.

The possession of information differs, as expected, by the educational levels of the workers. Over 50 per cent of illiterate workers have knowledge neither about job availability nor about the earnings of workers in other jobs, but around 13 per cent of them have a fair degree of such knowledge. Among those with primary education, 25 per cent are ignorant while 33 per cent are well posted on the job market. The percentage who are ignorant is still 25 among those with secondary school education, but the fairly knowledgeable increase to around 45 per cent. Among those who have gone to college, 13 per cent seem to have no information on the job market but 70 per cent revealed a "fair" or "good" degree of knowledge on the subject.

Recruitment agencies

In about 70 per cent of the cases the information about the job vacancies in the past was had from "friends and relatives". It suggests a predominance of informal channels and the absence of an equitable dissemination of information. An analysis of the agencies of recruitment revealed that the same informality and consequent inequity characterise the recruitment process as well. In 63 per cent of the cases the jobs were secured on the basis of "introduction by other worker" and this "other worker" was related to the incumbent by blood, kinship or community in 91 per cent of these cases. The recruitment system in the Ahmedabad labour market thus shows the characteristics of a predominantly and de facto "closed-shop" system. Here the "closed shop" is not a result of union policy but reflects the virtual absence of recruitment policy and procedures on the part of the managements who rely heavily on their existing employees. The latter naturally prefer their own kith and kin, thus making the entry of anybody else difficult. The system thus tends to be inequitable and renders the biases and preferences narrower than would have been the case even in closed-shop unionism. The employers are, however, unlikely to rely on

Table 6. Connection with employment agency used for number of jobs

Industry	Type of connection						
	Blood relation	Same caste	Same native place	Financial	Commission	Friends	Total
Food manufacturing (20)	16	17	4	-	-	5	42
Textiles (23)	184	222	55	2	5	16	484
Wood and cork (25)	43	25	11	-	-	7	86
Printing, publishing, etc. (28)	15	13	6	-	2	7	43
Rubber products (30)	8	9	2	-	-	4	23
Chemicals and chemical products (31)	4	5	2	-	-	1	12
Non-metallic mineral products (33)	5	17	7	-	2	4	35
Basic metal (34)	5	7	-	-	-	5	17
Metal products (35)	49	60	13	1	-	4	127
Machinery (36)	80	110	38	-	2	27	257
Transport equipment (38)	31	62	8	-	-	7	108
Miscellaneous manufacturing (39)	1	9	5	-	-	4	19
Total	441	556	151	3	11	91	1 253
Percentage	35.20	44.37	12.05	0.24	0.88	7.26	100.00

candidates recommended by other workers if they get "inferior"
workers in the bargain. From the viewpoint of efficiency, therefore, the predominantly informal system of recruitment which relies
on workers' caste and native place contacts may be presumed to be
harmless, if not preferable, but for considerations of equity and
fairness.

V. CONCLUDING REMARKS

The brief account of the characteristics and mechanism of the
Ahmedabad urban labour market presented in the preceding pages leads
one to two major conclusions. First, the local urban labour market
seems to be functioning more or less as the economic theory of the
labour market would suggest. In occupations where differentials are
high and a shortage prevails, job changes are found to be more frequent. And movements have been more or less consistently in the
direction of higher earnings. The wage structure, of course, is
characterised by significant differentials, higher among non-
competing groups than among competing ones. Inter-industry and
inter-plant deviations largely reflect occupational differentials and
the latter are explained mainly in terms of the cost of acquiring
skills. Thus, on the whole, mobility exists to the extent it is
warranted by the market and the wage structure shows signs of a stable
equilibrium.

Second, the functioning of the labour market does not show any
significant qualitative differences from the urban labour markets in
developed countries. At least in comparison with the organised sector of large-scale manufacturing in a developing country, the differences seem to be of degree rather than of kind.

These propositions do not, however, mean that no policy on and
institutional intervention in the labour market is required. The
neo-classical efficiency which a well-functioning labour market
brings need not necessarily be the ideal criteria. We have at
least three pieces of evidence out of the present study to suggest
that a serious conflict may arise between the "efficient" functioning
of the labour market and the goals of the system.

First, the continuing shortages in certain strategic occupations
could not be wiped out by the labour market changing wage relativi-
ties and inducing movements, for these shortages were real and not
mere results of labour market frictions. The individual units
refrained from an extensive programme of in-plant training on account
of the fear of losing hands once trained.

Second, the industry-wide arrangements for the rationalisation
and standardisation of the wage structure in the textile industry
provides an efficient alternative method of wage and personnel
administration to induce mobility - the rather painful process of
effecting changes in relative wages.

Third, the theoretical model would be indifferent between the
formal or informal method of recruitment as long as it ensures
supply in requisite quantity and quality. However, informal channels
raise questions concerning equity and fairness which cannot be set at
rest merely because we assume an employer interest in profit maximisation and efficiency.

A final qualification is in order. The present study is concerned only with the labour market for the factories and leaves out a large part of the urban labour market. Therefore, this exercise needs to be extended to the other segments of the urban labour market covering more aspects before generalisations useful for theoretical and policy purposes are drawn.[1]

---

[1] One such study on the Bombay labour market in its three major segments - casual workers, small establishments, and factories - is currently being undertaken by the author jointly with his colleague, Dr. L.K. Deshpande, under the sponsorship of the World Bank.

Training, position, and experience in the wage rates of specialised personnel in São Paulo's manufacturing firms

by
José Pastore,
University of São Paulo

Archibald O. Haller,
University of Wisconsin

Hernando Gomez Buendia,
Foundation for Higher Education and Development,
Bogotá

For some years now Brazil has been wholly committed to rapid economic growth. That it has been successful to date is attested by the recent growth rates. From 1968 through 1972, for example, the GNP per capita increased at an average rate of over 6 per cent per year. In an effort to maintain this momentum, the educational legislation was recently rewritten to revamp public education so as to train a more effective labour force. The new law clearly assumes that industrial productivity can be increased by providing the population with education appropriate for the occupations required by the economy of the region. The Government is especially concerned about the preparation of technical experts, managers and supervisors, and technical support personnel, here called "specialised personnel", required by the nation's factories.

The present research, conducted at the request of the Government of Brazil, was concerned with the evidence regarding the validity of this assumption. In 1970, when the project was begun, there was not much evidence regarding the effects of formal preparation on occupational productivity in Brazil or other developing countries. This is not to say, of course, that theory and some evidence were altogether lacking (Schultz, 1961; Morgan, David, Cohen and Brazer, 1962; Denison, 1966; Becker, 1967; and Blaug, 1970). But even in the richer countries, definitive multiple regression studies of the net effect of education, experience and other key variables on the income and/or wages of individuals have been appearing only within the last half-decade or so (Klevmarken, 1972; Mincer, 1974; Sewell and Hauser, 1975).

Yet even these cannot suffice to determine whether occupational preparation has a substantial effect on productivity. As Thurow (1973) has pointed out, education may operate merely to certify that the worker can learn the necessary skills once he has been hired; whether he actually learns any has yet to be shown. Indicators specifically designed to measure occupational preparation are needed. We also need better measures of productivity at the individual level in place of average or total earnings, the measure commonly employed, such as might be obtained by calculating the total monetary value of all the worker's wages and other benefits per unit time.

The present research was designed to estimate, in their proper causal order, the effects of occupational preparation, occupational position, job experience, age and seniority on standardised hourly wages, taken as a proxy for the productivity of individuals. Data obtained from a sample of specialised personnel in Brazil's manufacturing sector were subject to multivariate analyses.

In São Paulo, the State selected as the site, 20 per cent of Brazil's population produces 50 per cent of its GNP. Data were collected in 1970-71 on the 22,587 specialised workers in 688 industrial firms, which constitute a stratified random sample of

Note: The writers wish to thank the Foundation Institute of Economic Research of the University of São Paulo, the Graduate School and the College of Agricultural and Life Sciences of the University of Wisconsin, the Ford Foundation and the United States Agency for International Development for the support provided to this project. We also wish to thank T. Michael Carter, Tarcizio Rego Quirino, Ana Maria Bianchi and Dalcio Caron for statistical advice and computational assistance.

those with more than 20 employees in the 11 most productive
sectors. (For details see Pastore, Haller and Buendia, 1974.)
The sample included managerial, supervisory and support personnel,
amounting to 6 per cent of the total labour force of the firms.

The dependent variable is the worker's standardised hourly
wage, expressed in cruzeiros (W), the sum of his wages and benefits
divided by the number of hours worked during the year.

Occupational preparation (E), in approximate year equivalents,
is the first antecedent variable. It includes basic educational
attainment and occupationally specific training. These scores
range from 4 to 17, as follows: 4 - primary school plus in-
service training; 4 - some junior high school plus in-service
training; 8 - junior high school; 9 - junior high school plus
technical short courses (less than two years in length); 11 - high
school graduation; 12 - high school graduation plus technical
schooling appropriate to one's occupation; 13 - some university
education appropriate to one's occupation; 14 - a three-year
university degree in one's occupational speciality; 15 - same as
14, but four years; 16 - same as 14 but five years; and 17 - same
as 14 but six years. Note that the scale measures occupationally
relevant education rather than formal education in general.

Occupational influence level (I) is a measure of the rank of
the person's job (not necessarily the occupation for which he
trained) within the power hierarchy of his firm.[1] Combining span
and type of influence yields a six-point index: 6 - managers and
directors - wide, line; 5 - experts (scientists, attorneys,
engineers, etc.) - wide, staff; 4 - department heads and supervisors - medium, line; 3 - technicians - medium, staff; 2 - fore-
men - narrow, line; 1 - auxiliary office personnel - narrow, staff.

Age (A) in years (Reynolds, 1964; Mincer, 1974) is included
as a measure of the total accumulation of work experience.
Seniority (S), or years in the firm, is a second experience variable
which, net of age, measures one's knowledge of the firm's procedures. Years in the current job (J) is a third measure of accumulated experience variable, measuring one's knowledge of the
routines specific to a job.

Industrial sector is a control variable included to determine
the effects of the variables by sector.

Model. The five independent variables were incorporated into
a recursive "causal" model (Blalock, 1972) in which the standardised
hourly wage of the individual worker (W) is the dependent variable.
We posit that occupational influence level (I) has a direct effect
upon the dependent variable, and that indirectly it may transmit
part of the effects of training, seniority and age. Occupational
preparation (E), an exogenous variable, is taken as a measure of
trained competency, which, net of other variables, might directly
affect one's wage and might also do so indirectly by raising his
position in the firm. Age (A), indicating general experience,
might have direct and indirect effects by way of its impact on position in the firm and on job experience. These effects, too, would

----

[1] This concept is more fully explained in Pastore, Haller and
Buendia, 1974.

be net of those of all other variables.   It is also exogenous.
Seniority (S) too is exogenous, and affects the same variables as
age.   Years in the present job (J) is endogenous.   It is taken
to be partially determined by age and seniority (but not by occupational preparation or occupational influence level).   It may
only have direct effects on wages.

The estimation of effects assumes that the above sequence of
the variables is correct.   The total effect of an antecedent on
a subsequent variable is taken to be the sum of its indirect and
direct effects.   The direct effect of a variable is taken to be
its highest order partial beta weight on a dependent variable.
Its indirect effect is the product of its direct effect on an
intervening variable times the latter's direct effect on the dependent variable (Duncan, 1971;   Finney, 1972).

The main objective of this analysis is to present an intelli-
gible assessment and comparison of the network of effects of the
five antecedent variables on standardised wages and thus on productivity.   This leads to two key technical decisions.   First,
the common practice of analysing the lognormal transformation of
the wage variable is thus unnecessary and the dependent variable
was not transformed.   Second, path analysis requires linear
regression techniques.   Both for this reason and because a separa-
ate analysis showed that little was to be gained by allowing for
non-linear relations, all relations were assumed to be linear.

Results. A detailed summary of all the path analyses was prepared (Appendix A).[1]   The coefficients reported in the text are
taken from the total sample.

1.   Occupational influence (I), indicating the level in the
firm at which one exerts his influence on the company's operations,
is one of the most powerful variables affecting wages: $P_{WA} = 0.323$.
This means that in São Paulo's industries, wages are highly dependent upon the position the individual occupies in the power structure of the firm.   The higher one's position, the higher his
salary.   This variable is not merely an individual attribute;   it
is a position in the hierarchy of the firm.   In other words,
rewards accrue to persons because of their location in the institutional structure.

Disaggregating the effects of this variable on wages, we find
that 40 per cent of its total wage effect is due to the indirect
impact of occupational preparation, 20 per cent to age, and only
3 per cent to seniority.   In all, 63 per cent is thus due to the
combination of formal preparation and experience.   The remaining
37 per cent of its effect on wages is not relayed from any known

---

[1] Readers interested in the standardised multiple regression
equations for wages can form them by compiling the data in the
second column of Appendix A.   The five values for each sample (or
sector) are the partial beta (β) weights, or standardised regression
coefficients, of hourly wages on each variable.   Thus the estimated
standardised hourly wage level ($\hat{W}_T$) in the total sample may be
written as follows:

$$\hat{W}_T = .323I - .059J + .258A + .359E + .069S.$$

The standardised regression equations for the various sectors may
be formed analogously.

antecedent variable.   Yet the worker's occupational influence
level itself is largely determined by such other factors:
$R^2_{W.EAS}$ = 0.18.   Future research should attempt to determine what
these are.   In any case, the firm itself seems to take into
account a number of factors in allocating men to positions - line
and staff distinctions, span of control, etc., not to mention
individual characteristics.   One influences the operations of the
firm by his exercise of the powers inherent in his position,
together with whatever additional influence he can muster.   The
zero-order coefficient of determination provides an estimate of the
total effect of position on wages: r^2 = 0.24.   In other words,
about one-quarter of the variance in standardised wages is due to
one's power position.   Available theory on human capital tends to
ignore this aspect of the reward process, normally concentrating on
experience and education.

     2. Occupational preparation is one of the powerful factors
determining wage differentials.   Since it figures in the allocation of power positions, it plays a substantial indirect role.
Its indirect effect is $\pi_{WE(I)}$ = 0.130.   Its direct effect is
P_{WE} = 0.329, for a total effect of π_{WE} = 0.459.   This finding
appears to be consistent with the Brazilian policy of gearing
formal preparation to the occupational structure.   To the extent
that one's value to the firm is measured by his standardised
wage - an assumption which seems justified - it would appear that
occupationally specific formal preparation considerably enhances
it.

     In a rational economy it is to be expected that formal train-
ing for one's work will result in more effective performance.   Our
findings suggest that São Paulo's industrial system exhibits such
rationality.

     This finding is not, of course, inconsistent with previous
work showing large effects of education on income (Mincer, 1974).
Our main innovation (as opposed to much human capital research) is
the emphasis on occupational preparation rather than education as
such.

     3.   Age is a third important variable.   In this study its
effects are measured net of formal occupational preparation and of
seniority in the firm.   It thus seems reasonable to suppose that
its remaining wage effects are due to general work experience.
The large effect (total effect being 0.314) which it has on the
wages of these specialised industrial personnel implies that, at
least at this élite level of the firms, experience is a valuable
asset.   As we have just seen, a small part of its total wage
effect is relayed through occupational influence level, which it
influences to some extent.   Yet most of its effect is normally
direct.   In the over-all sample, for example, its direct effect
on wages is about 80 per cent of its total effect.

     4.   Seniority, years in the firm, is another measure, net of
formal preparation, age and time in the present job, experience
and knowledge, especially routines unique to the firm.   Perhaps
surprisingly, there is not one industrial sector in which this
variable has any substantial influence, although what little it has
is positive.   This seems to mean that the procedures of different
firms are so similar that it is not worth-while to use seniority as

anything more than a weak criterion for rewarding São Paulo's specialised industrial workers. Apparently, formal preparation and general work experience are far more important as sources of competency.

5. Net of the effects of the other variables which are sources of competence, job experience (years in the present job) goes unrewarded. Indeed, it has a small negative effect in most industrial sectors. The implication is that the more capable specialised workers do not stay in their jobs very long. They are evidently rewarded by being advanced into better-paying positions, leaving behind the less capable, who sometimes receive slightly lower salaries.

The above summaries seem generally appropriate for almost every industrial sector. The main exception is the clothing and shoe industry. This sector rewards occupational influence and age the least of all. It punishes longer job tenure most severely, and rewards seniority and occupational preparation the most highly. Perhaps it is significant that formal preparation counts most here where it is least available. That is, where trained people are especially abundant, training does not pay so well. The relationship between scarcity and impact on wages does not, however, hold for any of the other variables.

Conclusion. So far as we are aware, there are no other studies comparable to this one in which multiple regression methods are applied to the analysis of the effects of position, formal preparation, and experience on the standardised wages (or rewards) obtained by individual specialised workers in the industrial sector of a developing nation. Indeed, this project would appear to be unique in several respects: its use of total earnings standardised to an hourly basis; its adoption of an occupationally relevant measure of formal preparation; its use, under controlled conditions, of age, seniority and years on the job as measures of general work experience, experience in the firm and experience on the job; and its introduction of occupational influence level as a key variable. And it is almost unique (see Sewell and Hauser, 1975) in its application of path analysis as a method for assessing direct, indirect and total effects of antecedent variables on wages.

Beyond doubt, a more detailed discussion of the data presented herein would be profitable, although space limitations unfortunately will not permit it. In other publications, we intend to provide additional studies of them. But we hope that, by making the sectoral path analytic data and other basic statistics (Appendices B and C) available here, other researchers may be able to examine them fruitfully without waiting for further publications to appear.

The main general conclusion which we draw from the present examination is that the São Paulo industrial system appears to reward its most highly placed workers - here the top 6 per cent - according to national principles appropriate to the most highly industrialised countries. Even applying extremely restrictive constraints - linearity of relationships, measures of position, preparation and experience conceptually and operationally independent of each other, and an untransformed wage metric - we find that the five antecedent variables, reasonably placed in a causal order, account for about 36 per cent of the variance in hourly wage differentials. The most powerful of these are one's position in the firm's influence hierarchy, one's formal preparation for his occupation, and one's over-all work experience. Seniority in the firm and years on the job count for little in comparison.

We hope that the present work may make a small contribution
to the growing body of evidence regarding the determinants of wage
differentials in general and to the analysis of the productivity
of specialised industrial workers in developing nations in particular.   We also hope that similar research may be undertaken in
other countries, developing and developed, and in other strata of
the industrial labour force.   Such comparative studies may help
provide the basis by which untested myths about industry and
development may be replaced by solid research findings.

REFERENCES

Becker, Gary S.: Human capital and the personal distribution of
    income (Ann Arbor, University of Michigan Press, 1967).

Blalock, Hubert M.: Causal models in the social sciences (Chicago,
    Aldine, 1972).

Blaug, Mark: An introduction to the economics of education
    (London, Penguin Books, 1970).

Denison, Edward: "Measuring the contribution of education to the
    economic growth" in E.A.G. Robinson and J.E. Vaizey (eds.),
    The economics of education (London, Macmillan, 1966),
    pp. 202-260.

Duncan, Otis D.: "Path analysis: sociological examples" in
    Hubert M. Blalock (ed.), Causal models in the social sciences
    (Chicago, Aldine, 1971), pp. 115-138.

Finney, John M.: "Indirect effects in path analysis" (Sociological
    Methods and Research, 1, 1972), pp. 175-186.

Haworth, C.T. and Rasmussen, D.W.: "Human capital and inter-
    industry wages in manufacturing" (Review of Economics and
    Statistics, 53, Nov. 1971), pp. 376-380.

Klevmarken, Anders: Statistical methods for the analysis of earn-
    ing data (Stockholm, Sweden, Almqvist and Wiksell, 1972).

Mincer, Jacob: Schooling, experience, and earnings (New York,
    National Bureau of Economic Research and Columbia University
    Press, 1974).

Morgan, James, David, Martin, Cohen, Wilbur and Brazer, Harvey:
    Income and welfare in the United States (New York, McGraw-
    Hill, 1962).

Pastore, Jose, Haller, Archibald O., and Buendia, Hernando Gomez:
    "Determinants of wage differentials in São Paulo's industrial
    labour force" (presented at the annual meeting of the American
    Sociological Association, Montreal, Aug. 1974).

Reynolds, Lloyd G.: Labour economics and labour relations (New
    Jersey, Prentice Hall, 1964).

Schultz, Theodore W.: "Investment in human capital" (American
    Economic Review, 51, Mar. 1961), pp. 1-17.

Sewell, William H. and Hauser, Robert M.: Education, occupation, and earnings: achievement in the early career (New York, Academic Press Inc., 1975).

Thurow, Lester C.: "Education and economic equality" (The Public Interest, 28, Summer 1973), pp. 66-81.

APPENDIX A

Partitioned effects of independent and intervening variables on wages by industrial sector

Sector	Variable (i)	Total effect of the ith variable: π_{Wi}	Direct effect of the ith variable: P_{Wi}^1	$(P_{Ii} \times P_{Wi})$ ...		$+ (P_{Ji} \times P_{WJ})$ ...		Total indirect	$R^2_{W.IJAPE}$	Sample size
All sectors	I	0.323	(0.323)	-	-	-	-	-	0.363	22 587
	J	-0.059	(-0.059)	-	-	-	-	-		
	A	0.314	0.258	0.200	0.323	0.154	-0.059	0.056		
	E	0.459	0.329	0.401	0.323	0.552	-0.059	0.130		
	S	0.047	0.069	0.033	0.323	0.552	-0.059	0.022		
Food processing	I	0.316	(0.316)	-	-	-	-	-	0.330	1 341
	J	-0.103	(-0.103)	-	-	-	-	-		
	A	0.258	0.249	0.140	0.316	0.168	-0.103	0.027		
	E	0.482	0.347	0.427	0.316	0.531	-0.103	0.135		
	S	-0.033	0.007*	0.049*	0.316	0.531	-0.103	-0.040		
Clothing and shoes	I	0.253	(0.253)	-	-	-	-	-	0.389	183
	J	-0.107	(-0.107)	-	-	-	-	-		
	A	0.167	0.158	0.062*	0.253	0.066*	-0.107	0.009		
	E	0.541	0.433	0.428	0.253	0.809	-0.107	0.108		
	S	0.168	0.240	0.059*	0.253	0.809	-0.107	-0.072		
Textiles	I	0.343	(0.343)	-	-	-	-	-	0.330	1 578
	J	0.014	(0.014)	-	-	-	-	-		
	A	0.310	0.272	0.106	0.343	0.135	0.014*	0.038		
	E	0.426	0.279	0.427	0.343	0.659	-	0.147		
	S	-0.056	-0.062	-0.010*	0.343	0.659	0.014*	0.006		

Sector	Variable (i)	Total effect of the i-th variable: π_{Wi}	Direct effect of the i-th variable: P_{Wi}^l	Indirect effects of the i-th independent variable $(P_{Ii} \times P_{Wi})$		$+ (P_{Ji} \times P_{WJ})$		Total indirect	$R^2_{W.IJAPE}$	Sample size
Chemicals	I	0.311	(0.311)	-	-	-	-	-	0.420	1 418
	J	0.094	(0.094)	-	-	-	-	-		
	A	0.356	0.221	0.160	0.311	0.166	0.094	0.065		
	E	0.529	0.369	0.516	0.311	0.556	0.094	0.161		
	S	0.104	0.048*	0.014*	0.311	0.094	0.094	0.056		
Pharmaceuticals	I	0.457	(0.457)	-	-	-	-	-	0.412	1 354
	J	-0.014*	(-0.014)	-	-	-	-	-		
	A	0.314	0.197	0.263	0.457	0.255	-0.014*	0.117		
	E	0.386	0.220	0.363	0.457	0.494	-0.014*	0.166		
	S	-0.019	-0.042*	0.066	0.457	0.494	-0.014*	0.023		
Paper products	I	0.307	(0.307)	-	-	-	-	-	0.286	530
	J	-0.015*	(-0.015)	-	-	-	-	-		
	A	0.363	0.296	0.225	0.307	0.145	-0.015*	0.067		
	E	0.431	0.284	0.478	0.307	0.636	-0.015*	0.147		
	S	-0.004	0.023*	-0.055*	0.307	0.636	-0.015*	0.027		
Glass and cement	I	0.381	(0.381)	-	-	-	-	-	0.393	335
	J	-0.024*	(-0.024)	-	-	-	-	-		
	A	0.256	0.196	0.172	0.381	0.214	-0.024*	0.060		
	E	0.510	0.368	0.372	0.381	0.490	-0.024*	0.142		
	S	-0.035	-0.003*	-0.053*	0.381	0.490	-0.024*	-0.032		
Metals	I	0.321	(0.321)	-	-	-	-	-	0.401	2 561
	J	-0.047	(-0.047)	-	-	-	-	-		
	A	0.305	0.260	0.161	0.321	0.138	-0.047	0.045		
	E	0.537	0.386	0.470	0.321	0.536	-0.047	0.151		
	S	0.094	0.113	0.019*	0.321	0.536	-0.047	-0.019		

Sector	Variable (i)	Total effect of the i th variable: π_{Wi}	Direct effect of the i th variable: P_{Wi}[1]	Indirect effects of the i th independent variable: $(P_{Ii}$	x $P_{Wi})$	+ $(P_{Ji}$	x $P_{WJ})$	Total indirect	$R^2_{W.IJAPE}$	Sample size
Mechanical equipment									0.438	2 282
	I	0.422	(0.422)	-	-	-	-	-		
	J	0.026*	(0.026)	-	-	-	-	-		
	A	0.347	0.253	0.214	0.422	0.137	0.026*	0.094		
	E	0.463	0.309	0.365	0.422	-	-	0.154		
	S	0.058	0.065	-0.051	0.422	0.586	0.026*	-0.007		
Electrical equipment									0.482	3 620
	I	0.360	(0.360)	-	-	-	-	-		
	J	-0.044	(-0.044)	-	-	-	-	-		
	A	0.345	0.274	0.213	0.360	0.138	-0.044	-0.071		
	E	0.509	0.351	0.440	0.360	-	-	0.158		
	S	0.119	0.126	0.051	0.360	0.572	-0.044	-0.007		
Motor vehicles									0.343	7 853
	I	0.301	(0.301)	-	-	-	-	-		
	J	-0.011*	(-0.011)	-	-	-	-	-		
	A	0.336	0.274	0.211	0.301	0.143	-0.011*	0.026		
	E	0.393	0.297	0.320	0.301	-	-	0.096		
	S	0.102	0.078	0.092	0.301	0.409	0.011*	0.024		

[1] Coefficients in this column are the β coefficients corresponding to those of the standardised multiple regression of wages on the five other variables.

W: Wages (cruzeiros per hour)

I: Occupational Influence level

J: Job experience (years in the job)

A: Age (in years)

E: Education (in year equivalents)

S: Seniority (years with the firm)

*: $P > .05$

APPENDIX B

Zero-order correlations among variables
for each industrial sector

		A	E	S	J	I	W
				All sectors (N = 22 517)			
Food processing (N = 1 341)	A	–	-0.139	0.447	0.401	0.159	0.271
	E	-0.267	–	-0.243	-0.162	0.365	0.403
	S	0.502	-0.313	–	0.621	0.025	0.076
	J	0.434	-0.213	0.616	–	-0.016	0.029
	I	0.051	0.374	-0.014	-0.055	–	0.486
	W	0.132	0.418	-0.044	-0.081	0.464	–
				Clothing and shoes (N = 183)			
Textiles (N = 1 578)	A	–	-0.154	0.319	0.325	0.015	0.137
	E	-0.153	–	0.050	0.019	0.422	0.525
	S	0.377	-0.223	–	0.831	0.101	0.249
	J	0.383	-0.145	0.710	–	0.062	0.168
	I	0.037	0.414	-0.066	-0.094	–	0.456
	W	0.224	0.391	-0.035	0.002	0.470	–
				Chemical (N = 1 418)			
Pharmaceutical (N = 1 354)	A	–	-0.080	0.546	0.469	0.127	0.301
	E	0.021	–	-0.269	-0.144	0.495	0.479
	S	0.521	-0.258	–	0.646	-0.036	0.119
	J	0.508	-0.039	0.624	–	-0.083	0.149
	I	0.305	0.351	0.107	0.128	–	0.512
	W	0.312	0.396	0.043	0.110	0.588	–
				Paper and paper products (N = 530)			
Glass and cement (N = 335)	A	–	-0.317	0.549	0.494	0.042	0.224
	E	-0.185	–	-0.336	-0.295	0.426	0.318
	S	0.466	-0.245	–	0.716	-0.093	0.051
	J	0.443	-0.170	0.590	–	-0.119	0.027
	I	0.078	0.353	-0.064	-0.005	–	0.441
	W	0.145	0.471	-0.041	-0.004	0.529	–
				Metals (N = 2 561)			
Mechanical equipment (N = 2 282)	A	–	-0.214	0.439	0.373	0.068	0.231
	E	-0.152	–	-0.267	-0.172	0.431	0.447
	S	0.419	-0.292	–	0.596	-0.036	0.084
	J	0.382	-0.201	0.643	–	-0.052	0.034
	I	0.137	0.347	-0.068	-0.071	–	0.504
	W	0.301	0.393	0.069	0.072	0.558	–
				Electrical equipment (N = 3 620)			
Motor vehicles (N = 7 385)	A	–	-0.058	0.419	0.378	0.209	0.365
	E	-0.086	–	-0.229	-0.156	0.416	0.463
	S	0.388	-0.190	–	0.629	0.040	0.147
	J	0.301	-0.110	0.464	–	-0.014	0.079
	I	0.218	0.285	0.112	0.017	–	0.569
	W	0.341	0.345	0.156	0.081	0.454	–

APPENDIX C

Means and standard deviations

Sectors	Hourly wage (W)	Occupational influence level (I)	Job experience (J)	Age (A)	Education (E)	Seniority (S)
			Means ($\overline{X}$)			
All sectors	8.514	3.196	3.173	35.541	11.048	6.509
Food processing	7.366	3.491	3.613	36.754	10.896	7.368
Clothing and shoes	6.524	3.169	4.789	37.896	9.174	7.071
Textiles	7.615	3.146	5.384	39.904	9.988	8.755
Chemicals	8.755	3.338	4.816	37.161	11.447	9.377
Pharmaceuticals	8.434	3.279	3.329	34.682	11.969	6.979
Paper products	8.056	3.374	4.557	37.298	10.811	7.358
Glass and cement	7.423	3.200	4.116	38.281	9.904	8.051
Metals	8.281	3.311	3.335	36.150	10.901	6.513
Mechanical equipment	7.098	3.053	3.397	34.757	10.396	6.023
Electrical equipment	8.193	3.199	2.756	34.022	11.253	5.358
Motor vehicles	9.692	3.103	2.175	34.428	11.325	5.804
			Standard deviations (σ)			
All sectors	6.159	1.488	4.022	9.728	3.586	6.763
Food processing	5.718	1.529	4.683	10.471	3.820	8.286
Clothing and shoes	6.427	1.465	5.898	10.175	3.761	7.230
Textiles	5.960	1.484	6.473	11.476	3.905	9.426
Chemicals	6.592	1.408	4.695	10.201	3.783	7.982
Pharmaceuticals	6.259	1.726	4.302	10.227	3.200	7.469
Paper products	6.812	1.464	5.208	11.131	4.021	8.044
Glass and cement	5.739	1.439	5.026	10.396	4.061	8.329
Metals	6.279	1.545	4.073	9.634	3.907	7.099
Mechanical equipment	4.942	1.392	3.655	9.551	3.881	6.191
Electrical equipment	5.374	1.489	3.202	9.033	3.438	5.433
Motor vehicles	6.566	1.448	2.669	8.793	3.163	5.382

The operation of urban labour markets in Kenya

by
Henry Rempel,
Department of Economics, University of Manitoba

William J. House,
Department of Economics, University of Nairobi

INTRODUCTION

This paper examines some of the factors that the investigator of urban labour markets in LDCs would be required to consider. It summarises some of the conclusions derived by the authors from their on-going research and pleads for more survey work of informal sector activities so that further data might be generated with which to extend the quantitative analysis of urban labour markets.

The statements in our general survey are not to be taken as verified facts or tested theories. Rather, prevalent assumptions and postulated causal relationships are laid bare in the hope that they will be challenged and tested.

THE EXTENT OF URBANISATION

Regardless of what definition of urbanisation is adopted, at least 90 per cent of the population was rural at the time of the 1969 census. The urban scene is dominated by Nairobi, accounting for 4.6 per cent of the population and, to a lesser extent, by Mombasa which accounts for half as much as Nairobi. In addition, there are nine other towns with populations in excess of 10,000. If desired, urbanisation can be expanded to include some 23 other towns which had a minimum of 2,000 people according to the 1962 census. These small towns contain just over 1 per cent of Kenya's population and the growth between 1962 and 1969 was only slightly higher than the growth rate for Kenya's population.

The average annual rate of growth of the African population in all urban centres over 10,000 was just under 9 per cent between 1962 and 1969, with above average growth evident in Nairobi. The age-specific selective nature of the urban in-migration has caused the urban labour force to grow at a faster rate than the urban population.[1] With very limited urbanisation evident in Kenya, this rate of growth of the towns has not reduced the absolute size of the rural population. During the inter-censal period it has been estimated that rural-urban migration has removed no more than one of every four new entrants to the rural labour force.[2] Within the towns, the rate of growth has exceeded the rate of growth of formal sector jobs. This would indicate that a growing proportion of the urban population, either by choice or by necessity, is looking to the informal sector as a means of existence.

THE URBAN WAGE AND EMPLOYMENT STRUCTURE

According to economic theory, under competitive conditions wage differences between occupations would be "equalising", merely covering the extra cost of acquiring the necessary skills.

---

[1] Rempel, H.: "An estimate of Kenya's labour force" (University of Nairobi, Institute for Development Studies, Working Paper No. 159, 1974).

[2] Rempel, H.: "The extent and nature of the population movement into Kenya's towns" (University of Nairobi, Institute for Development Studies, Working Paper No. 160, 1974).

Similarly the industrial wage structure would provide equal pay for workers of the same skill in different industries.

Using a large body of unpublished data from Kenya's Annual enumeration of employees, the authors examined the occupational and the industrial wage structures, both at the national level and for each of the 11 towns. By means of extensive standardisation exercises it was possible to attribute differences in average modern sector earnings in each town to differences in occupational mix, differences in industry mix and differences because similarly classified occupations and industries pay different wages in certain towns.[1]

Between 1964 and 1972 average earnings per worker of the ten largest towns increased relative to Nairobi, with the coefficient of variation of average earnings declining from 44.7 per cent in 1964 to 38.5 per cent in 1972.[2] However, all the towns had average earnings well below Nairobi with Nakuru and Nanyuki being first and last in the average earnings league relative to Nairobi. Nakuru's average earnings were 77 per cent of Nairobi's and Nanyuki's 44 per cent in 1972.[3]

The results of the standardisation exercises suggest that Nairobi's relatively higher earnings per worker are explained primarily by a favourable occupational mix, according to 12 job descriptions from the Annual enumeration of employees for 1972, and by similarly classified industries paying more in Nairobi than elsewhere. However, a three-digit classification of an "industry" can encompass a wide spectrum of industrial activities. Possibly the more capital intensive are located in Nairobi, requiring a higher level of skilled labour. If so, the products and techniques of production are quite likely to be different in any one industry in Nairobi, compared with the other urban centres. This would help explain the results obtained from occupational data, that the skill make-up of the labour force is higher in Nairobi and makes a relatively large contribution to its high average earnings because the industrial structure is truly different.

---

[1] The standardisation technique was used by Hanna and Denison for analysing inter-state income differences in the United States. Hanna, F.A.: Inter-state income differentials, 1919-1954 (Durham, Duke University Press, 1959); Denison, E.F.: "Comment", in F.A. Hanna (ed.), Regional income; studies in income and wealth (Princeton, Princeton University Press, 1957), pp. 161-179. Subsequently, the technique was used by House to explain inter-provincial wage differences in Kenya. House, W.J.: "Earnings per worker differentials in the provinces of Kenya, 1963-1970", in Journal of Developing Areas, Apr. 1975.

[2] The coefficient of variation is defined as:

$$\frac{\sqrt{\frac{1}{n-1} \sum_i (Y_i - \overline{Y})^2}}{\overline{Y}}$$

where Y_i is the average earnings in town i, $\overline{Y}$ is

Nairobi's average earnings and n is the number of towns.

[3] This information is based on total three-digit ISIC industry earnings which include the earnings of casual workers.

These results indicate that labour market segmentation is not particularly marked in Kenya's urban labour markets. For the unskilled, which one expects is a reasonably homogeneous group, the degree of inter-urban earnings inequality is well below that of all workers. The coefficient of variation for unskilled earnings for the ten towns, relative to Nairobi, was 21 per cent in 1972.

DETERMINANTS OF AND CHANGES IN THE
URBAN WAGE AND EMPLOYMENT STRUCTURE

Although knowledge of the nature of the wage structure is important, the more crucial questions for research are the determinants of the structure and the nature of the cause-and-effect relationships between wage levels and changes in wage levels reflecting the levels of and changes in the demand for and supply of labour.

Various theories have been proposed. According to one theory the high wage industries are characterised by advanced technology and oligopolistic product market conditions. The combination of these factors provides an ability to pay wages above the existing supply price of labour as such wage increases can be passed on in the form of higher prices and technological choice is exogenous. An alternative position emphasises the role of institutional wage determination which reflects the upward pressures via the market power of unions, labour legislation and vocal civil servants.[1]

A third position focuses attention on a unit of labour productivity which need not be equated with one person because of variations in the quantity and type of human capital embodied in each person.[2] Such variations in the quality of labour can account for variations in wages paid. More importantly, much of the human capital is obtained through on-the-job training. To the extent that such skills are not specific to the one firm only, the firm must pay the marginal product of the employee to retain his services and to maximise its return on the training costs embodied in the employee. Therefore, the existence of unemployed labour need not indicate wages are too high because the two types of labour, the employed versus the unemployed, are not substitutes for each other.

Because the need for skilled labour is most evident in capital-intensive industries and upper-level civil service positions, the productivity determinant of wages cannot be distinguished readily from either the ability to pay or the institutional determinants. As the skills in question are primarily the experience gained on the

---

[1] Both of these positions have been developed in greater detail in House, W.J., and Rempel, H.: "The determinants of and changes in the structure of wages and employment in the manufacturing sector of the Kenya economy" (University of Nairobi, Institute for Development Studies, Discussion Paper No. 207, 1974).

[2] Harris, H.R.: "Wage rate determination with limited supplies of labour in developing countries: a comment", in Journal of Development Studies, Jan. 1971, pp. 197-200.

job (versus formal education) and oligopolistic firms can, within
limits, pass on wage increases through higher prices, as can
Government in the form of higher taxes, it is worth examining
whether such firms and Government have bid up wages artificially in
an effort to keep key personnel.

Using the information from the <u>Annual enumeration of employees,</u>
the authors examined changes in the industrial wage structure
during 1967-72.   Since most of the manufacturing activities are
conducted in urban areas of Nairobi and Mombasa, we were essentially
dealing with the urban sector.   The coefficient of variation calculated for average earnings per worker for all employees and for
unskilled workers for 42 three-digit industries increased from 41 per
cent in 1967 to 52 per cent in 1972, and from 31 per cent to 41 per
cent respectively.   Clearly the inter-industry wage structure in
Kenya is diverging and has reached a relatively high level of dispersion by international standards.

Using multiple regression analysis the authors found that
differences in wages paid by manufacturing industries in Kenya are
explained rather successfully by various measures of relative differences among industries in their respective abilities to pay wages
above the supply price of labour; and by such institutional factors
as industry differences in the proportion of the labour force
employed in Nairobi and in government enterprises.[1]

The responsiveness of the wage structure to changes in the
demand for different types of labour was examined for various sub-
periods between the years 1968-72.   Whether expanding industries
were required to raise wages to attract additional labour of various
qualities or whether this could be done within the existing wage
structure was explored.   Our results suggest that it was not
necessary, in general, for industries to raise wages to fill vacancies that occurred.[2]   The employment opportunities expanded fastest
in the high-wage industries, and these vacancies were filled by the
existing wage structure without the need for additional increases in
wages.   In contrast, the initial low-wage industries responded
competitively by granting above-average increases to their skilled
employees.

The influence of changes in the supply of labour on wages has
recently been examined by the authors, using a simultaneous equation
system and data at the district level for Kenya.   Initial results
suggest that supply changes play little role in dampening the tendency for wages to increase because of demand changes.[3]   At a later
time the authors plan to test the model using data for the 34 towns
of Kenya with a population of more than 2,000.

---

[1] House and Rempel, loc. cit.

[2] ibid.

[3] Rempel, H., and House, W.J.: <u>The Kenya employment problem:</u>
<u>the impact of growth in the labour supply on the modern sector wage</u>
<u>structure</u>.   Final Report of Research Project to the World Employ-
ment Programme Research Branch, Employment Planning and Promotion
Department, International Labour Office, Geneva, 1975.

Such statistical exercises throw light on[1] the degree of segmentation of urban labour markets in Kenya,[1] segmentation with respect to inter-urban markets, inter-occupation immobility and inter-firm (large versus small, foreign versus indigenous) separation of markets. An estimate of differential turnover rates for skilled and unskilled labour would be revealing here. However, little reliable information on labour turnover is available in Kenya and there would seem to be an urgent need for a large-scale survey of modern sector firms to gather information on patterns of recruitment, reward systems and fringe benefits amongst firms of different size, industry, ownership and market power.[2]

Of further interest is the degree of segmentation of the modern sector unskilled labour market from the urban traditional or informal sector labour market. Are labourers in the informal sector ready substitutes for unskilled modern sector workers or are these markets non-competing? A survey to gather information on informal sector earnings is essential to gauge the extent of segmentation of these labour markets. Little is known at present of inter-sectoral wage differences. However, it is hoped that a further test of our model will suggest the extent to which excess supply of urban unskilled labour exerts downward pressure on wages in the modern sector.

We also need a more systematic examination of firms identified as having an ability to pay above the opportunity cost of labour and of the concentration of so much economic activity in a few urban centres. According to the ILO Kenya mission, the key determinant of such aspects of the employment situation is the concentration of income and wealth in the hands of a very small proportion of the population.[3] This rich minority has taste preferences very different from that of the vast majority of other Kenyans. This wealthy minority dominates production decisions by demanding many goods and services requiring technology and capital beyond the capability of existing or potential Kenyan businessmen. Foreign firms have been invited to supply the required technology and capital with protection against imported goods provided as an inducement where required. The infrastructure provided for these firms, in turn, induces other firms and Government to want to locate in these places. These firms are characterised by high wages and low employment per

---

[1] For an introduction to the theory of segmented labour markets see Reich, M., Gordon, D.M. and Edwards R.C.: "A theory of labour market segmentation", Papers and Proceedings of the Eighty-fifth Annual Meeting of the American Economic Association, May 1973; Vietorisz, T. and Harrison, B.: "Labour market segmentation: positive feedback and divergent development", Papers and Proceedings of the Eighty-fifth Annual Meeting of the American Economic Association, May 1973; Harrison, B.: "Ghetto economic development, a survey", in The Journal of Economic Literature, Mar. 1974.

[2] A recent attempt has been made to gather information on some of these practices from a sample of five manufacturing firms. Henley, J.S.: "Employment relationships and economic development: the Kenyan experience", in The Journal of Modern African Studies, Dec. 1973.

[3] ILO: Employment, incomes and equality: a strategy for increasing productive employment in Kenya (Geneva, 1972).

unit of output.   The existence of these "high-wage" employment
opportunities in a few places has been a key determinant of both
rural-to-urban migration and the demand for a particular type of
formal education to the detriment of general human capital development and rural development.[1]

This interpretation of the employment situation places the
origin of the problem in the nature of the colonial situation in
Kenya.   It is not surprising to observe that, with the exception
of Malindi, all urban centres are located either in the former
"white highlands" or served as the seaport and the terminal point
of the railroad.   Ten years of independence have brought drastic,
commendable changes in Kenya, but this structure of the economy
inherited from the colonial period has not changed significantly
except for the racial composition of the controlling minority.   The
unresolved question is whether long-term development, designed to
encompass the total labour force in productive employment, can
occur without a radical transformation of this structure.

The urban informal sector

Research on the informal sector is only starting now so there
is very little that can be said about its role and potential in the
economy.   One position is that the low cost output of the informal
sector is essential to the profitable existence of the formal sector.[2]   Although it is true that the unskilled employees could not
exist in Nairobi without relying on the informal sector for their
day-to-day needs, it would be very difficult to demonstrate that
either the existence or the profitability of the foreign firms
"requires" the existence of an informal sector.   Rather, the ILO
report's interpretation of the informal sector as a competitive
threat to aspects of the formal sector appears more realistic.
The setting of town boundaries well beyond the actual town plus a
variety of health, licensing, wage and training regulations within
these boundaries has served to protect the formal sector from competition from the informal sector.

Still unresolved is the development potential of the informal
sector.   One extreme possibility is that the bulk of the daily non-
agricultural needs of the vast majority of Kenya's urban population
are met by production within the informal sector.   The validity of
this position can be determined only by detailed analysis of expen-
diture patterns.   Where and why are particular purchases being
made and the degree of substitutability between informal and formal
sector output are basically empirical questions.

From the standpoint of labour market analysis there is a real
need to determine the motivation of the participants in the informal
sector.   To what extent do people in the informal sector see in it

---

[1] This interpretation of the nature of the problem and its
impact on education and rural development appears to be evident in
the Government's response to the ILO report.   Republic of Kenya,
Sessional paper on employment, May 1973, pp. 8-11.

[2] Leys, C.: Underdevelopment in Kenya: the political economy
of neo-colonialism, 1964-1971 (London, Heinemann Educational Books
Ltd., 1975), p. 267.

their present and future. well-being? Or are they there primarily
because they are waiting for formal sector opportunities to open up?
It is likely that the latter constitute the majority. If so, it
will be difficult to obtain in the informal sector: (a) any sem-
blance of a stable labour force, a characteristic of segmented
labour markets;[1] (b) the investment of current income to build up
a stock of productive assets; (c) an "Adam Smith" approach to
developing indigenous technology via constant attempts to change the
nature of one's productive endeavour; and (d) the social attitude
required for group effort to improve the employment and living situation in which people find themselves.

ADDITIONAL RESEARCH REQUIRED

We append below a partial list of research priorities which
need to be met to enable us to shed more light on the issues raised
in this paper. In formulating these here, it is our hope to
encourage other researchers in other countries to pursue similar
queries and to stimulate a dialogue on these points.

The formal sector and Kenya's development potential

(a) To determine the feedback effects of the high wage, low employ-
     ment nature of the formal sector on aspirations for formal
     education.

(b) To determine the feedback effects of the current formal sector
     on rural development efforts. This would include the extent
     and nature of formal sector demand for rural output as well as
     the effects of out-migration and other transfers from the rural
     sector.

(c) To determine the impact of the extensive separation of family
     members in the formal sector because of housing and other prob-
     lems for the urban workers.

The operation of the informal sector

(a) To determine the nature of the market for informal sector acti-
     vities.

(b) To ascertain its labour productivity, efficiency, ability to
     innovate and growth potential. This would include the dynamics
     of the impact of the competition and regulation emanating from
     the formal sector.

(c) To determine the motivation and intentions of employers and the
     self-employed to enable an assessment of the development poten-
     tial of the current participants given the nature of the social,
     political and economic conditions under which they operate.

---

[1] Harrison, loc. cit.

(d)   To determine the attitudes of the informal sector employees
      to assess such factors as labour force stability, extent of
      perceived labour exploitation, human capital accumulation, and
      the impact of the formal sector wage and employment structure.

(e)   To determine the extent of on-the-job training taking place
      currently in the informal sector, to assess its value and to
      enable the formulation of policy designed to build on such
      training possibilities.

(f)   To determine the longer run impact of existence in the condi-
      tions of the informal sector on the development of either a
      "culture of poverty" or an "urban ghetto" mentality.

Migration, the informal sector, and the urban labour market in developing countries: The case of Jakarta

by
S. V. Sethuraman,
World Employment Programme,
International Labour Office

It is common knowledge now that many developing countries in the world are currently experiencing an unprecedented rate of urbanisation. It is also fairly clear from the accumulated empirical evidence that the process of urbanisation presently taking place in the Third World is not so much due to rapid industrialisation; rather it is the consequence of growing population pressure on land in the countryside. No doubt the introduction of high-yielding varieties during the last decade or so has helped to alleviate this pressure to a small extent by raising labour productivity and increasing employment opportunities in agriculture, but its impact has not been sufficiently large to arrest the rural exodus. As a result, migration from rural to urban areas continues, leading to substantial additions to the urban labour force. Although the formal sector of the urban economy and the government sector have shown an impressive rate of labour absorption, the rate has been far from adequate to absorb all the additions to the urban labour force. Thus the new entrants to the urban labour force are forced to seek either self-employment opportunities or wage employment in what is called the informal sector or remain unemployed.

These changes have profound implications for urban labour market policies in developing countries. The purpose of the paper is to illustrate the kind of labour market adjustments that are currently taking place in many developing countries, with special reference to Jakarta city in Indonesia.[1]

THE JAKARTAN REGIONAL ECONOMY AND POPULATION

Jakarta, the largest city in the most overpopulated island of the Indonesian archipelago, is located in the northern coastal plain of the island of Java, and is the capital of Indonesia with an area of about 590 square kilometres. Being the capital city, Jakarta is the seat of the central Government, and since it is also a province by itself, it houses the provincial Government as well. With about 100,000 persons employed in the central government offices located in the city and 30,000 persons with the regional Government, the Government plays a major role in the economy. The manufacturing sector in the Jakarta regional economy is relatively less important; its share in the regional gross domestic product varied between 7 and 8 per cent in recent years and, in terms of employment, it was only 10 per cent in 1971. Large- and medium-scale manufacturing accounted for only half of the employment in this sector. Agriculture has a relative contribution to the regional income comparable to that of manufacturing. By far the most important distinguishing feature of Jakarta is the dominance of the tertiary sector, particularly the trade and the service sectors, generating over half of the regional income.

---

[1] The author alone is responsible for the views expressed in the paper. The reader interested in further details and sources of data is referred to S.V. Sethuraman: Urbanisation and Employment in Jakarta, Urbanisation and Employment Research Project, Working Paper No. 6 (ILO, Geneva, 1974).

The Jakarta regional gross domestic product seems to have grown at an annual rate of 6 to 7 per cent at least in recent years. The most important sectors contributing to growth were the trade and the services sectors. Besides the labour absorptive character of economic growth, Jakarta has been successful in attracting a lion's share of the approved domestic and foreign investment in the country in recent years. The reasonably good performance of the regional economy did not, however, lead to a substantial rise in the standard of living for a large majority of the population, owing to rapid urbanisation in Jakarta, as we shall see below. The case of Jakarta is therefore one of urbanisation without industrialisation.

The population of Jakarta increased from about 533,000 in 1930 to 2.91 million in 1961 and to 4.55 million in 1971, implying an annual rate of growth of 5.6 per cent between 1930 and 1971 or 4.6 per cent between 1961 and 1971. Since the natural rate of growth in population in Java was well under 2 per cent per year, the bulk of the annual increase in population in Jakarta would appear to be the result of migration.

The population growth in Jakarta between 1961 and 1971 was accompanied by some significant structural changes such as the following. In 1971, there were fewer males per 1,000 females in the age group 15-24; and the proportion of unmarried population over 10 years of age was significantly higher than in 1961. Population increase in the 10-19 age group far exceeded the over-all increase during the decade. Also, population in Jakarta increased faster than all other urban areas in Indonesia.

Population in the working age group (above 10 years) increased as fast as the total during the 1960s. The average number of years of schooling for this population group showed a substantial rise: from 3.42 to 4.74 for males and 1.90 to 3.21 for females between 1961 and 1971. As compared to 17 per cent in 1961, there were 29 per cent of males above 10 years in 1971 who had over six years of schooling. Population with more than 6 years of schooling and above 10 years increased at an annual rate of 10 per cent or so during the last decade.

Even though the population above 10 years of age increased at 4.5 per cent or so per year in Jakarta during the 1960s, the corresponding rate of growth in the labour force was only 3.2 per cent per year (2.9 per cent per year for males and 4.4 per cent per year for females) because of a reduction in the labour force participation rate between 1961 and 1971. The reduction is particularly striking for males: from 77 per cent in 1961 to 66 per cent in 1971; much of the reduction was concentrated in the 15-24 age group; because of the large weight attached to this age group, the labour force below 24 years increased at only 1.6 per cent per annum. A breakdown of the data by schooling level shows that the bulk of the decline in the labour participation rate occurred among the young males with under 6 years of schooling. These findings, based on the population censuses, are puzzling and they contradict some of the findings pertaining to migration, which has played an important role. Nevertheless, the labour force according to the censuses increased by 360,000 in 10 years or at an annual rate of 36,000 persons. The changes in the level and structure of population and labour force imply a virtual doubling of the number of new entrants to the Jakarta labour force in recent years in comparison with earlier periods.

MIGRATION AND THE URBAN LABOUR MARKET

What is the role of migration in this context?   It is
estimated that the increase in population due to migration during
the 1960s might be of the order of 860,000 or about 86,000 per
year; if we exclude children below 10 years, then the annual
increase might be of the order of 53,000 persons per year,
virtually all of them in the age group 10-29 years.   Since the
labour force participation rate for this age bracket is very high
and since a greater proportion of migrants tend to participate in
the labour force, it follows that a large majority of the 53,000
persons did participate in the labour force;   in other words,
migration played a dominant role in causing shifts in the supply
of labour in Jakarta.   Since the typical migrant is around
20 years of age at the time of migration, it implies that migration
influences the supply of labour particularly in the younger age
brackets.

The data on migration also suggest that nearly 75 per cent of
the migrants had below 6 years of schooling;   in fact, one quarter
of all the migrants had no schooling at all.   Only a relatively
small proportion of persons migrating to Jakarta seems to have had
over 10 years of schooling.   Further, female migrants have fewer
years of schooling than males.

What is the significance of such additions to the labour
force to the functioning of the labour market in Jakarta?   Quite
naturally, the massive migration into Jakarta contributed to a
substantial rise in the rate of unemployment, measured as a percentage of the labour force, from 7.4 in 1961 to 12.8 in 1971.   The
rate of increase in employment between 1961 and 1971 was greater
among (a) persons over 24 years of age;   (b) females; and (c) persons with over six years' schooling, as compared to their counterparts - 3.3 per cent, 3.4 per cent and 9.7 per cent per year
respectively as against 0.8 per cent, 2.3 per cent and 0.7 per cent
per year.   Nevertheless, the rate of unemployment increased over
the decade for all these categories of labour force: for persons
below 24 years - from 13.4 per cent to 19.4 per cent for males,
from 17.2 per cent to 22.9 per cent for females;   for persons over
24 years - from 3.4 per cent to 7.8 per cent for males, from 8.2
per cent to 16.5 per cent for females;   from 6.4 per cent to
10.8 per cent for all males, from 11.3 per cent to 19.0 per cent
for all females;   and for persons with over six years' schooling -
from 6.7 per cent to 11.6 per cent for males;   from 11.2 per cent
to 20.7 per cent for females;   and for those having under six years'
schooling - from 6.4 per cent to 10.5 per cent for males, and
from 11.3 per cent to 18.6 per cent for females.   What about the
structure of unemployment?   In 1971, only 48 per cent of the
unemployed were below 24 years as compared to 67 per cent in 1961.
In other words, more than half of the unemployed in 1971 were above
24 years even though this group experienced a higher rate of
employment growth.   Only 15 per cent of the males unemployed in
1961 had over six years of schooling as compared to 34 per cent in
1971;   the corresponding figures for females were respectively
11 per cent and 21 per cent.   To put it another way, there was a
relative decrease in the number unemployed below 24 years of age
and having fewer than six years' schooling.

Since the bulk of the migrants also belong to the age group
below 24 years and have fewer than six years of schooling, it is
surprising that there were relatively fewer unemployed persons in

these groups in 1971 than in 1961.   These findings seem to
suggest that the migrants have been relatively more successful in
finding jobs as compared to the natives.   This conclusion is
also consistent with the fact that the number of unemployed in
Jakarta increased from 73,000 in 1961 to 172,000 in 1971 or an
absolute increase of about 100,000 persons in ten years (i.e.
about 10,000 persons per year), which is a fraction of the
increase in the labour force due to migration.   There is also
evidence from other sources such as a sample survey of migrants
in Jakarta city to support this conclusion: in spite of the fact
that a larger fraction of the migrant population participated in
the labour force after migration than before, the rate of
unemployment among migrants was lower after migration than before.

The implication of the above findings is that the demand for
labour has been responding sympathetically to the shifts in the
supply of labour in Jakarta.   Other available information based
on survey data further suggests that the average period of waiting is significantly smaller for the migrants than for the
natives.   For example, among males with some work experience,
only 44 per cent of the unemployed migrants had been unemployed
for longer than ten weeks as compared to 61 per cent of the
unemployed natives.   Corresponding figures for males without
work experience were 72 per cent and 86 per cent.   Somewhat similar findings are reported for females as well.   Thus the waiting
period for migrants is significantly smaller for the migrants
than for the natives.   What emerges from the foregoing is that
the labour market is functioning fairly efficiently in Jakarta
even in the presence of massive migration.   Nevertheless, there
are good reasons to be concerned with the emerging situation in
Jakarta, as we shall see below.

JAKARTA'S INFORMAL SECTOR

One of the interesting features of the structure of employment in Jakarta is the dominance of employment in the informal
sector.   First, a word about the informal sector.   The concept
was first introduced in the ILO employment mission report[1] on
Kenya which described the informal sector as follows: ease of
entry for new enterprises; reliance on indigenous resources;
family ownership of enterprises; small scale of operation;
labour-intensive and adapted technology; skills of workers
acquired outside the formal school system; and unregulated and
competitive markets.   Further, informal sector enterprises
largely rely on their own sources of capital or on borrowings
from friends and relatives.

In the case of Jakarta, however, data considerations dictated
the following definition - all unregistered enterprises.   This
definition seems to be a conservative one because many small enterprises having the characteristics stated above are excluded from
the informal sector simply because they are registered.   According to the available data, close to half a million employed

---

[1] International Labour Office: Employment, incomes and
equality: a strategy for increasing productive employment in
Kenya (Geneva, 1972).

persons were dependent on the informal sector for employment as
compared to an estimated total workforce of 1 million persons in
1967.   Indications are that this number has continued to swell in
recent years as well, notwithstanding a substantial rise in
employment in the formal sector.

There is also evidence to support the view that a large
majority of the migrants to the city who succeed in securing a job
depend on the informal sector for employment opportunities.
According to a recent migration survey, it is estimated that only
about 16 per cent of the fresh migrants seem to take up jobs in
administration, finance and government-related activities, the
rest being employed as petty traders, hawkers, vendors, barbers,
tailors, repair and maintenance workers, shop assistants, taxi
drivers, betjak (or tricycle) drivers and so on.   A small percentage of the latter is also employed as daily labourers.   The proportion of persons becoming house-helpers is of course much
greater among female migrants than among males.   These findings
suggest that a majority of the new entrants to the labour force
become self-employed.   It is not clear from the available data
whether it reflects the preference for self-employment or whether
it is due to lack of wage employment opportunities.   But from the
limited evidence available, it would appear that both the low
level of earnings and the lack of job security in wage employment
may have discouraged many from seeking wage employment opportunities.   In any case, the evidence quoted above together with other
available scattered evidence provide some support to the classical
Say's law that "supply creates its own demand".   That the labour
market in Jakarta is working fairly efficiently should not therefore come as a surprise.

The presence of a spongy informal sector in Jakarta has no
doubt considerably minimised the adjustment problems in the labour
market resulting from massive migration.   But at the same time it
has elevated the concern for equity.   For one thing, the slum and
squatter areas, where most of the participants in the informal
sector live, have become more glaring.   This in turn has drawn
attention to the low incomes and earnings of individuals in the
informal sector.   The available data suggest that there are wide
disparities in the productivity of labour, particularly between
the formal and the informal sectors, as reflected in the earnings
of workers in the two sectors.   Many participants in the informal
sector, according to scattered evidence, receive significantly
lower earnings and the earnings are also subject to uncertainty.

Interestingly enough, low earnings cannot be attributed to
fewer hours of work per day (or week or month) since the unemployment surveys suggest that more than half of the employed persons
work for over 44 hours per week, irrespective of their monthly
income, and that only a negligible proportion work for under
15 hours per week.   And only 21 per cent of those employed seem
to want more work.   Among persons having wage employment, a large
majority seems to be employed on a daily basis, presumably because
it is advantageous to the employer: he does not have to pay wages
to the worker when he is not working.   Further, by paying wages
on a daily basis it is easy to replace workers.   As a result,
many of these workers not only receive low earnings but also lack
job security.   No doubt this situation is mainly the consequence
of the general labour surplus situation vis-à-vis the weak bargaining position of the worker.   While these factors are important in
explaining the concern for equity, they tell only a part of the

story. To explain the disparities in wages and productivity
between the formal and the informal sectors one must go further and
examine why the formal sector wages are higher and why there is no
tendency for the wage differential between the two sectors to narrow
through labour mobility in the appropriate directions.

INFORMAL-FORMAL SECTOR EARNINGS AND MOBILITY

One of the factors relevant in this context is the prevailing
wage structure in the Government, which more or less influences, if
not determines, the wage structure in the formal sector. "In many
of the less-developed countries, independence from colonial rule
was followed by a great expansion in government employment, partly
to replace former expatriate staff, and partly in the belief that
a much larger role for government was needed for economic and
social development ... Generally, salaries paid were somewhat below
the levels formerly enjoyed by the expatriate staff but, at least
in the higher grades, very high compared with average incomes in
the rest of the country."[1] " ... the difficulty of measuring the
productivity of workers engaged in public administration has led to
salaries being fixed in terms of educational level of the workers
rather than in relation to the jobs they have to do or even to the
specialisation of their education".[2] It is further observed that:

> The wage system which evolved in Indonesia after indepen-
> dence was from the beginning weighted towards social security
> objectives. Inflation, especially the great inflation of the
> mid-1960s, strengthened this tendency. Among the features of
> the Indonesian wage system which illustrate this social policy
> role, the most important are: (a) the payment of a high pro-
> portion of wages in kind; (b) the practice of relating a
> high proportion of wages, especially of the wages paid in
> kind, to the "needs" of the worker, e.g., the number of his
> dependants; (c) the payment of a wide variety of allowances
> and fringe benefits; (d) manpower regulations designed to pro-
> tect job security by limiting employers' right of dismissal.[3]

It would, therefore, appear that the prevailing wage structure is
far from optimal in the sense that it fails to reflect the true
scarcity for different categories of labour. Public sector pay
policies and their role as norms to be followed by other large
enterprises, coupled with the regulation restricting the right of
the enterprise to dismiss workers, would appear to have discouraged
labour mobility between the formal and the informal sectors.

---

[1] See H.W. Arndt and R.M. Sundrum: "Wages, salaries and
incentives", paper presented at the Panel discussion of wages and
salaries and unemployment in Indonesia, held in May 1974, p. 51.

[2] ibid.

[3] ibid., pp. 29-30. See also ILO, Asian Regional Team for
Employment Promotion: Manpower and related problems in Indonesia
(Bangkok, 1972) for further discussion on this topic.

In addition, lack of appropriate skills among the informal
sector participants and barriers to skill formation together with
poor substitution possibilities between different kinds of skills
have acted as a deterrent to labour mobility.   Typically, the
participant in the informal sector has three or four years of
schooling or even less.   The available data on migrants also show
that they were mostly in the occupational category "agriculture,
livestock and fishing", and the next most important group belonged
to "traders and vendors".   For example, 58 per cent of the
migrants with no schooling were employed in agriculture and related
activities before they came to Jakarta, but after migration 36 per
cent were in trading and vending activities, 16 per cent were
domestic servants, 14 per cent were daily labourers, 10 per cent
were in production and transport-related activities, and the rest
in miscellaneous activities.   In contrast, less than 10 per cent
of the migrants with over six years of schooling were employed in
agriculture and related activities before they came to Jakarta,
but after migration a large majority of them found jobs in administration, finance, government and other professional occupations.
It is therefore clear that skill is a major constraint which prevents the informal sector participants from entering the formal
sector.

An important barrier to labour mobility from the informal to
the formal sector is the requirement of a residence and work permit.
Such permits are difficult to obtain if the worker is a migrant to
the city.   The Governor of Jakarta officially declared in 1970
that the city is "closed" with a view to discouraging migration
into Jakarta.   Even though it is widely recognised that this
policy has been ineffective in arresting migration owing to inherent weaknesses in such a policy, the permit system would appear to
have discouraged migrants from entering the formal sector and
encouraged them to enter the informal sector, over which the
Government has little control, if any.

Nevertheless, the migrants have been responding to opportunities, particularly within the informal sector.   Data based on the
migration survey show that these individuals do try to move towards
more preferred occupations as their length of stay in Jakarta
increases.   A greater proportion of those who migrated some time
ago, for example, are taxi drivers, as compared to the recent
migrants, presumably because over a period of time they could
acquire the necessary skills and access to a vehicle.   Likewise
there is a sharp decline in the proportion of daily labourers and
those engaged in trade, among male migrants, with an increase in
the length of their stay in Jakarta.   In the case of female
migrants, the proportion employed as domestic servants decreases
from over 40 per cent for recent migrants to under 20 per cent
among those who migrated five years earlier;   but correspondingly
the proportion entering the professional occupations and the trading
and vending business shows a rise.   Such changes in the occupational pattern are also correlated with the level of education of
the migrant.

The evidence quoted above clearly suggests that there is some
mobility between occupations;   but such mobility seems to be largely
confined to the informal sector rather than being towards the formal
sector occupations.   It is not clear from the data whether such
mobility is due to (a) better labour market information;   or
(b) ready response from individuals to acquire the necessary skills;
or (c) greater access to credit and other facilities;   or (d) a

combination of the above reasons.   This is an area for further
research which can lead to appropriate policies in increasing the
efficiency of the labour market and improving the income distribution.

The case of Jakarta is not atypical of other urban centres in
many developing countries.   It shows that migration towards urban
areas is an important factor contributing to the additions to the
urban labour force.   Either owing to lack of adequate employment
opportunities in the formal sector and the Government, or due to
lack of ability among the new entrants to the labour force to
exploit such opportunities successfully, many of them are forced to
seek opportunities for work in the informal sector.   Even though
there is a preference for wage employment, many of them choose to
become self-employed either because such wage employment is not
easily available or because the working conditions, including
earnings, are not sufficiently attractive.   By virtue of the
characteristics of the informal sector, it has been possible to
avoid excessive unemployment rates in urban areas.   Nevertheless,
the urbanisation process has elevated the concern for equity;
besides the mushroom growth of slum areas with inadequate urban
services, it has contributed to the swelling number of low-income
earners.

Some of the key questions that emerge from the evidence presented above are as follows.   First, there is a need to improve the
working conditions of workers in the informal sector as well as
their earnings through appropriate policies and action-oriented programmes.   Second, there is a need to understand the factors
impeding labour mobility between the informal and the formal sectors.   This involves considerable research on the changes in the
occupational pattern and the factors governing the change in order
to discover the appropriate policies leading to greater labour
mobility.   In particular, one must examine the opportunities for
skill acquisition by the informal sector participants, the scope
for increasing their earnings through such skill formation, the
cost of imparting the necessary skills, and so on.   Equally important is an appraisal of the existing institutional barriers to
labour mobility.   Finally, there is an urgent need to examine the
rationality of the wage structure in the Government and the formal
sector and modify it, particularly with a view to facilitating
labour mobility between the informal and formal sectors and thereby
improving the distribution of income.

Manpower planning and labour markets: the Yugoslav case

by

H. Thomas,
Institute of Social Studies, The Hague

INTRODUCTION

In this chapter we shall investigate methods of manpower planning in relationship to labour markets. The Yugoslav labour situation will be used to substantiate the necessity for examining "institutional" realities before deciding on an appropriate method of manpower planning. This will be done by analysing two methods of manpower planning with a given assumption as to substitution possibilities between categories of labour.

To begin with, we will argue that the usual regression analyses of the cross-sectioned relationships between wages and employment based on poor aggregative data are not very meaningful and may even be misleading.

Workers' self-management is accorded high priority and constitutional sanction in Yugoslavia. In theory, this should have a strong impact on the Yugoslav labour market, and we shall examine how far this is so. The importance of these institutional insights for model specification and for the interpretation of findings on the elasticity of substitution between categories of labour will be demonstrated. Finally, our empirical work, which makes use of new data, indicates that there are considerable possibilities for substitution.

I. ISSUES OF MANPOWER PLANNING

The role of manpower planning has changed considerably during the past two decades. In West European countries, for example, new questions are raised with respect to graduate unemployment, skill patterns of migrant workers and the length of graduate studies, as well as their relevance to society at large; in poor countries more emphasis is now given to basic education, provision of elementary skills, new views on curriculum development, and to recurrent and adult education.[1] New questions need new answers, and in this respect manpower planning seems to be a suitable tool with which to clarify the linkages between the expense of training and education and the labour markets.

Manpower planning is usually associated with attempts to assess the educational requirements of changing economies. Attempts are made to forecast the long-run skill requirements of society; this often means skill preferences as expressed by a

---

Note: H. Thomas, Senior Lecturer (Labour Economics), Institute of Social Studies, The Hague. This paper is based on Chapter III of "Personal income distribution in Yugoslavia: a human capital approach to the analysis of personal income differences in the industry of a labour-managed market economy" (unpublished Ph.D. dissertation, Cornell University, 1973), by Hendrik Thomas.

[1] Organisation for Economic Co-operation and Development: The residual factor and economic growth (Paris, OECD, 1964); Mark Blaug: An introduction to the economics of education (England, Allen Lane Penguin Books, 1970), pp. 61-100; Lester Thurow: Investment in human capital (California, Wadsworth Publishing Company Inc., 1970), pp. 1-28.

small industrialising sector, since only the required input-output
matrices are available with any degree of reliability.   It is
easier to collect prospective data on the formal than on the informal sector, on commercial agricultural holdings than small individual farms and on large service organisations than street peddlars.
This being so, it is only one step further to develop manpower
planning techniques that will fit the available data.

     The fixed requirements approach towards manpower planning has
followed this pattern of analysis.[1]   On the base of a perspective
plan, long-term goals are set for gross domestic product distributed over the main branches of the economy.   Next, the sectoral
targets through occupational matrices and educational components
are translated into future educational requirements.   Depending on
the gestation period, policy makers will then implement measures
such as investing in building, setting up teachers' training programmes, and guaranteeing enrolment figures to achieve the stated
goals.

     This is a rather mechanical exercise designed to spot "sur-
pluses" and "shortages" of skills at an early stage without taking
into account the operations of the labour markets.   Since the
data requirements of this manpower planning method are relatively
modest and its explanatory claims are high without demanding
excessive professional skills on the part of policy makers, it has
been widely used.   However, after a considerable period in which
experience of using this method has been accumulated, the time for
evaluation has now arrived, and predictive records prove to be
dismal.[2]

     Another method of manpower planning, the rate of return
approach, views educational expenses as investments in human capital.[3]   Benefit-cost analysis is applied to expenses for training
and education incurred by public agencies and by individuals;
rates of return and net present values indicate the profitability
of planned outlays in this field and permit comparability with
public expenditures in entirely different fields.   This method
meets with huge problems of an analytical and empirical nature
since it is necessary to define the nature of future benefits, both
social and private, and these in turn must be measurable.   Standard practice has been to consider before- and after-tax wages as
an approximation of social and private benefits.   The rate of
return approach is thus clearly related to labour market behaviour.
In spite of huge data problems, this method has been widely applied
and rate of return studies, usually referring to small sectors of
society, are presently available for some 30 countries.[4]   There is

---

     [1] Bashir Ahamad and Mark Blaug, eds.: The practice of manpower
forecasting: a collection of case studies (Amsterdam, Elsevier
Scientific Publishing Company, 1973).

     [2] Ahamad and Blaug, ibid.

     [3] See also Blaug, op. cit., and Thurow, op. cit., on education
as an investment in human capital.

     [4] George Psacharopoulos: "Rates of return to investment in
education around the world", in Comparative Education Review, Feb.
1972, pp. 54-67; M. Carnoy: Schooling, income, the distribution of
income and unemployment: a critical appraisal (Paris, OECD, Oct.
1973, restricted).

ample scope for further development by including probability, risk, and socio-economic variables. Despite weaknesses, it is acceptable because it attempts to integrate manpower planning into labour markets as illustrated by Thurow's work on the American labour markets, and by the studies of Carnoy and Thias, and Shortlidge, which yield new insights into the functioning of labour markets in situations of underdevelopment.[1]

By now, it should be sufficiently clear that the fixed requirements approach and the rate of return approach are vastly different instruments of manpower planning. Labour economists will need to specify the circumstances under which each approach is valid and applicable for policy making. A testing device is available since the two methods assume opposite possibilities of substitution between skill categories. Substitution in response to adjustment of wage structures is lacking (zero) in the fixed requirements approach,[2] whereas this is limitless (infinite) in the rate of return approach.[2] The elasticity of substitution, the technical concept that measures this responsiveness, ranges between zero and infinity, and is a highly suitable instrument for manpower planning based on labour market realities. The technical matrices of the fixed requirements approach allow no scope for the inclusion of labour market variables such as changing wage structures. The rate of return approach takes the opposite position: small changes in wage structure are followed by perfect substitution by one skill category or another, and vice versa. It should therefore be possible to discard the fixed requirements approach if econometric analysis could prove that the elasticity of substitution between categories of manpower differs significantly from zero. Such empirical testing, however, encounters major difficulties. Within the same socio-economic and labour market framework, wage and employment data by category of labour should ideally be available with which to estimate the elasticity of substitution. So far, Dougherty's study on the USA based on time series is the only one which rejects the null hypothesis.[3] There are indications that elsewhere the degree of substitution is also considerable, as Psacharopoulos shows in a survey article. There are also a few studies which use cross-sectional analysis with aggregate wage and employment data. The estimated values for elasticity of substitution are invariably different from zero; however, definite conclusions cannot be drawn since such aggregate analysis suggests that labour demand curves are identical in different countries.[4]

---

[1] M. Carnoy and Hans Thias: "Educational planning with flexible wages: a Kenyan example", in Economic Development and Cultural Change, Apr. 1972, pp. 438-473; Richard Lynn Shortlidge, Jr., "The employment and earnings of agricultural graduates in India: a benefit-cost case study of GB Pant College of Agriculture and Technology" (unpublished Ph.D. dissertation, Cornell University, 1973).

[2] George Psacharopoulos: "Substitution assumption versus empirical evidence in manpower planning", in De Economist, 1212, Nr. 6, 1973, pp. 609-625.

[3] C.R.S. Dougherty: "Estimates of labour aggregation functions", in Journal of Political Economy, Nov./Dec. 1972, pp. 1101-1119.

[4] Psacharopoulos, op. cit., pp. 619-623; and Jan Tinbergen: "Substitution of graduate by other labour", in Kyklos, Vol. XXVII, 1974, pp. 217-226, report how other studies have dealt with "shifting variables".

We shall test the same hypothesis in the Yugoslav institutional framework, as Yugoslav manpower planners have been making exclusive use of the fixed requirements approach,[1] and the labour situation possesses unique features which may be expected to influence the substitution between skill categories.   The next section will focus on Yugoslav political economy characteristics (neither "capitalist" nor "command" types) that are relevant for an understanding of the specific features of the Yugoslav labour market.

II.   WORKERS' SELF-MANAGEMENT: THE CASE OF YUGOSLAVIA

Workers' participation in management and ownership has become a significant issue of political and economic interest.   Among non-capitalist countries, the outstanding experiment is taking place in Yugoslavia, where participation and self-government are an integral part of the national constitution as well as of company law in the social sector of the economy;   the country is rightly named the "laboratory" of workers' self-management and self-government.   But various forms of workers' participation have also been introduced in less-developed countries;   broad evidence of this has been reported in the proceedings of a conference organised by[2] the ILO on workers' participation in decisions within undertakings.   These countries show a similar range of concepts and issues: from modest schemes of having workers participate in issues of their immediate concern and interest to developments in Peru where, in the span of less than five years, participation has expanded to include a com-plete social property sector designed according to the well-established theory of participatory economics.[3]   The political and economic constraints in Peru, perhaps in Chile prior to September 1973, and in Yugoslavia, are so different from those in the West European situation that some social scientists argue in favour of a third model of self-government as a point of reference.

We are concerned with the impact of this third system, especially of workers' participation, on the elasticity of substi-tution between categories of manpower, as a prelude of our econo-metric research.

Fortunately, the economics of participation, as a complete general economic theory for a third system of political economy, is already highly developed.   Ward, Domar and Robinson have done

---

[1] Institut za Ekonomiku Investicija: "Projekcija Dugorocnih Potrebah u Kadrovima Sr. Srbije u Perspecktivi do 1986 Godine (Belgrade, Institut za Ekonomiku Investicija, 1971);   also Amartya K. Sen: "Models of educational planning and their applica-tions", Journal of Development Planning, No. 2, 1970, pp. 11-18.

[2] International Labour Organisation: Symposium on Workers' Participation in Decisions within Undertakings, Oslo, 20-30 Aug. 1974 (ILO, Geneva, unpublished documents, 1974).

[3] Working papers by Tom E. Davis, Fernando Collazo, Jaroslav Vanek (Ithaca, NY, Cornell University, 1974).

pioneering work in this respect, and Vanek's design of key characteristics of the system will be described in the following paragraphs.[1]

A participatory enterprise is distinguished by the following features:

(a) Decision-making procedures within the enterprise follow majority rule and democratic procedures in which only those take part who actually work in the enterprise. Self-management structures with respect to policy making and control, and managerial operational efficiency with respect to policy execution, are key notions in this model of industrial organisation. The excellent growth record of the Yugoslav economy during the last 20 years sufficiently indicates that democracy need not imply chaos and anarchy.[2]

(b) A participatory society needs to introduce "social ownership" of the means of production. Social ownership implies an innovative legal concept wherein "society" - the State, planning agencies, banks, or private individuals - own equipment, factories, means of production, without any control over the internal operations of the enterprise.[3] Workers' associations in turn obtain the usufruct - the yields of the means of production - but have to compensate "society" by setting aside amounts for depreciation and by paying an annual scarcity price for use of the capital.

(c) It follows logically that the net revenue - gross revenue minus costs of material, services rendered by third parties, depreciation, and user costs of means of production - is entirely at the disposal of the workers' collectives. These will share total labour income, a large part being paid out as "wages", and the remainder invested or used for collective consumption or set aside for emergencies.

(d) The three characteristics so far described imply the need for decentralised decision-making together with central intervention to allocate capital when new workers' associations are established. The market is the main co-ordinating mechanism, whereas multi-level planning - the labour-managed agency according to Vanek - assumes a major role with respect to capital allocation and the provision of expert technical services.[4]

---

[1] Jaroslav Vanek: The general theory of labour-managed market economies (Ithaca, NY, Cornell University Press, 1970).

[2] See for an excellent statement on the internal organisation of a self-managed enterprise: Autoriteit en Democratie by Rob Boonzajer Flaes and Joop Ramondt (Rotterdam, Universitaire pers, 1974).

[3] Social ownership thus is not identical with nationalisation.

[4] We might mention here the role which Caja Laboral Popular plays with respect to the Mondragon producers' co-operatives, and the national labour-managed agency in Peru, as cases in which banks have been transformed and now stimulate and initiate new projects. On Mondragon producers' co-operatives we find useful information in Les Coopératives industrielles de Mondragon By Quintin Garcia (Paris, Editions Economie et Humanisme, 1968/1969).

(e) The last main characteristic concerns the freedom of workers
     to leave an enterprise and to associate in order to form a new
     one, thus laying the foundation for a new concept of labour
     market under workers' self-management.

Having identified these five characteristics, Vanek next
argues that maximisation of labour income per employed worker
rather than the maximisation of profit is the motivating principle:
labour income is made up of monetary and non-monetary rewards,
which also include collective consumption and long-term provisions.[1]

The model has immediate implications for labour markets and
thus for the relationship between these markets and manpower planning. Firstly, unlike labour markets in the traditional or neo-
classical setting, in a labour-managed market economy workers
associate in enterprises and strive after maximisation of average
labour income. New employment will be offered as long as average
income has not reached the maximum, but not to the point where
falling marginal value product equalises the market wage rate.
The worker-managed enterprises thus determine a point on the demand
schedule corresponding to the desired maxima, rather than search
for an otpimum with regard to some externally determined market
wage rate.   The absence of a traditional labour market thus calls
for action by planning agencies to stimulate the formation of new
associations by unemployed workers who cannot obtain employment by
offering to work at a lower wage at "the gates of the enterprise".
The least to be said is that the widespread unemployment which has
occurred in recent years in Yugoslavia does not contradict this
theoretical consideration.[2]

Secondly, workers will probably be extremely reluctant to dismiss their colleagues in times of depression, but will be highly
motivated to guarantee employment and stable take-home incomes.
Horvat's interesting study on business cycles provides strong empirical evidence to substantiate this point: during the downward
wave of cycles employment remains stable and inventories accumulate
rapidly.[3]

A third aspect, of more theoretical importance, concerns the
low supply elasticity of labour.   Under certain conditions negative
elasticities may occur and unstable equilibria may result.[4]
Fourthly, workers, including managers, do not receive "wages" as
distinct from "profits" but obtain legal title to the entire surplus
value.   Accounting techniques have to be adjusted and comparisons
with wages in other systems are not directly possible.   Fifthly, it
may be expected that democratic processes of decision-making, along
with other features of workers' self-management, influence a wide
range of labour problems such as wage structures, the allocation of

---

[1] Vanek, op. cit., and also Boonzajer Flaes and Ramondt, op.
cit.

[2] Thomas, op. cit., Ch. II, surveys the employment situation in
Yugoslavia.

[3] Branko Horvat: Business cycles in Yugoslavia (New York,
International Arts and Sciences Press, 1971).

[4] Vanek, op. cit., Ch. 4.

resources to skill formation and training, the distinction between general and specific training, hierarchical structures, and finally the degree of substitution between categories of labour.

Together with Vanek, Boonzajer Flaes and Ramondt,[1] we conclude that Yugoslavia reasonably fits the third system of political economy and that the theoretical labour market considerations mentioned above apply to Yugoslav enterprises.

For econometric reasons it is important to know whether relative wages or the level and composition of employment is the dependent variable in demand functions.   The earlier description of "labour markets" in Yugoslavia indicates that wages are a dependent variable as workers' assemblies frequently decide on this, taking into account changing scarcity relationships.   The skill composition, however, is largely determined by expansion of the enterprise, the chosen technology, and the funding of training programmes, each of which relates to some characteristic of the system of workers' self-management.

We must also expect workplace hierarchies to develop as workers are assigned to different job and work classifications in accordance with experience, on-the-job training and formal education.   But this will proceed in accordance with the needs of democratic structures.   We expect greater substitution than in other systems of organisation, since workers will be cautious in giving colleagues higher responsibilities along with increased incomes.

The institutional framework of worker-managed enterprise thus has consequences for model specification from which the elasticity of substitution is derived.   Estimates would be biased if this dimension was ignored in regression analysis.   Furthermore, the elasticity of substitution under worker management may be expected to assume higher values than have been found in non-participatory enterprises.

III.   EMPIRICAL RESEARCH ON THE DEGREE OF SUBSTITUTION BETWEEN CATEGORIES OF LABOUR IN YUGOSLAVIA

To measure the response of educational wage differentials to changes in skill composition of labour, one needs data on wages and employment by categories of education on a large scale, and such data rarely exist.   Fortunately we have been able to collect, from various sources, sufficient data that permit us, first, to apply time-series analysis to the period 1956-70 with aggregate data of the entire social sector of the Yugoslav economy and, second, to apply cross-sectional analysis to the period 1967-70 with data for each of the eight regions of Yugoslavia.[2]

---

[1] Vanek, op. cit., and other publications; Boonzajer Flaes and Ramondt, op. cit., p. 12.

[2] Thomas, op. cit., Ch. III; in this chapter, a detailed report is found on employment data in Yugoslavia.

These data refer to two systems of classification: one based on education and the other on occupational categories. We shall report here on these classifications and on the estimated values of the elasticity of substitution between either education or occupational classes; some comments on model specification are given in the Appendix. Elasticity is defined as a percentage change of relative wages in response to a 1 per cent change in the relative employment figures of the classes concerned. The educational classification is divided into eight categories. Four white-collar classes are assigned to workers with primary or secondary education or with bachelor's or master's degrees; blue-collar classes are assigned among the very highly skilled, highly skilled, semi-skilled and unskilled workers, representing different formal levels of technical education.[1]

With all eight categories in one regression analysis we obtain an elasticity of 50 (t-value is 99). Next, the same parameter is estimated separately for white-collar workers and for blue-collar workers: in the first case the elasticity amounts to 10 (t-value 3.2), while we did not succeed in obtaining a statistically significant estimate for blue-collar workers. Finally, we further divided the white-collar workers, and found a value of 16 (t-value 1.2) for the degree of substitution between workers with primary and those with secondary education; and of 8 (t-value 3.4) for substitution between graduates with a bachelor's degree and those with a master's degree.

The second classification divides the same labour force into seven occupational classes that are based both on formal education and experience; the estimates relate to the period 1956-70.[2] The occupational categories comprise three classes of white-collar workers with primary, secondary and university education, and four classes of blue-collar workers from very highly skilled to the unskilled.

In this case we first estimate for the entire labour force a value of 4 (t-value is 8.6) for the elasticity of substitution between occupational classes; next, with separate estimates for white- and blue-collar workers, we obtain a value of 5.5 (t-value 2.9) for white-collar workers and of 4 (t-value 3.2) for blue-collar workers.[3]

The null hypothesis that assumes absence of substitution possibilities is, therefore, convincingly rejected. The fixed requirements approach will need to be discarded by Yugoslav manpower planners because workers' associations substitute "abundant" skills for "scarce" ones rather than wait until the latter are "produced" by the educational system. It is also striking that the elasticity of

---

[1] Psacharopoulos: "Substitution Assumption", for a comparison with classifications that are available in other studies.

[2] Classes based on both formal and information education must, from an efficiency viewpoint, be more homogeneous than just educational classes.

[3] See footnote 1 above. This explains why the values for the elasticity have to be smaller with this classification. Part of substitution, now, is already included in the occupational classes.

substitution assumes high values, thus underscoring our second hypothesis that, in a labour-managed market economy, substitution possibilities will be greater than in other types of industrial organisation. All things not being equal, direct comparison with estimates made by other researchers is not possible.

In addition to our observations on the two hypotheses that were tested, we must reiterate that the model from which the estimated values were derived - on which we briefly report in the Appendix - was carefully designed to take into account the features of the Yugoslav labour situation.

IV. CONCLUSIONS

Within the limits of this chapter it has not been possible to do full justice to the institutional issues and econometric problems faced in our research into the relationship between manpower planning and labour markets in Yugoslavia. We have elaborated on the unique features of the Yugoslav participating economy and labour situation and briefly discussed the econometric problems in the Appendix.

As the focal point of the relationship, we have emphasised the "elasticity of substitution between skill categories of labour", tailoring the empirical investigations to the Yugoslav institutional framework. The estimated parameters clearly show that existing methods of manpower planning in Yugoslavia are based on an unrealistic assumption, namely the absence of substitution possibilities between skill categories. The opposite would seem to be the case since our findings indicate high values of this elasticity as compared to those reported in a non-participatory context.[1]

Although labour markets in a system of workers' self-management generally tend to adjust slowly to disequilibria - see in particular the first characteristic mentioned on page 196 above - it appears that internal adjustments are made more swiftly than in non-participatory industrial organisations. Our findings add a new dimension to the concept of "dual labour markets" which Miller and Zaidi have written about with specific reference to the "Piore-Doeringer model".[2] The labour-managed sector would be characterised by low viscosity between enterprises but by well-functioning market mechanisms internally.

---

[1] Psacharopoulos, "Further Assumptions" contains information on other studies.

[2] Richard U. Miller and Mahmood A. Zaidi: "The relevance of two sector models for the study of labour absorption and mobility in the urban labour markets of developing countries", paper presented at the Research Conference on Urban Labour Markets in Developing Areas, International Institute for Labour Studies, Geneva, September 1974.

It follows that the internal dynamics of worker-managed enterprises deserve considerable attention. Vanek has emphasised the role of effort, along with time, as inputs into production processes, and recent interest in wage structures, shown for example by Wan, Marglin and Klevmarken, almost yields an agenda for research to be undertaken in worker-managed enterprises.[1] Such research should include experiments such as the Scott Baader co-operatives, work-classification schemes in Mondragon producers' co-operatives, and the internal dynamics of worker-managed enterprises in the social property sector in Peru.

Although the focus in this study is on the well-developed Yugoslav system of self-management, it is clear that econometrics can be separated from institutional dimensions only at the risk of harming both aspects.

APPENDIX

Model specification

The theoretical foundation for estimation of the elasticity of substitution between categories of labour was laid by Sato, when he developed a two-level constant-elasticity-of-substitution production function.[2] He also proved that there was no difficulty in expanding the analysis to third-level and fourth-level CES production functions. From these production functions, under neo-classical conditions, are then directly derived demand functions for categories of labour, which yield an estimate of substitution elasticity. We have argued that the labour force should be an independent variable, whereas the wage structure is the dependent variable, in the following manner:

$$\ln w_i = \ln a_i + (k - 1) \ln L_i + (\ln L^{1-k} \cdot df/dL) \qquad (1)$$

in which w_i is the wage of category i, a_i is the weight given to the i-th category of skill, L and L_i stand for the total labour force and the skill categories, and df/dL is the marginal product of total labour services; Ln is the natural logarithm. The elasticity of substitution between the categories of labour then is $-1/((k-1))$.

---

[1] Henry Y. Wan, Jr.: "A general theory of wages, employment and human capital - an application of semi-competitive equilibrium", Working Paper No. 51, Department of Economics, Cornell University, 1973; Stephen A Marglin: "What do bosses do? The origins and functions of hierarchy in capitalist production", in The Review of Radical Political Economics, Vol. VI, No. 2, Summer 1974, pp. 60-112; Anders Klevmarken: Statistical methods for the analysis of earnings data (Stockholm, Almqvist and Wiksell, 1972).

[2] K. Sato: "A Two-Level Constant-Elasticity-of-Substitution Production Function", in Review of Economic Studies, Apr. 1967, pp. 201-218.

Dougherty has offered an elegant solution for the shifting
variables by including dummy variables in his time-series analysis
for the American labour market.[1]   In our cross-section analysis we
included dummy variables for regions and time for the same purpose.
For the time-series analysis we included as a shifting variable
gross domestic product per labourer because the dummy variable
method would cause undue loss of degrees of freedom.

In the time-series analysis we faced auto-correlation, which
disappeared after we included changing weights for each of the
occupational classes by substituting $(\ln a_i + b_i \cdot K/L)$ for $(\ln a_i)$
in equation (1), in which K/L is a capital-labour ratio.

Excessive capital intensities thus lead to distortions in the
structure of the labour market.   In our study we found that the
weights of workers with secondary education and university degrees
increase with growing capital intensity, and of workers with technical skills become less.   This supports earlier findings on
capital-skill complementarities by Griliches.[2]

---

[1] Dougherty, op. cit., pp. 1101-1105.

[2] Zvi Griliches: "Capital-skill complementarity", in Review
of Economics and Statistics, Nov. 1969, pp. 465-468.

PART V

Urban labour markets in developing areas: selected bibliography

by
Teshome Mulat,
(formerly) Haile Selassie University, Addis Ababa;
International Institute for Labour Studies, Geneva

INTRODUCTION

Major sources used for compiling this bibliography include the
Journal of Economic Literature, computer printouts of ILO library
documents on the subject and many other sources from developing
countries.

Since studies on urban labour markets in developing areas are
of relatively recent origin (even in the advanced countries of the
West) no special effort was made to look for materials published
before 1960.   We have also referred to very few sociological
research studies relating to urban planning.   The focus has been
on the workings of urban labour markets in developing countries.
As a result we have emphasised topics such as employment, wage
determination, labour mobility and labour market information.   Even
on these topics we do not claim to have provided the reader with an
exhaustive list.

Abercrombie, K.C.: "Agricultural mechanisation and employment in Latin America", International Labour Review, July 1972.

Adams, D.W.: "Rural migration and agricultural development in Colombia", Economic Development and Cultural Change, 17(4), July 1969, pp. 527-539.

Agarwala, N.: "Disguised unemployment, unlimited supply of labour and the wage gap", Indian Economic Journal, Jan.-Mar. 1972, pp. 387-403.

Ahluwalla, M.S.: "Taxes, subsidies and employment", Quarterly Journal of Economics, Aug. 1973.

Allsbrook, O.O.; Delorme, C.D.: "More on wage rate determination in underpopulated, underdeveloped rural areas", Economica Internazionale, Aug.-Nov. 1971.

Alonso, W.: "Urban and regional imbalances in economic development", Economic Development and Cultural Change, 17(1), Oct. 1968, pp. 1-14.

Andrews, F.M.; Phillips, G.W.: "The squatters of Lima: Who they are and what they want", The Journal of Developing Areas, 4(2), Jan. 1970.

Angi, G.; Coombe, T.: "Training programmes and employment opportunities for primary school leavers in Zambia", Manpower and Unemployment Research in Africa (Montreal), Nov. 1969, pp. I-12.

Annable, J.E.: "Internal migration and urban unemployment in low-income countries: A problem in simultaneous equations", Oxford Economic Papers, 24(3), Nov. 1972, pp. 399-412.

Arles, J.P.: "Emergency employment schemes", International Labour Review, 109(1), Jan. 1974, pp. 69-88.

Ashenfelter, O.: "Changes in labour market discrimination over time", The Journal of Human Resources, Winter 1971.

Ashenfelter, O.; Rees, A. (eds.): Discrimination in labour markets. Princeton University Press, 1973.

Baali, F.: "Social factors in Iraqi rural-urban migration", American Journal of Economics and Sociology (New York), 25(4), Oct. 1966, pp. 359-364.

Baer, W.; Herve, M.E.A.: "Employment and industrialisation in developing countries", Quarterly Journal of Economics, 80(1), 1966.

Bairoch, P.: Urban unemployment in developing countries: The nature of the problem and proposals for its solution. Geneva, ILO, 1973.

Banks, F.E.: "Fiscal measures to improve employment in developing countries: A comment", Public Finance, 7(4), 1972, pp. 473-476.

Barbero, G.: "Agricultural mechanisation and employment in South Italy", International Labour Review, Nov. 1972.

Barker, R.: "Employment and technological change in Philippine agriculture", International Labour Review, Aug.-Sept. 1972.

Bartsch, William H.: Problems of employment creation in Iran. Employment Research Papers, Geneva, ILO, 1970, 86 pp.

Behrman, J.: "Sectoral elasticities of substitution between capital and labour in a developing economy: Time-series analysis in the case of postwar Chile", Econometrica, Mar. 1972.

Bell, D.: "Occupational discrimination as a source of income differences: Lessons of the 1960s", American Economic Review, May 1972, pp. 363-372.

Bell, R.T.: "Migrant labour: Theory and policy", South African Journal of Economics, Dec. 1972.

Beller, I.: "Latin America's unemployment problem", Monthly Labour Review, 93(ii), Nov. 1970, pp. 3-10.

Benveniste, Guy.; Ilchman, Warren F.: Agents of change: professionals in developing countries. New York, Praeger, 1969, 252 pp.

Berreman, G.D.: "Social categories and social interaction in urban India", Reprint of Centre for South and South-east Asia Studies, University of California, Berkeley, from: The American Anthropologist (74), 1972, pp. 567-586.

Berry, R.A.: "Factor proportions and urban employment in developing countries", International Labour Review, Mar. 1974, pp. 217-233.

Beyer, John C.: "High growth, unemployment and planning in Venezuela: Some observations", Economic Development and Cultural Change, 1970, pp. 267-273.

Beyer, G.M. (ed.): The urban explosion in Latin America. New York, Cornell University Press, 1967.

Bienefeld, M.A.: The self-employed of urban Tanzania. Institute of Development Studies at the University of Sussex, May 1974, IDS discussion paper No. 54.

Bhagoliwal, T.N.: Economics of labour and social welfare: An authoritative account of labour problems in India and other countries of industrial importance. Agra, Shaitya Bhavan, 1966.

Bhagwat, A.: "Main features of the employment problem in developing countries", International Monetary Fund Staff Papers, 20(1), Mar. 1973, pp. 78-99.

Bhagwati, J.; Dellafar, W.: "The brain-drain and income taxation", World Development, Jan.-Feb. 1973.

Bhalla, A.S.: "Choosing techniques: Hand-pounding versus machine milling of rice: An Indian case", Oxford Economic Papers, Mar. 1965.

___ "The role of services in employment expansion", International Labour Review, May 1970.

Bhalla, A.S.: "Self-employment in the less-developed countries: Some aspects of theory and policy", in K. Wohlmuth (ed.), Employment creation in developing economies. New York, Praeger, 1971.

___ "Implications of technological choice in African countries", Africa Spectrum (Hamburg), 1, 1973.

___ "A disaggregative approach to employment in LDCs", The Journal of Development Studies, Oct. 1973.

Bhatt, B.J.: Labour market behaviour of factory workers in Bombay: A case study. Madison, Industrial Relations Research Institute, Wisconsin University, 1969.

Bjerke, K.: "Income and wage distributions - Part I: A survey of the literature", Review of Income and Wealth, Sept. 1970, pp. 235-252.

Black, J.: "Foreign trade and real wages", Economic Journal, Mar. 1969.

Blaug, M.: Causes of graduate unemployment in India. London, Penguin Press, 1969.

___ "Educated unemployment in Asia: A contrast between India and the Philippines", Philippine Economic Journal, first semester 1972, pp. 33-57.

___ "Employment and unemployment in Ethiopia", International Labour Review, Aug. 1974.

Blueston, B.: "The tripartite economy: Labour markets and the working poor", Poverty and Human Resources, July-Aug. 1970.

Bonnin, J.M.; Davis, W.Y.: "Labour force responsiveness to short-run variation in economic opportunity", Southern Economic Journal, Oct. 1971.

___ "Estimated seasonal components in recorded unemployment in 1970", Industrial and Labour Relations Review, Apr. 1972.

Boserup, Ester: Woman's role in economic development. New York, St. Martins Press, 1970, 283 pp.

Bowey, A.: "Labour stability curves and a labour stability index", British Journal of Industrial Relations, Mar. 1969.

Bowles, S.: Planning educational systems for economic growth. Cambridge, Harvard University Press, 1969.

Bowles, Samuel; Nelson, V.I.: "The 'inheritance of IQ' and the intergenerational reproduction of economic inequality", The Review of Economics and Statistics, 56(1), Feb. 1974, pp. 39-51.

Breese, G. (ed.): The city in newly developing countries. Englewood Cliffs, Prentice Hall, 1969.

Brown, E.H.P.: "Levels and movements of industrial productivity and real wages (Internationally compared 1860-1970)", Economic Journal, Mar. 1973.

Brunn, Stanley; Thomas, R.N.: "Socio-economic environments and
    internal migration: The case of Tegucigalpa, Honduras",
    Social and Economic Studies, Dec. 1972.

Bruton, H.J.: "Elasticity of substitution in developing countries",
    Research Memoranda - 45, Williams College, Department of
    Economics, Apr. 1972.

___   "Economic development and labour use", World Development, Dec.
    1973.

Burki, Shahid J.: "Employment creation urban public works pro-
    grammes: Outline of a strategy", Pakistan Development Review,
    Autumn 1973.

Burton, J.F.; Benham, L.K.; Vaughn, W.M.; Flanagan, R.J.:
    Readings in labour market analysis.   New York, Holt, Rinehart
    and Winston, 1971.

Burton, J.; Parker, J.: "Interindustry variations in labour
    mobility", Industrial and Labour Relations Review, Jan. 1969.

Bussey, E.M.: The flight from rural poverty - How nations cope.
    D.C. Heath and Company, 1973.

Caldwell, J.C.: "Determinants of rural-urban migration in Ghana",
    Population Studies, London, 22(3), Nov. 1968, pp. 361-377.

Carnoy, M.: Schooling, income, the distribution of income and
    unemployment: A critical appraisal.   Paris, OECD, Oct. 1973.

Carnoy, M.; Thias, Hans: "Educational planning with flexible wages:
    A Kenyan example", Economic Development and Cultural Change,
    Apr. 1972, pp. 438-473.

Cebula, R.J.: "The city as a source of regional economic disparity
    in Latin America: A comment", Review of Social Economy, Apr.
    1973.

Centre for Developing-Area Studies, McGill University: Manpower and
    unemployment research in Africa: A newsletter, 7(1), Apr. 1974.

Chakravorti, B.N.; Chatterjee, K.D.; Chellaswami, T.: Incomes of
    agricultural workers in India.   A survey report. ·New Delhi,
    1968.

Ghandavarkar, A.G.: "More growth, more employment? A challenge for
    the less-developed countries", Financial Development, 9(2),
    June 1972, pp. 28-35.

Chapin, G.L.; Vedder, R.K.; Gallaway, L.D.: "The determinants of
    emigration to South Africa, 1950-1967", South African Journal
    of Economics, Dec. 1970, pp. 374-381.

Ghaudhuri, Pramit (ed.): Aspects of Indian Economic Development.
    London, George Allen and Unwin, 1971, 288 pp.

Christopher, A.J.: "Urban encroachment on a large farm in Rhodesia",
    Land Economics, Aug. 1972.

Clague, K.: "Capital-labour substitution in manufacturing in under-
    developed countries", Econometrica, July 1969.

Clark, D.H.: "Manpower planning in Singapore", <u>Malayan Economic Review</u>, Oct. 1971.

Clark, D.H.; Pang, Eng Fong: "Returns to schooling and training in Singapore", <u>Malayan Economic Review</u>, Oct. 1970.

Clayton, E.S.: "Mechanisation and employment in East African agriculture", <u>International Labour Review</u>, Apr. 1972.

Clowes, G.A.: "The analysis of labour turnover", <u>Journal of Royal Statistical Society</u>, Series A, 135, 1972.

Cole, Robert E.: "The theory of institutionalisation: Permanent employment and tradition in Japan", <u>Economic Development and Cultural Change</u>, Oct. 1971, pp. 47-70.

___ <u>Japanese blue collar: The changing tradition</u>. Berkeley, University of California Press, 1971, 300 pp.

Committee on Education and Total Employment: <u>Educated unemployment in India; challenges and responses: Study report</u>. Delhi, Hindustan Publ. Corp., 1972.

Comitas; Lambros; Lowenthal, D. (eds.): <u>Work and family life: West Indian perspectives</u>. New York, Doubleday and Company, 1973, 422 pp.

Conning, A.M.: "Rural community differentiation and the rate of rural-urban migration in Chile", <u>Rural Sociology</u> (Brookings), Sept. 1971, pp. 296-314.

Conroy, J.D.: "Urbanisation in Papua, New Guinea: A development constraint", <u>Economic Record</u>, Mar. 1973, pp. 76-88.

Costa, E.: "Maximising employment in labour-intensive development programmes", <u>International Labour Review</u>, Nov. 1973.

Crisostomo, C., et al.: "New rice technology and labour absorption. in Philippine agriculture", <u>Malayan Economic Review</u>, Oct. 1971.

Cumper, G.E.: "Lewis' two-sector model of development and the theory of wages", <u>Social and Economic Studies</u>, 12(1), Mar. 1963.

Daniels, M.R.: "Differences in efficiency among industries in developing countries", <u>American Economic Review</u>, Mar. 1969.

Dasgupta, B.: "Calcutta's informal sector", <u>Bulletin, Institute of Development Studies</u> (Brighton), Oct. 1973, pp. 53-75.

Davies, D.G.: "A critical discussion of International Labour Office Report on Employment in Kenya", <u>Pakistan Development Review</u>, XII(3), Autumn 1973, pp. 283-292.

Davis, K.: <u>World urbanisation 1950-1970 (Vol. 2), analysis of trends, relationships and development</u>. Berkeley, California University, Institute of International Studies, 1972. Population Monograph Series, No. 9.

Davis, S.M.; Goodman, L.W. (eds.): <u>Workers and managers in Latin America</u>. Lexington, Mass., D.C. Heath and Company, 1972.

Dayal, S.: "Wage policy in India: A critical evaluation", Indian Journal of Industrial Relations, Oct. 1970, pp. 149-170.

Debeauvais, M.: Analysis of the earnings patterns of diploma holders: Main aspects of a programme of studies by the development centre. OECD, Feb. 1973.

Denti, E.: "Sex-age patterns of labour force participation by urban and rural populations", International Labour Review, 98(6), Dec. 1968, pp. 525-550.

Department of Labour and Industrial Relations (Malaya): Report on employment, unemployment and underemployment, 1962. Kuala Lumpur, 1963.

Department of Statistics (Malaya): Report on employment and unemployment in metropolitan towns. Kuala Lumpur, 1966.

De Vortez, D.J.: "Migration in a labour surplus economy", Philippine Economic Journal, first semester 1972, pp. 58-80.

Dholakia, J.: "Some aspects of unemployment among the educated in Gujarat", Artha-Vikas, 6(2), July 1970, pp. 79-87.

Diejomaoh, V.P.; Orimalade, W.A.T.: "Unemployment in Nigeria: An economic analysis of scope, trends and policy issues", Nigerian Journal of Economic and Social Studies, 13(2), 1971.

Dietz, H.: "Urban squatter settlements in Peru: A case history and analysis", Journal of Inter-American Studies (Coral Gables), 11(3), July 1969, pp. 353-370.

Doeringer, P.B.; Piore, M.J.: Internal labour markets and manpower analysis. Mass., Lexington Books, 1971.

Dougherty, C.R.S.: "Substitution and the structure of the labour force", Economic Journal, Mar. 1972, pp. 170-182.

Dougherty, C.; Selowsky, M.: "Measuring the effects of misallocation of labour", The Review of Economics and Statistics, 55(3), Aug. 1973, pp. 386-390.

Dwyer, D.J. (ed.): The city as a centre of change in Asia. Hong Kong, Hong Kong University Press, 1972.

Eames, E.: "Urbanisation and rural-urban migration in India", Population Review, 9(1-2), 1965.

Edwards, E.O.; Todaro, M.P.: "Educational demand supply in the context of growing unemployment in less-developed countries", World Development, Mar.-Apr. 1973, pp. 107-117.

Elizaga, J.C.: "The participation of women in the labour force of Latin America", International Labour Review, May-June 1974.

Elkan, W.: "Urban unemployment in East Africa", International Affairs (London), 46(3), July 1970, pp. 517-528.

Emmerij, L.: "Research priorities of the World Employment Programme", International Labour Review, 105(5), May 1972, pp. 411-423.

Emmerij, L.: "Education and employment: Some preliminary findings and thoughts", International Labour Review, Jan. 1973.

Epstein, D.G.: "Genesis and function of squatter settlements in Brasilia", Anthropology of urban environments, by the Society for Applied Anthropology (Washington), 1968, pp. 51-58.

Eriksson, J.R.: "Wage change and employment growth in Latin American industry", Research Memoranda - 36, Williams College, Department of Economics, July 1970.

Evsinkov, I.: "Migration of the population from the countryside to the city (problems of analysis and forecasting", Problems of Economics, June 1973, pp. 14-25.

Eze, J.O.N.: "Career opportunities for Nigerian graduates", The Educationist, I(3), 1972, pp. 12-18.

Fair, R.C.: The short-run demand for workers and hours. Amsterdam, North Holland, 1969.

Falae, S.O.: "Unemployment in Nigeria", Nigerian Journal of Economic and Social Studies, 13(1), 1971.

Farooq, G.M.: The people of Karachi - economic characteristics. Karachi, Pakistan Institute of Development Economics, 1969. Monograph No. 15.

___ "Economic growth and changes in the industrial structure of income and labour force in Pakistan", Economic Development and Cultural Change, Jan. 1973, pp. 293-308.

Fei, J.C.; Renis, G.: "Development and employment in open dualistic economy", Malayan Economic Review, Oct. 1971.

Fields, G.S.: Rural-urban migration, urban unemployment and job-search activity in LDCs. Yale University. Economic Growth Centre. Centre Discussion Paper No. 168.

___ Private returns to investment in higher levels of education in Kenya. Centre for Research on Economic Development, University of Michigan, Ann Arbor, Mar. 1972. Discussion Paper 19.

Firestone, O.J.: "Educational and economic instability", Canadian Journal of Agricultural Economics, Feb. 1972.

Fisk, E.K.: "Labour absorption capacity of subsistence agriculture", Economic Record, Sept. 1971, pp. 366-378.

Fleisher, B.M.: "The economics of labour force participation: A review article", Journal of Human Resources, Spring 1971, pp. 139-148.

Flinn, W.L.: "The process of migration to a shantytown in Bogotá, Colombia", Inter-American Economic Affairs (Washington), 22(2), Autumn 1968, pp. 77-88.

Flinn, W.L.; Converse, J.W.: "Eight assumptions concerning rural-urban migration in Colombia: A three shantytowns test", Land Economics, 46(4), Nov. 1970, pp. 455-466.

Fogel, W.; Lewin, D.: "Wage determination in the public sector",
    Industrial and Labour Relations Review, 27(3), Apr. 1974,
    pp. 410-431.

Fonseca, A.: "Need-based wage and its implementation", The Indian
    Journal of Industrial Relations, 4(4), Apr. 1969.

Form, W.H.: The internal stratification of the working class:
    System involvements of autoworkers in four countries.
    Illinois (n.d.), Illinois University, Institute of Labour and
    Industrial Relations.   Reprint Series, No. 237.

Frank, C.R.: "Urban unemployment and economic growth in Africa",
    Oxford Economic Papers, July 1968.

___   Problems of urban unemployment in Africa.   Princeton, 1970.
    Discussion Paper No. 16.

Frankman, M.J.: "Labour migration in less-developed countries:
    Comment", Manpower and employment research in Africa, 5(1),
    1972.

Frankmann, M.; Charle, E.: "Employment in the service sector in
    sub-Saharan Africa", The Journal of Modern African Studies,
    11(2), 1973.

Freeman, R.B.: "Decline of labour market discrimination and
    economic analysis", American Economic Review, May 1973.

Friedmann, J.; Sullivan, F.: "The absorption of labour in urban
    economy: The case of developing countries", Economic Develop-
    ment and Cultural Change, 22(3), Apr. 1974.

Friedmann, J.; Lackington, T.: "Hyperurbanisation and national
    development in Chile", Urban Affairs Quarterly, 2(4), 1967.

Fuchs, C.J.; Landsberger, H.A.: "'Revolution of rising expecta-
    tions' or ' traditional life ways'? A study of income
    aspirations in a developing country", Economic Development and
    Cultural Change, 21(2), Jan. 1973, pp. 212-226.

Gagala, K.: "The dual urban labour market blacks and whites",
    American Economist, Spring 1973.

Galenson, W. (ed.): Essays on Employment.   Geneva, International
    Labour Office, 1971.

Galfung, J.: "On the relationship between human resources and
    development: Theory, methods, data", Journal of Development
    Studies, Apr. 1972, pp. 137-154.

Gallaway, L.E.; Cebula, R.J.: "Differentials and indeterminacy in
    wage rate analysis: An empirical note", Industrial and Labour
    Relations Review, 26(3), Apr. 1973, pp. 991-995.

Gaude, J.: "Agricultural employment and rural migration in a dual
    economy", International Labour Review, Nov. 1972.

Geertz, G.: Peddlers and princes: Social and economic modernisa-
    tion in two Indonesian towns.   Chicago, University of Chicago
    Press, 1963.

Gellner, C.E.: "Occupational characteristics of urban workers", Monthly Labour Review, Oct. 1971, pp. 21-32.

Ghosh, B.N.: "A note on 'work-making' and 'work-stretching' aspects of disguised unemployment", The Indian Economic Journal, Jan. 1972.

Ginnold, R.E.: "The ILO plan for solving the job crisis in Colombia", Monthly Labour Review, 94(3), Mar. 1971, pp. 32-40.

Ginzberg, Eli: Manpower for development: Perspectives on five continents. New York, Praeger Publishers, 1971, 331 pp.

Glaser, W.A.: Brain-drain and study abroad. Bureau of Applied Social Research, Columbia University, Jan. 1974.

Godfrey, E.M.: "Labour surplus models and labour-deficit economies - the West African case", Economic Development and Cultural Change, 17(3), Apr. 1969, pp. 382-391.

___ "Economic variables and rural-urban migration: Some thoughts on the Todaro hypothesis", The Journal of Development Studies, 10(1), Oct. 1973.

Godfrey, U.N.: "A broader role for national provident funds: The Zambian experience", International Labour Review, Feb. 1974.

Goldfarb, R.S.: "A model of wage setting and wage diversity in local labour markets", Western Economic Journal, Mar. 1973.

Goldstein, G.S.; Moses, L.N.: "A survey of urban economics", Journal of Economic Literature, June 1973.

Goldstein, M.: "The trade-off between inflation and unemployment: A survey", International Monetary Fund Staff Papers, Nov. 1972.

Gollas, M.: "Surplus labour and economic efficiency in the traditional sector of a dual economy: The Guatemalan case", Journal of Development Studies, July 1972.

Gordon, D.M.: Theories of poverty and underemployment: Orthodox, radical and dual labour perspectives. Lexington, Mass., D.C. Heath, 1972.

Gordon, R.J.: "Wage-price controls and the shifting Philipps curve", Brookings Papers on Economic Activity, (2), 1972.

Gouverneur, J.: Productivity and factor proportions in less-developed countries: Case of industrial firms in the Congo. New York, Oxford University Press, 1971.

Grant, J.P.: "Marginal men: the global unemployment crisis", Foreign Affairs, Oct. 1971, pp. 112-124.

Greenhalgh, C.: "Income differentials in the eastern region of Ghana", Economic Bulletin of Ghana, 2(3), 1972.

Greenstreet, M.: "Employment of women in Ghana", International Labour Review, Feb. 1971.

Greenwood, M.J.: "A regression analysis of migration to urban
areas of a less-developed country: The case of India",
Journal of Regional Science, Aug. 1971.

Gregory, R.G.; James, D.W.: "Do new factories embody best
practice technology?", Economic Journal, Dec. 1973.

Guha, S.: "Contribution of non-farm activities to rural employment
promotion: Experience in Iran, India and Syria", International
Labour Review, Mar. 1974, pp. 235-250.

Gujarati, D.: "The behaviour of unemployment and unfilled vacancies",
Economic Journal, 82(325), Mar. 1972, pp. 195-204.

Gulati, I.S.; Krishnan, T.N.: "Fiscal measures to improve employment in developing countries - a comment", Public Finance,
27(4), 1972, pp. 477-482.

Gulliver, P.H. (ed.): Tradition and transition in East Africa:
Studies of the tribal element in the modern era. Berkeley and
Los Angeles, University of California Press, 1969, 378 pp.
(Economic Development and Cultural Change, Oct. 1972, 200 pp.)

Gupta, J.R.: "Growth of unemployment with particular reference to
underemployment in India (1951-1966)", Economic Affairs, Dec.
1971, pp. 529-534.

Gupta, S.: "Shadow price of labour", Indian Economic Journal, Jan.-
Mar. 1972, pp. 420-431.

Gutkind, P.C.W.: "The energy of despair - social organisation of
the unemployed in two African cities, Lagos and Nairobi; a
preliminary account", Civilisations, 17(3), 1967, pp. 186-214
and 17(4), 1967, pp. 380-405.

_____ "From the energy of despair to the anger of despair; the
transition from social circulation to political consciousness
among the urban poor in Africa", Canadian Journal of African
Studies, 7(2), 1973, pp. 179-198.

Ham, E.: "Urbanisation and Asian lifestyles", Annals of American
Academy of Political and Social Sciences, Jan. 1973.

Hamermesh, D.S.: "Price and quantity adjustment in factor markets",
Western Economic Journal, Mar. 1973.

Hamermesh, D.S.; Portes, R.D.: "The labour market central planning:
the case of Hungary", Oxford Economic Papers, July 1972.

Handy, L.J.; Papola, T.S.: "Wage policy and industrial relations
in India: a reappraisal", The Economic Journal, 84(333), Mar.
1974.

Hanna, W.J.; Hanna, J.L.: Urban dynamics in Black Africa, an
interdisciplinary approach. Chicago: Aldine-Atherton, 1971,
390 pp.

Hansen, B.: "Employment and wages in rural Egypt", American
Economic Review, June 1969.

Harberger, A.C.: "On measuring the social opportunity cost of
labour", International Labour Review, June 1971.

Harewood, J.: "Changes in the demand for and supply of labour in the Commonwealth Caribbean 1946-1960", Social and Economic Studies, Mar. 1972.

Harris, J.R.: "Wage rate determination with limited supplies of labour in developing countries: A comment", Journal of Development Studies, Jan. 1971, pp. 197-200.

Harris, J.R.; Todaro, M.P.: "Urban unemployment in East Africa - an economic analysis of policy alternatives", Eastern Africa Economic Review, 4(2), Dec. 1968, pp. 17-36.

_____ "Wages, industrial employment and labour productivity", East African Economic Review, 1969.

Harrison, B.: Education, training and the urban ghetto. Baltimore, Johns Hopkins University Press, 1972.

_____ "Additional thoughts on the dual labour market", Monthly Labour Review, Apr. 1972.

_____ "Education and underemployment in the urban ghetto", American Economic Review, Dec. 1972.

Hart, K.: "Small-scale entrepreneurs in Ghana and development planning", Journal of Development Studies, July 1970.

_____ "Informal income opportunities and urban employment in Ghana", The Journal of Modern African Studies, II(1), 1973, pp. 61-89.

Hart, R.A.: "The economic influences on internal labour force migration", Scottish Journal of Political Economy, June 1972.

Harvey, M.: "Implications of migration to Freetown: A study of the relationship between migrants, housing and occupation", Civilisations (Brussels), 18(2), 1968, p. 247-269.

Hassan, M.F.: "High growth, unemployment and planning in Venezuela: a reply", Economic Development and Cultural Change, Jan. 1970, pp. 274-277.

_____ "Unemployment in Latin America: causes and remedies", American Journal of Economics and Sociology, Apr. 1973, pp. 179-190.

Hassan, R.: "Population change and urbanisation in Singapore", Civilisations, 19(2), 1969.

_____ "Class, ethnicity and occupational structure in Singapore", Civilisations, 20(4), 1970, pp. 496-515.

Hauser, P.M. (ed.): Urbanisation in Latin America. Paris, UNESCO, 1961.

Helfgott, R.B.: "Multinational corporations and manpower utilisation in developing nations", Journal of Developing Areas, Jan. 1973.

Helmer, J.: "Labour market segmentation: Positive feedback and divergent development", American Economic Review, May 1973.

Helmer, J.; Harrison, B.: The economic development of Harlem. New York, F.A. Praeger Publishers, 1970.

Helmer, J. (ed.): Urbanman, the psychology of urban survival.
    New York, Freepress, 1973.

Herrick, B.: Urban migration and economic development in Chile.
    Cambridge, Mass., MIT Press, 1965.

_____ "Urbanisation and urban migration in Latin America: An
    economist's view", in Latin American Urban Research, ed. by
    F.F. Rabinovitz and F.M. Trueblood, USA, Sage Publications,
    1971.

Hicks, U.K.: "Urban problems in underdeveloped countries",
    Pakistan Economic and Social Review, Dec. 1972.

Hoerr, O.D.: "Education, income and equality in Malaysia",
    Economic Development and Cultural Change, Jan. 1973,
    pp. 247-273.

House, W.J.: "Wages, employment and productivity in Kenya",
    Eastern Africa Economic Review, 5(1), June 1973.

_____ "Market structure and industry performance: The case of
    Kenya", Oxford Economic Papers, 1973.

Howe, C.: Employment and economic growth in urban China.   New
    York, Cambridge University Press, 1971.

Hsieh, C.: "Measuring the effects of trade expansion on employ-
    ment: A review of some research", International Labour
    Review, Jan. 1973.

Hunter, G.: "Employment policy in tropical Africa: The need for
    radical revision", International Labour Review, Jan. 1972,
    pp. 35-57.

Hutton, C.R.: Aspects of urban unemployment in Uganda.   Kampala,
    East African Institute of Social Research Conference Papers,
    1966.

_____ Reluctant farmers?   A study of unemployment and planned
    rural development in Uganda.   Nairobi, East African Publish-
    ing House, 1973.

International Labour Office: "Unemployed youth.   An African
    symposium", International Labour Review, 87, 1963, pp. 183-205.

_____ "Back to the land - the campaign against unemployment in
    Dahomey", International Labour Review, 93(1), Jan. 1966,
    pp. 29-49.

_____ Minimum wage fixing and economic development.   Geneva,
    International Labour Office, 1969, 217 pp.

_____ Towards full employment: A programme for Colombia.   Prepared
    by an inter-agency team organised by the International Labour
    Office, Geneva, ILO, 1970, 471 pp.

_____ Problems of employment promotion in Pakistan.   Geneva, ILO,
    1971.

_____ Matching employment opportunities and expectations - a pro-
    gramme of action for Ceylon.   Geneva, ILO, 1971, 251 pp.

International Labour Office: <u>Fiscal measures for employment promotion in developing countries</u>. Geneva, ILO, 1972.

___ <u>Automation in developing countries</u>. Geneva, 1972, 246 pp.

___ <u>Youth training and employment schemes in developing countries</u>. Geneva, ILO, 1972, 109 pp.

___ <u>Employment, incomes and equality - a strategy for increasing productive employment in Kenya</u>. Geneva, ILO, 1972, 600 pp.

___ <u>Report to the Government of India on the employment market information programme</u>. Geneva, 1972. (Confidential.)

___ <u>Employment and income policies for Iran</u>. Geneva, ILO, 1973.

___ World Employment Programme: Research project on urban employ-<u>ment problems in developing countries - Progress Report No. 2</u>. Geneva, ILO, Oct. 1973 (mimeo.).

___ <u>Population and labour</u>. A popular account of the implications of rapid population growth for the training, employment and welfare of workers.

___ <u>Industrialisation and wages in Japan</u>. Geneva, ILO, 1973.

Ingham, G.K.: <u>Size of industrial organisation and worker behaviour</u>. London, 1970.

Innkain, I.: "Farm mechanisation, output and labour input: A case study in Thailand", <u>International Labour Review</u>, 101(5), May 1970, pp. 453-473.

Isbister, J.: "Urban employment and wages in a developing economy: The case of Mexico", <u>Economic Development and Cultural Change</u>, Chicago, Oct. 1971, pp. 24-46.

Jackson, D.: "Income differentials and unbalanced planning: The case of Botswana", <u>Journal of Modern African Studies</u>, London, Dec. 1970, pp. 553-562.

___ "Wage policy and industrial relations in India", <u>Economic Journal</u>, Mar. 1972, pp. 183-194.

Jackson, D.; Turner, H.A.: "How to provide more employment in a labour-surplus economy", <u>International Labour Review</u>, 107(4), Apr. 1973, pp. 315-338.

Jakobson, L.; Prakash, V. (eds.): <u>Urbanisation and national development</u>. South and South-east Asia Urban Affairs Annuals, 1, California, Sage Publications, 1971.

Japan Institute of Labour: <u>Industrialisation and manpower policy in Asian countries</u>. The Japan Institute of Labour, 1973, 359 pp.

Johnson, G.E.; Whitelaw, W.E.: "Urban-rural income transfers in Kenya: An estimated-remittance function". <u>Economic Develop-ment and Cultural Change</u>, 22(3), Apr. 1974.

Johnson, G.E.: <u>The determination of individual hourly earnings in urban Kenya</u>. Ann Arbor, Michigan. University. Centre for Research on Economic Development, 1972. Occasional paper 21.

Johnson, G.E.: "The structure of rural-urban migration models", Eastern Africa Economic Review, 3(1), June 1971, pp. 21-28.

Johnston, J.: "A model of wage determination under bilateral monopoly", Economic Journal, Sept. 1972.

Johri, C.K.: Unionism in a developing economy: A study of the interactions between trade unionism and government policy in India, 1950-1965. Bombay, Asia Publishing House, 1967.

Johri, C.K.; Agrawal, N.C.: "Inter-industry wage structure in India, 1950-1961: An analysis", Indian Journal of Industrial Relations, Apr. 1966.

Johri, C.K.; Misra, U.N.: "Regional labour mobility: An inter-industry analysis", Indian Journal of Industrial Relations, 8(2), Oct. 1972.

____ "Wage payment systems, wage differentials and incomes policy", Indian Journal of Industrial Relations, July 1973.

Johri, C.K.; Pandey, S.M.: "Employment relationship in the building industry", Indian Journal of Industrial Relations, Apr. 1969.

Jolly, R.; Dekadt, E.; Singer, H.; Wilson, F. (eds.): Third World employment problems and strategy. London, Penguin Education, 1973.

Jones, A.: "Prices and incomes policy", Economic Journal, Dec. 1968.

Kahil, R.: "The absorption of manpower by the urban and rural sectors of Brazil", Oxford Bulletin of Economics and Statistics, 27(1), Feb. 1965, pp. 45-53.

Kannappan, S.: "The economics of structuring an industrial labour force", British Journal of Industrial Relations, Nov. 1966.

____ "Unlimited labour supply and the problems of shaping an industrial labour force in India", Economic Development and Cultural Change, Apr. 1968, pp. 451-469.

____ "The brain-drain and the developing countries", International Labour Review, July 1968, pp. 1-26.

____ "Flexible approaches to manpower planning", Manpower Journal, IV(3), 1968-1969, pp. 13-30.

____ "Some problems in the development of advanced and research manpower in India", Asian Survey (Berkeley), Oct. 1969.

____ "Labour force commitment in early stages of industrialization", Indian Journal of Industrial Relations, 5(3), Jan. 1970.

____ "Implications of educational expansion for equality of opportunities", paper presented at the Association for Asian Studies, Apr. 1970, pp. 1-29.

Kao, C.H.C.: Brain-drain: A case study of China. Taiwan, Mei Ya Publications Inc., 1971.

Kasper, H.: "The asking price of labour and the duration of unemployment", Review of Economics and Statistics, May 1967.

Kee, W.S.: "The causes of urban poverty", The Journal of Human Resources, 4(1), Winter 1969.

Kerton, Robert R.: "An economic analysis of the extended family in the West Indies", Journal of Development Studies, July 1971.

Kessel, D.: "Non-white wage increases and inflation in South Africa", South African Journal of Economics, Dec. 1972.

Kim, S.: "Rural-urban migration and technological changes in the agriculture of a developing country", Economic Record, Mar. 1973, pp. 15-23.

King, J.R.: "Wages, employment and productivity in Kenya: A comment", East African Economic Review, June 1972.

Kleiman, E.: "Wages and plant size: A spillover effect?: Reply", Industrial and Labour Relations Review, Oct. 1971, pp. 125-126.

Klitgaard, R.E.: "The dual labour market and manpower policy", Monthly Labour Review, Nov. 1971, pp. 45-48.

Knight, J.B.: "Rural-urban income comparisons and migration in Ghana", Bulletin, Oxford, University Institute of Economics and Statistics, May 1972, pp. 199-228.

Koll, M. (ed.): African urban development. Düsseldorf, Bertelsmann Universitätsverlag, 1972, 215 pp.

Kotliar, A.; Kirpa, I.: "Demographic aspects of employment in cities with differing industrial structures", Problems of Economics, Apr. 1973.

Kregel, J.A.: Rate of profit, distribution and growth. London, Macmillan, 1972.

Kuhnen, F.: Problems of employment promotion in Pakistan. Geneva, ILO, 1971. Employment Research Papers.

Lal, D.: "Disutility of effort, migration and the shadow wage rate", Oxford Economic Papers (London), Jan. 1973, pp. 112-126.

Lakhoua, F.: Cost benefit analysis of Tunisian emigrant workers. (Unpublished Ph.D. thesis, Michigan State University.)

——— "Structure of wages in LDCs: Theory and empirical evidence". (Forthcoming, Revue Tunisienne de Sciences Sociales.)

Landes, W.M.: "The economics of fair employment laws", Journal of Political Economy, July/Aug. 1968.

Leijohhufvud, A.; Buchanan, J.M.: "The backbending supply curve of labour comment", History of Political Economy, Spring 1973.

Leiserson, M.W.: "Employment perspectives and policy approaches in Indonesia", International Labour Review, Apr. 1974.

Lester, R.A.: "Manipulation of the labour market", article in Twenty-Fifth Anniversary Volume, Industrial Relations Research Association, May 1973.

Levi, J.F.S.: "Migration from the land and urban unemployment in Sierra Leone", Oxford Bulletin of Economics and Statistics, Nov. 1973.

Levine, S.B.: "Labour markets and collective bargaining in Japan", in The State and economic enterprise in Japan, W.W. Lockwood (ed.), Princeton University Press, 1965.

Levine, S.B.; Somers, G.G.: "Youth and employment and wages in Japan", in Youth Unemployment and Minimum Wages, Bulletin 1957, US Department of Labour, Bureau of Labour Statistics, 1970.

Levy, M.B.; Wadycki, W.J.: "The influence of family and friends on geographical labour mobility", Review of Economics and Statistics, 55(2), May 1973, pp. 198-203.

___ "What is the opportunity cost of moving?   Reconsideration of the effects of distance on migration", Economic Development and Cultural Change, 22(2), Jan. 1974.

Lewis, W.A.: "Economic development with unlimited supplies of labour", The Manchester School of Economic and Social Studies, 1954.

___ "Summary: The causes of unemployment in less-developed countries and some research topics", International Labour Review, 101(5), May 1970, pp. 547-554.

___ "Unemployment in developing countries", World Today (London), 23(1), Jan. 1967, pp. 13-22.

Lindbeck, A.: "On the transmission mechanism of wage change", Swedish Journal of Economics, Sept. 1971, pp. 273-293.

Lockwood, W.: "Employment, technology and education in Asia", The Malayan Economic Review, XVI(2), Oct. 1971.

Lofchie, M.F. (ed.): The state of the nations: Constraints on development in independent Africa.   Berkeley, University of California Press, 1973, 305 pp.

Lubell, H.: "Urban development and employment in Calcutta", International Labour Review, 108(1), July 1973.

___ Calcutta: Its urban development and employment prospects. Geneva, ILO, 1974.

Mabro, R.: "Employment and wages in dual agriculture", Oxford Economic Papers, Nov. 1971, pp. 401-417.

Mabry, B.D.; Kompor, T.P.: "Manpower imbalances in Thailand", Western Economic Journal, Dec. 1972.

MacEwen, A.M.: "Stability and change in a shantytown: A summary of some research findings", Sociology (Oxford), 6(1), Jan. 1972, pp. 41-57.

MacDonald, J.S.; MacDonald, L.D.: "Jobs and housing: Alternative developments in the Venezuelan Guayana", Journal of Inter-American Studies and World Affairs, 13(3-4), July/Oct. 1971, pp. 342-366.

McCabe, J.L.: <u>Unemployment as a social-welfare problem in urban</u>
<u>Zaire</u>. Yale University, Economic Growth Centre, 1972.

――― <u>Employment in the Congo: A preliminary investigation</u>. Yale
University, Economic Growth Centre, 1972.

McFarquhar, A.M.M.; Evans, G.B.A.: <u>Employment creation in primary</u>
<u>production in less-developed countries</u>. Paris, OECD, 1972,
Employment Series No. 6.

McGee, T.G.: <u>The urbanisation in the Third World</u>. London, G. Bell,
1972.

――― "Peasants in the cities: a paradox, a most ingenious paradox",
<u>Human Organisation</u>, 32(2), Summer 1973.

McQueen, A.J.: "Unemployment and future orientations of Nigerian
school-leavers", <u>Canadian Journal of African Studies</u>, 3(2),
1968, pp. 441-461.

Macisco, J.J.; Bouvier, L.F.; Weller, R.H.: "The effect of labour
force participation on the relation between migration status
and fertility in San Juan, Puerto Rico", <u>Milbank Memorial Fund</u>
<u>Quarterly</u> (New York), 48(1), Jan. 1970, pp. 51-70.

Madaiah, M.: "Disguised unemployment and economic growth - a
diagramatic representation", <u>Indian Economic Journal</u>, 19(1),
July-Sept. 1971, pp. 74-84.

Maddox, R.C.: <u>Wage differences between United States and Guatemalan</u>
<u>industrial firms in Guatemala</u>. Austin, Texas, 1971. (Texas
University. Graduate School of Business. Bureau of Business
Research. Studies in Latin American Business No. 10.)

Magee, S.: "Factor market distortions, production and trade: A
survey", Oxford Economic Papers, Mar. 1973.

Maikov, A.: "Redistribution of rural labour resources", <u>Problems of</u>
<u>Economics</u>, Nov. 1972.

Maital, S.: "Targets, trade-offs and economic policy. A
generalized Phillips curve", <u>Public Finance Quarterly</u>, Jan. 1973.

Maitha, J.K.: "A short-term employment function for Kenyan manufacturing", <u>East African Economic Review</u>, 4(2), Dec. 1972,
pp. 67-72.

Mangin, W.: "Latin American squatter settlements: A problem and a
solution", <u>Latin American Research Review</u>, Summer 1967.

Mann, M.: <u>Workers on the move: The sociology of relocation</u>. New
York, Cambridge University Press, 1973.

Mardsen, K.: "Progressive technologies for developing countries",
<u>International Labour Review</u>, May 1970.

Marsh, Robert M.; Mannari, H.: "A new look at 'lifetime commitment'
in Japanese industry", <u>Economic Development and Cultural Change</u>,
July 1972, pp. 611-630.

Mason, R.H.: "Level of economic development and performance of
United States direct investments abroad", <u>Review of Economics</u>
<u>and Statistics</u>, 50(4), Nov. 1968.

Mason, R.H.: "Some observations on the choice of technology by multinational firms in developing countries", Review of Economics and Statistics, Aug. 1973.

Mattila, J.P.: "The effects of extending minimum wages to cover household maids", The Journal of Human Resources, Summer 1973.

Mazumdar, D.: "The marginal productivity theory of wages and disguised unemployment", Review of Economic Studies, June 1959.

___ "Underemployment in agriculture and the industrial wage rate", Economics, Nov. 1959.

___ "Labour supply in early industrialisation: The case of the Bombay textile industry", Economic History Review, Aug. 1973.

Mehmet, O.: "Manpower planning and labour markets in developing countries: A case study of West Malaysia", Journal of Development Studies, Jan. 1972, pp. 277-288.

Meier, G.M.: "Development without employment", Quarterly Review, Banca Nazionale del Lavoro (Rome), Sept. 1969, pp. 309-319.

Merrick, T.: "Study of the labour market in a growing urban area", CEDEPLAR (University Minhas Gerais Issues), June 1974.

Metcalf, J.P.: "From economic growth to total development: A strategy for Liberia", International Labour Review, Feb. 1974.

Miller, F.: "Return and non-return immigration", Growth and Change, Jan. 1973.

Miller, R.U.: "Labour legislation and Mexican industrial relations", Industrial Relations, 7(2), Feb. 1968.

___ "Statutory wages and employment: Stabilization in developing countries: Some observations in Latin America", in D. Chaplin (ed.), Population Policies and Growth in Latin America, D.C. Heath, 1972.

___ "The relevance of surplus labour theory to the urban labour markets of Latin America", Bulletin, International Institute for Labour Studies, 8, 1971, pp. 220-245.

___ "Theory of surplus labour markets", Paper for the International Industrial Relations Association, Geneva, Sept. 1970.

Minami, R.: "Transformation of the labour market in post-war Japan", Hitotsubashi Journal of Economics, June 1972.

Minocha, A.C.: "Unemployment in a dual economy - a critique of Lewis' model of growth", Asian Economic Review, 8(3), May 1966, pp. 308-321.

Miracle, M.P.; Fetter, B.: "Backward-sloping labour-supply functions and the African economic behaviour", Economic Development and Cultural Change, Jan. 1970, pp. 240-251.

___ "Two causal models of African economic conduct: A reply", Economic Development and Cultural Change, Oct. 1972, pp. 171-173.

Mitra, A.: "Housing the urban poor: The case of Calcutta", Economic and Political Weekly, 6(30-32), 1971. (Special No.)

Mitra, P.: "The vicious circles of Indian economic policy", South Asia Review, Jan. 1974.

Modigliani, F.; Tarantelli, E.: "A generalisation of the Phillips curve for a developing country", Review of Economic Studies, Apr. 1973, pp. 203-223.

Mohindru, R.K.: "The structural unemployment controversy resisted", Journal of Economics and Business, Winter 1973.

Moller, B.: Employment approaches to economic planning in developing countries. Lund, Sweden, Studentlitteratur, Scandinavian Institute of Asian Studies Monograph Series, 1972, 305 pp.

Morawetz, D.: "Employment implications of industrialisation in developing countries: A survey", The Economic Journal, Sept. 1974.

Morse, R.M.: "Recent research on Latin American urbanisation: A selective survey with commentary", Latin American Research Review, 1(1), 1965, pp. 35-75.

Moss, Milton (ed.): The measurement of economic and social performance. National Bureau of Economic Research. New York, Columbia University Press, 1973, 605 pp.

Mouly, J.: "Some remarks on the concept of employment, under-employment and unemployment", International Labour Review, Feb. 1972.

Mueller, P.; Zevering, K.H.: "Employment promotion through rural development: A pilot project in Western Nigeria", International Labour Review, Aug. 1969, pp. 111-130.

Mulat, Teshome: The changes in the level and structure of employment in developing countries. (Unpublished Ph.D. thesis, University of Manchester, 1971.)

Mulvey, C.; Trevithick, J.A.: "Trade unions and wage inflation", Economic and Social Review, Jan. 1973.

Muthuchidambaram, S.: "Commitment and motivation of blue-collar workers in India", Indian Journal of Industrial Relations, 7(4), Apr. 1972.

Nachane, D.M.: "A note on optional development in a labour surplus economy", Indian Economic Journal, Jan./Mar. 1972, pp. 404-407.

Nagi, M.H.: Labour force and employment in Egypt: A demographic and socio-economic analysis. New York, Praeger Publishers, 1971, 285 pp.

Nair, P.A.: Employment market in an industrial metropolis - A survey of educated unemployment in Bombay. Bombay, Lativani Publishing House, 1968.

Nakamura, T.: "The labour market under economic growth",
    Industrialization and manpower policy in Asian countries.
    Proceedings of the 1973 Asian Regional Conference on Industrial
    Relations, Tokyo, Japan, 1973.   The Japan Institute of Labour,
    1973.

Naseem, S.M.: "Mass poverty in Pakistan: Some preliminary find-
    ings", The Pakistan Development Review, XII(4), Winter 1973.

Nath, V.; Prasad, A.: "Impact of irrigation on intensity of
    cropping and labour utilization - A case study", Economic
    Affairs, Dec. 1971, pp. 543-548.

National Manpower Policy Task Force: Adapting labour market statis-
    tics to policy needs. A policy statement by the National Man-
    power Policy Task Force. Washington, D.C., Jan. 1974.

Nelson, J.M.: Migrants, urban poverty and instability in developing
    nations. Centre for International Affairs, Harvard University,
    1969. Occasional Papers in International Affairs, No. 22.

_____ "The urban poor - disruption or political integration in Third
    World cities", World Politics (Princeton), 22(3), Apr. 1970,
    pp. 393-414.

Noll, R.: "Metropolitan employment and population distribution and
    the conditions of the urban poor", Urban Affairs Annual Review,
    4, 1970.

Ohadike, P.O.: "The nature and extent of urbanization in Zambia",
    Journal of African and Asian Studies, Apr. 1969.

O'Herlithy, C.St.J.: "Capital/labour substitution and the develop-
    ing countries: A problem of measurements", Oxford University
    Bulletin, 34(3), Aug. 1972, pp. 269-280.

Oliver, R.; Sabolo, Y.: "Simultaneous planning of employment pro-
    duction and education", International Labour Review, Apr. 1973.

Oshima, H.T.: "Income inequality and economic growth: The postwar
    experience of Asian countries", Malayan Economic Review, Oct.
    1970.

_____ "Labour-force 'explosion' and the labour-intensive sector in
    Asian growth", Economic Development and Cultural Change, Jan.
    1971, pp. 161-183.

_____ "Labour absorption in East and South-east Asia: A summary with
    interpretation of postwar experience", Malayan Economic Review,
    Oct. 1971, pp. 55-77.

_____ "Seasonality and underemployment in Monsoon Asia", Philippine
    Economic Journal, first semester 1971, pp. 63-97.

Oyejide, T.A.: "Fiscal measures to improve employment in developing
    countries: A comment", Public Finance, 27(4), 1972, pp. 483-488.

Pack, H.: "Employment and productivity in Kenyan manufacturing",
    East African Economic Review, 4(2), Dec. 1972, pp. 29-52.

Pack, H.; Todaro, M.: "Technological transfer, labour absorption and economic development", <u>Oxford Economic Papers</u>, Nov. 1969, pp. 395-403.

Paine, S.: "Lessons for LDCs from Japan's experience with labour commitment and subcontracting in the manufacturing sector", <u>Bulletin of the Institute of Economics and Statistics</u>, May 1971, pp. 115-133.

Pang, Eng Fong: "Inter-industry mobility in a city economy: A test of some hypotheses", in <u>Industrialisation and manpower policy in Asian countries</u>, Proceedings of the 1973 Asian Regional Conference on Industrial Relations, Tokyo, Japan, 1973, pp. 35-49.

_____ "A note on labour under-utilization in Singapore", <u>Malayan Economic Review</u>, XVIII(1), Apr. 1973.

_____ "Returns to schooling and training in Singapore", <u>Malayan Economic Review</u>, XV(2), Oct. 1970.

_____ "Economics of labour market", in <u>Labour Research in India</u>, ed. by Singh, U.B., for ISLE, Bombay, Popular Prakashnan, 1970.

_____ <u>Principles of wage determination: An empirical study</u>. Bombay, Somaiya Publications, 1971.

Papola, T.S.; Bharadwaj, V.P.: "Dynamics of industrial wage structure: An inter-country analysis", <u>The Economic Journal</u>, Mar. 1970.

Papola, T.S.; Subrahmanian, K.K.: <u>Structure of a local labour market: A study in Ahmedabad</u>. Economic and Political Weekly Annual Number, Feb. 1973.

Papola, T.S.: "Regional wage differentials in Indian industry", <u>Anvesak</u>, I(1), June 1971.

Parsons, D.O.: "Specific human capital: An application to quit rates and layoff rates", <u>Journal of Political Economy</u>, Nov./Dec. 1972.

Peacock, A.; Shaw, G.K.: <u>Fiscal policy and the employment problem in less-developed countries</u>. Development Centre Studies, Paris, OECD, 1971. Employment Series No. 5.

_____ "Fiscal measures to create employment: the Indonesian case", <u>Bulletin of International Fiscal Documentation</u>, Nov. 1973.

_____ "Fiscal measures to improve employment in developing countries - A reply", <u>Public Finance</u>, 27(4), 1972, pp. 487-490.

Peel, D.A.: "The kinked demand curve - The demand for labour reconsidered", <u>Récherches Economiques de Louvain</u>, Sept. 1972.

Peil, M.: "Unemployment in Tema: The plight of the skilled worker", <u>Canadian Journal of African Studies</u>, 3(20), Summer 1969, pp. 409-419.

_____ <u>The Ghanan factory worker: Industrial man in Africa</u>. New York, Cambridge University Press, 1972. African Studies Series No. 5.

Perrakis, S.: "The labour surplus model and wage behaviour in Mexico", <u>Industrial Relations</u>, Feb. 1972.

Perry, G.L.: <u>Inflation and unemployment</u>. The Brookings Institute, Washington, D.C., 1970, Reprint 188.

Peston, M.: "Unemployment: why we need a new measurement", <u>Lloyds Bank Review</u>, Apr. 1972, pp. 1-7.

Pettiss, S.: "A study of social consequences of internal migration of youth from rural to urban areas in three African countries", <u>Manpower and Unemployment Research in Africa</u>, Montreal, Nov. 1969, pp. 39-42.

___ <u>Social consequences of rural-urban youth migration in two African countries: Nigeria and Kenya</u>. Mass., Brandes University, Florence Heller Graduate School for Advanced Studies in Social Welfare, 1971.

Piore, M.J.: "Fragments of a sociological theory of wages", <u>American Economic Review</u>, May 1973, pp. 377-584.

Polzin, P.E.: "Urban employment models: Estimation and interpretation", <u>Land Economics</u>, May 1973, pp. 226-232.

Porter, R.C.: <u>Labour migration and urban unemployment in less-developed countries: Comment</u>. Ann Arbor, Michigan University. Centre for Research on Economic Development, 1973. Discussion Paper 29.

Pournarakis, E.: "Development with labour surplus and 'aid through trade': A neo-classical approach", <u>Journal of Business and Economics</u>, Winter 1971-1972, pp. 1-12.

Prattern, C.F.: "How higher wages can cause unemployment", <u>Lloyds Bank Review</u>, Jan. 1972, pp. 12-24.

Rakowski, J.: "Is labour mobility a substitute for trade?", <u>Economic Journal</u>, Mar. 1969.

Ramos, J.R.: <u>Labour and development in East Africa: Studies of the tribal element in the modern era</u>. Berkeley, University of California Press, 1969, 378 pp.

Ranis, G.: "Industrial sector labour absorption", <u>Economic Development and Cultural Change</u>, Apr. 1973, pp. 387-408.

Rao, V.R.: "Educated unemployment", <u>Indian Labour Journal</u>, Apr. 1972, pp. 537-550.

Raswi, J.A.: <u>Measures to fight unemployment in Iraq</u>. Baghdad, 1965.

Redcliff, M.R.: "Squatter settlements in Latin American cities: The response from government", <u>The Journal of Development Studies</u>, Oct. 1973, pp. 92-109.

Reddaway, W.B.: "The development of the labour market in Kenya", <u>Economic Development and Cultural Change</u>, ed. by I.G. Steward. Edinburgh, Edinburgh University Press, 1969.

Rees, A.: "On equilibrium in labour markets", <u>Journal of Political Economy</u>, Mar.-Apr. 1970, pp. 306-310.

Rees, A.; Schultz, G.P.: Workers and wages in an urban labour market. Chicago, University of Chicago Press, 1971.

Rehovot Conference: On urbanisation and development in developing countries: Conference papers. Rehovot, Israel, Continuation Committee of the International Conference on Science in the Advancement of New States in Co-operation with the Settlement Study Centre, 1971.

Reich, M.; Gordon, D.M.; Edwards, R.G.: "A theory of labour market segmentation", American Economic Review, proceedings, 1973.

Rempel, H.: Labour migration into urban centers and urban unemployment in Kenya. Madison, University of Wisconsin, 1971.

___ The extent and nature of the population movement into Kenya's towns. (Copyright pending Africana Publishing Corp., 1974.)

Reynolds, L.J.: "Wages and employment in a labour surplus economy", American Economic Review, Mar. 1965. The results were later incorporated into a book: L.G. Reynolds and P. Gregory, Wages, productivity and industrialization in Puerto Rico. Illinois, Richard D. Irwin, 1965.

Reynolds, L.G.: "Economic development with surplus labour: Some complications", Oxford Economic Papers, Mar. 1969.

Richards, P.J.: Employment and unemployment in Ceylon. Paris, OECD, 1971.

___ "Job mobility and unemployment in the Ceylon urban labour market", Oxford Bulletin of Economics and Statistics, Feb. 1973.

Richards, S.F.: "Geographical mobility of industrial workers in India", in D.S. Dwyer (ed.), The city as a centre of change in Asia. Hong Kong University Press, 1972.

Riddell, J.B.; Harvey, M.E.: "The urban system in the migration process: An evaluation of step-wise migration in Sierra Leone", Economic Geography, July 1972.

Ridker, R.G.; Lubell, H. (eds.): Employment and unemployment problems of the Near East and South Asia, Vols. I and II. London, Vikas Publications, 1971, 862 pp.

Robinson, D. (ed.): Local labour markets and wage structures. London, Gower Press, 1970.

Robinson, W.C.: "The economics of work in peasant agriculture", Economic Development and Cultural Change, Oct. 1971, pp. 131-141.

Romm, J.: Urbanization in Thailand. International Urbanisation Survey, The Ford Foundation.

Roussel, L.: "Employment problems and policies in the Ivory Coast", International Labour Review, 104(5), Dec. 1971, pp. 505-525.

___ "Measuring rural-urban drift in developing countries - A suggested method", International Labour Review, Mar. 1970, pp. 229-246.

Ruchlin, H.S.: "Education as a labour market variable", Industrial
     Relations, Oct. 1971, pp. 287-300.

Sadove, R.: "Urban needs of developing countries", Finance and
     Development, June 1973.

Sandbrook, R.: "The working class in the future of the Third World",
     World Politics, XXV(3), Apr. 1973.

___   "Workers, unions and development in Africa", Journal of Modern
     African Studies, XI,· Sept. 1973.

___   Proletarians and African Capitalism: The Kenyan Case, 1960-1972.
     Cambridge University Press, 1974.

Sandbrook, R. (co-author and co-editor): Towards an African working
     class: Studies in class formation and action. Toronto,
     University of Toronto Press, Jan. 1975.

Schultz, T.P.: "Rural-urban migration in Colombia", Review of
     Economics and Statistics (Cambridge), 53(2), May 1971,
     pp. 157-163.

Schumacher, E.F.: "The work of the intermediate technology develop-
     ment group in Africa", International Labour Review, July 1972.

Scoville, J.G.: "Afghan labour markets - A model of interdependence",
     Industrial Relations, Oct. 1974.

___   "The occupational structure of employment, 1960-1980", in
     Sectoral aspects of projection for the world economy, III,
     United Nations, 1969.

___   "Remuneration in Afghan industry", International Labour Review,
     Apr. 1969.

Seers, D.: "New light on structural unemployment lessons of a
     mission to Ceylon", International Labour Review, Feb. 1972.

Sethuraman, S.V.: "Prospects of increasing employment in Indian
     manufacturing", in H. Lubell and R.G. Ridker (eds.), Problems
     of employment and unemployment in Near East and South Asia, II,
     New Delhi, 1971.

___   "Towards a definition of the informal sector", WEP 2-19, Draft
     for comment, Jan. 1974.

___   Urbanization and employment in Jakarta: Summary and conclusions
     of a case study. Working papers, World Employment Programme
     Research. Geneva, ILO, May 1974.

___   "Employment and labour productivity in India since 1950",
     Economic Development and Cultural Change, June 1974.

Sharir, S.: "On the relationship between durations, flows, and
     stocks of unemployment and vacancies: A comment", Journal of
     Human Resources, Fall 1971, pp. 528-532.

Sheffield, J.R. (ed.): Education, employment and rural development.
     Nairobi, East African Publishing House, 1967.

Shoo, B.: "Approach to the problem of unemployment in India", Economic Affairs, 15(6-8), Aug. 1970, pp. 329-339.

Siddigi, A.H.: "Urbanization in Asia", Land Economics, Nov. 1971, pp. 389-400.

Siegel, P.H.: "The location of industry and job participation: An econometric study", Economic Affairs (Annual 1973).

Singh, V.B. (ed.): Patterns of economic development. Bombay, Allied Publishers, 1970, 576 pp.

Sinha, J.N.: "Agrarian reforms and employment in densely populated agrarian economies", International Labour Review, Nov. 1973.

Slighton, R.L.: Urban unemployment in Colombia: Measurement characteristics and policy problems. Santa Monica, Rand Corporation, 1968.

Smith, A.D. (ed.): Wage policy issues in economic development. Proceedings of a symposium held at Egelund, Denmark, by the International Institute for Labour Studies. London, Macmillan, 1969.

Sobel, I.; Folk, H.: "Labour market adjustments by unemployed workers", in Employment, policy and the labour market, A.M. Ross (ed.), Berkeley, University of California Press, 1965.

Solo, R.A.; Rogers, E.M. (eds.): Inducing technological change for economic growth and development. East Lansing, Michigan State University Press, 1972, 238 pp.

Sovani, N.V.: "The analysis of over-urbanization", Economic Development and Cultural Change, 12(2), Jan. 1964, pp. 113-122.

Spandau, S.: "South African wage board policy: An alternative interpretation", South African Journal of Economics, Dec. 1972.

Speare, A., Jr.: "Urbanisation and migration in Taiwan", Economic Development and Cultural Change, 22(2), Jan. 1974.

Spence, A. Michael: Market signalling informational transfer in hiring and related screening processes. Cambridge, Mass., Harvard University Press, 1974.

Spitz, A.A.: Development change: An annotated bibliography. Lexington, University Press of Kentucky, 1969, 316 pp.

Standing, G.; Taira, K.: "Labour market effects of multinational enterprises in Latin America", Nebraska Journal of Economics and Business, 12(4), Autumn 1973, pp. 103-117.

Stanley, E.: Planning occupational education and training for development. New York, Praeger Publishers, 1971, 181 pp.

Sternlieb, S.; Bauman, A.: "Employment characteristics of low-wage workers", Monthly Labour Review, July 1972.

Stigler, G.: "Information in the labour market", Journal of Political Economy, Oct. 1962.

Stiglitz, J.E.: "A note on technical choice under full employment in a socialist economy", Economic Journal, Sept. 1968.

_____ "Rural-urban migration, surplus labour, and the relationship between urban and rural wages", East African Economic Review, 12(6), Dec. 1969, pp. 58-67.

_____ "Wage determination and unemployment in LDCs", Quarterly Journal of Economics, May 1974.

Stoikow, V.: "The structure of earnings in Japanese manufacturing industries: A human capital approach", Journal of Political Economy, Mar.-Apr. 1973.

Sundrum, R.M.: "Manpower and educational development in East and South-east Asia: A summary of conference proceedings", The Malayan Economic Review, XVI(2), Oct. 1971.

Sussman, Zvi: "The determination of wages for unskilled labour in the advanced sector of the dual economy of mandatory Palestine", Economic Development and Cultural Change, 22(1), Oct. 1973.

Sween, J.; Clignet, R.: "Urban unemployment as a determinant of political unrest: The case study of Duala, Cameroon", Canadian Journal of African Studies, Summer 1969, pp. 463-487.

Taber, S.R.: "Economic opportunity and urban orientation as factors in Uganda migration", Geography Papers, University of East Africa, Makerere Institute of Social Research (Kampala), 1968/1969, pp. 29-42.

Taira, K.: Economic development and the labour market in Japan. New York, Colombia University Press, 1970.

_____ "Industrial dualism in Japan", Economic Development and Cultural Change, Jan. 1970, pp. 278-284.

_____ "The labour market in Japanese development", British Journal of Industrial Relations, July 1964.

_____ "The relation between wages and incomes from self-employment", The Manchester School, May 1966.

_____ "Unemployment, labour markets and wage differentials in Asian countries", Industrialisation and Manpower Policy in Asian Countries. Proceedings of the 1973 Asian Regional Conference on Industrial Relations, Tokyo, Japan, 1973. The Japan Institute of Labour, 1973.

_____ "Wage differentials in developing countries: A survey of findings", International Labour Review, Mar. 1966.

Tandon, M.L.: "Rural-urban wage differentials and rationalisation of employment pattern: A case study", The Indian Journal of Economics, I(198), Jan. 1970.

Taylor, D.P.: "Discrimination and occupational wage differences in the market for unskilled labour", Industrial and Labour Relations Review, Apr. 1968, pp. 375-390.

Taylor, L.: Survey of employment planning methodology: An
evaluation of planning models used in the past. Presented at
the conference on planning for income distribution and employment, sponsored by the IBRD and the Institute of Development
Studies, Sussex, in Bellagio, Italy, Apr. 1973.

Thillainathan, R.: "The second Malaysia Plan - Issues relating to
the employment strategy", EKONOMI (a publication of the
University of Malaya Economic Society), 12(2), 1972.

Thirlwall, A.P.: "An extension of Sen's model of the valuation of
labour in surplus labour economies", Pakistan Development
Review, Autumn 1970, pp. 393-396.

____ "The valuation of labour in surplus labour economies: A
synoptic view", Scottish Journal of Political Economy, Nov.
1971, pp. 299-314.

Thomas, H.: "Literacy without formal education: A case study in
Pakistan", Economic Development and Cultural Change, 22(3),
Apr. 1974.

Thomas, R.D.: The adjustment of displaced workers in a labour surplus economy: A case study of Trinidad and Tobago. Institute
of Social and Economic Research, University of West Indies,
Jamaica, 1972.

Thorbecke, E.: "The employment problem: Critical evaluation of
four comprehensive country reports", International Labour
Review, May 1973.

Tiano, A.: "Human resources investment and employment policy in the
Maghreb", International Labour Review, Feb. 1972.

Tidrick, G.M.: Wages, output and the employment lag in Jamaica.
Williamstown (Mass.), Williams College, Centre for Development
Economics, 1970.

____ Wage spill-over and unemployment in a wage-gap economy: The
Jamaican case. Williams College, Mass. Centre for Development
Economics. Research Memorandum No. 47, 1972.

Todaro, M.P.: "The urban employment problem in less-developed
countries. An analysis of demand and supply", Yale Economic
Essays, Fall 1968.

____ "A model of labour migration and urban unemployment in less-
developed countries", American Economic Review, 59(1), Mar.
1969, pp. 138-148.

____ "Income expectations, rural-urban migration and employment in
Africa", International Labour Review, Nov. 1971, pp. 387-413.

Truu, M.L.: "On the micro-economics of 'stagflation'", South
African Journal of Economics, Sept. 1971.

Turner, R. (ed.): India's urban future. Berkeley, University of
California Press, 1962.

Turner, H.R.; Jackson, D.A.S.: "The determination of the general
wage level - A world analysis or 'unlimited labour forever'",
Economic Journal, Dec. 1970.

Turnman, D.: The employment problem in less-developed countries: A review of evidence. Paris, OECD, 1971, 154 pp.

Ulman, L.: "Labour markets and manpower policies in perspective", Monthly Labour Review, Sept. 1972.

United Nations Economic Commission for Latin America: Development problems in Latin America. Austin, University of Texas Press, 1970, 318 pp.

United Nations Institute for Training and Research: The brain-drain from five developing countries. Cameroon, Colombia, Lebanon, the Philippines, Trinidad and Tobago. New York, 1971 (UNITAR Research Report No. 5).

US Department of Labor - Bureau of Statistics: Labour developments abroad. Special issue on labour migration, Apr./May 1971.

Vanderkamp, J.: "Migration flows, their determinants and the effects of return migration", Journal of Political Economy, 79(5), Sept./Oct. 1971, pp. 1012-1031.

Vanek, J.: The general theory of labour-managed market economies. Ithaca, New York, Cornell University Press, 1970.

Verma, P.: "Regional wages and economic development: A case study of manufacturing wages in India, 1950-1960", The Journal of Development Studies, 10(1), Oct. 1973.

Vietorisz, T.; Harrison, B.: "Labour market segmentation; positive feedback and divergent development", American Economic Review, May 1973, pp. 366-376.

Vincens, J.; Robinson, D.: Research into labour market behaviour. Paris, OECD, 1974.

Wachtel, H.M.; Betsey, C.: "Employment at low wages", Review of Economics and Statistics, May 1972.

Wachter, M.L.: "Wage determination in a local labour market: A case study of the Boston labour market", The Journal of Human Resources, 7(1), Winter 1972.

___ "A new approach to the equilibrium labour force", Economica, 41(161), Feb. 1974, pp. 35-51.

Wackstein, R.: "Unemployment and development planning", (International Technical Co-operation Centre), ITCC Review (Tel Aviv), July 1973, pp. 16-19.

Wallace, T.: "Young and unemployed - who is and what does it mean?", East African Journal, 9(11), 1972.

Walliman, S.: "Conditions of non-development: The case of Lesotho", Journal of Development Studies, Jan. 1972.

Walter, J.P.: "The city as a source of regional economic disparity in Latin America", Review of Social Economy, Apr. 1973.

Warriner, D.: "Problems of rural-urban migration: Some suggestions for investigation", International Labour Review, 101(5), May 1970, pp. 441-451.

Warriner, D.: "Employment and income aspects of recent agrarian reforms in the Middle East", International Labour Review, June 1970.

Watanabe, I.: "Improvement of labour quality and economic growth - Japan's postwar experience", Economic Development and Cultural Change, Oct. 1972, pp. 33-53.

Watanabe, S.: "Exports and employment: The case of the Republic of Korea", International Labour Review, Dec. 1972.

___ "Constraints on labour-intensive export industries in Mexico", International Labour Review, Jan. 1974.

Waters, A.R.: "Migration remittances and the cash constraint in African smallholder economic development", Oxford Economic Papers, 25(3), Nov. 1973, pp. 435-454.

Watts, H.W.; Cain, G.G.: Basic labour supply response findings from the urban experiment (New Jersey-Pennsylvania). A report presented at the annual meeting of the American Economic Association, 30 Dec. 1973.

Weeks, J.F.: "Unemployment, rising wages and underdeveloped countries: A theory of wage determination", (mimeo.).

___ "Wage policy and the colonial legacy: a comparative study", Journal of Modern African Studies, Oct. 1971.

Welch, Finis: "Labour market discrimination: An interpretation of income differences in the rural south", Journal of Political Economy, June 1967, pp. 225-240.

Wilde, J.C.: "The manpower and employment aspects of selected experiences of agricultural development in tropical Africa", International Labour Review, Nov. 1971, pp. 35-44.

Willmott, W.E. (ed.): Economic organisation in Chinese society. Stanford, California, Stanford University Press, 1972, 461 pp.

Winston, G.C.: "On the inevitability of factor substitution", Research Memoranda - 46, Williams College, Department of Economics, Apr. 1972.

Witte, A.D.: "Employment in the manufacturing sector of developing economies: A study of Mexico and Peru", The Journal of Development Studies, 10(1), Oct. 1973, pp. 33-49.

Wohlmuth, K. (ed.): Employment creation in developing societies. Praeger Publishers, 1973.

Youssef, N.H.: "Differential labour force participation of women in Latin American and Middle Eastern countries: The influence of family characteristics", Social Forces, 51(2), Dec. 1972, pp. 135-153.

Zaidi, M.A.: "The impact of new industrial towns on the labor market: The Mexican experience". Minneapolis, 1970, 64 pp. (ITS: Working Paper 71-02.)

___ "Economic development, structural change and employment potential", The Journal of Development Studies. Special Issue on Employment and Income Distribution, Vol. XI, No. 2, Jan. 1975.

Zaidi, M.A.: "Labour mobility, wage sensitivity, and human resource development in a new industrial town", Paper presented at the December 1973 meeting of the Econometric Society, New York, (with Calvin D. Siebert). IRC Working Paper No. 74-02.

Zucker, A.: "Minimum wages and the demand for low-wage labor", Quarterly Journal of Economics, May 1973.